Equality in
Liberty and Justice

Equality in Liberty and Justice

Antony Flew

With a new introduction by the author

Transaction Publishers
New Brunswick (U.S.A.) and London (U.K.)

Library of Congress Catalog Number: 00-051199
ISBN: 0-7658-0734-3
Printed in the United States of America

Library of Congress Cataloging-in-Publication Data

Flew, Antony, 1923-
    Equality in liberty and justice / Antony Flew ; with a new introduction by the author.
        p.cm.
    Second edition.
    Includes bibliographical references and index.
    ISBN: 0-7658-0734-3 (pbk.: alk. paper)
        1. Equality. 2. Liberty. 3. Justice. I. Title.

JC575 .F56 2000
172'.2—dc21

00-051199

Il y a en effet une passion mâle et légitime pour l'égalité qui excite les hommes à vouloir être tous forts et estimés. Cette passion tend à élever les petits au rang des grands; mais il se rencontre aussi dans le cœur humain un goût dépravé pour l'égalité, qui porte les faibles à vouloir attirer les forts à leur niveau, et qui réduit les hommes à préférer l'égalité dans la servitude à l'inégalité dans la liberté.

Alexis de Tocqueville:
Democracy in America, ch. III *ad fin.*

Contents

Introduction to the Transaction Edition   xi

Part I

1 The logic of liberty   3
  1. Political freedom   4
  2. Freedom of the will   9
  3. Deny freewill and disdain political liberty   14
  4. Liberties and democracies   19

2 Could there be universal natural rights?   27
  1. The objectivity of natural rights   28
  2. The groundedness of all rights   33
  3. The reciprocities of rights   36
  4. Rights and compulsions   39
  5. The road to a rationale   43

3 Social Contract or General Will?   47
  1. Sources of misunderstanding   49
  2. Popular absolutism   56
  3. Vanguards and voluntarism   63

4 'Freedom is slavery!': slogan for philosopher
  kings   69
  1. What is to be examined   70
  2. Misunderstanding the meaning of 'liberty'   74
  3. Suggesting senses of 'freedom'   77
  4. Miscellaneous anti-liberal misconceptions   85

5 Choices and wants: discrediting the actual   90
    1. Plato, delinquency, and disease   93
    2. Agents' actions or symptomatic spasms?   96
    3. Disease, disability, and dissidence   102
    4. The logic of wants and needs   108

Part II

6 The geography of justice   119
    1. Justice as a particular virtue   121
    2. Plato and (social) justice   126
    3. Aristotle and (distributive) justice   134
    4. Procrusteanism, or justice?   142

7 Annihilating the individual   144
    1. Individual differences and (social) justice   146
    2. Individual deserts and 'genetic inheritances' 150
    3. Actual entitlements, but not deserved   156
    4. Everywhere different, yet born identical?   161

8 Equal outcomes, or equal justice?   165
    1. Hayek's last mission   168
    2. Three ideals of equality   174

9 Enemies of poverty, or of inequality?   182
    1. Procrusteans, or Good Samaritans?   183
    2. Procrusteanism and monopoly provision   191
    3. Distracting aims within the Poverty Lobby   195
    4. A sting in the tail   208

   Bibliography   210

   Name index   221

Acknowledgements

What follows is a new book rather than a collection of papers. It does nevertheless contain a lot of material recycled from various previous publications. Thanks are therefore owed, and gladly given, to all the editors and publishers who have granted their permission for this reuse. In the cases of chapters two, three, four, and nine there were single articles which can now be regarded as first drafts. These were 'Could there be universal natural rights?', published in volume 6 of the *Journal of Libertarian Studies* (Summer/Fall 1982); 'Particular liberties against the general will', contributed to the *Festschrift* for Murray Rothbard sponsored by the Ludwig von Mises Institute but at the time of writing not yet in print; ' "Freedom is Slavery": a slogan for our new philosopher kings' published in A. P. Griffiths (ed.) *Of Liberty* (Cambridge: Cambridge University Press, 1983); and 'Good Samaritans become procrusteans', published in C. Jones and J. Stevenson (eds.) *The Yearbook of Social Policy in Britain 1982* (London and Henley: Routledge & Kegan Paul, 1983).

Both in these four chapters and elsewhere there are bits and pieces, amounting perhaps in total to almost the equivalent of another chapter, which have been drawn from my *The Politics of Procrustes* (London and Buffalo, NY: Temple Smith and Prometheus, 1981). This book remains in print only in the USA. Other articles from which substantial quantities of material have been recycled here were 'Justice: real or social?', published in volume 1 of *Social Philosophy and Policy* (Autumn 1983); 'The mirage of social justice', published in E. Butler (ed.) *Hayek and the Fabric of Human Society* (London: Adam Smith Institute, 1987); 'Four kinds of equality', published in *Reason Papers No. 8*

(Santa Barbara, Calif.: Reason Foundation, 1982); and 'The concept, and conceptions of justice', published in the *Journal of Applied Philosophy* for 1985. A paper on 'The philosophy of freedom', extracted from chapter one, is to be given in Colombo in July 1988, and simultaneously published there by the sponsoring Martin Wickramasinghe Trust.

Equality in Liberty and Justice was wholly composed in the Social Philosophy and Policy Center at Bowling Green State University, Ohio. Fred Miller, Ellen and Jeffrey Paul, and John Ahrens have, with a strong support staff, created an ideal environment to encourage such work. Excellently equipped, friendly, alive, and in a most salutary way untroubled by any distracting temptations, this Center is all that a think-tank ought to be. I am especially grateful to Mrs Linda Brown who, while still meeting all the engaging demands of Miss Lorna Brown, managed to transform my legible yet untidy manuscript into a typescript looking better than perhaps it is.

Antony Flew
Bowling Green State University, Ohio
April 1988

Introduction to the Transaction Edition

The writing of the present book was completed at the Social Philosophy and Policy Center in Bowling Green State University, Ohio during the spring semester of 1988, and it was first published in 1989. The intervening twelve years have seen great political changes, the most happy being the peaceful winning of the Cold War by the United States and its allies, and the subsequent more or less successful attempts to establish democratically elected governments and prosperous market economies in both the constituent republics of the former Soviet Union and in the republics in Eastern Europe formerly associated with it. Younger readers may therefore need some help if they are to understand illustrative references that at the time of writing were topical. But before attempting here to meet that need, I want first to add various things that I have come to realize should have been included from the beginning.

Thus, whereas chapter 2 asks the question 'Could there be universal natural rights?' and proceeds to argue for an affirmative answer without attempting to actually identify any specimens of such universal natural rights, I now contend that the rights to life, liberty, and the pursuit of happiness proclaimed in the American Declaration of Independence do actually constitute three specimens of such universal natural rights.

If this contention is to be sustained in a secular age then we cannot argue, as the words of that Declaration might suggest, that our endowment with these rights is the result of an arbitrary exercise of Divine power. Instead, we have to claim that these three rights are firmly grounded in the peculiar nature of the species of which we are all members. We are, that is to say, all members of a kind of creatures who can, and therefore cannot but, make choices between various possible alternative courses of action or inaction, choices some of which will be made of the agents' own free will and others under various kinds and degrees of constraint. Another peculiarity of our peculiar kind of creatures is that we are all rational beings—rational as opposed of course not to irrational but to non-rational—beings which can have reasons both for acting in the ways in which we choose to act (practical reasons) and reasons for believing what we do believe (theoretical reasons). All individual creatures of this peculiar kind can surely be assumed in their own interests implicitly to have made with all other members of their kind a tacit social contract. This tacit social contract, which it is in everyone's interest to accept, endows each and everyone with these three moral rights—providing, of course, that all accept their consequent reciprocal duty to respect the corresponding rights of everyone else.

Next, it should surely be noticed here that although the first Continental Congress had approved a Bill of Rights calling for the protection of 'life, liberty, and property,' Mr. Jefferson in drafting the Declaration for the second Continental Congress substituted the expression 'the pursuit of happiness' for the word 'property.' It is not known why. But it is certain that everyone in that period claiming a right to liberty believed this right to be necessarily connected with a right to property.[1] Somewhat later James Madison wrote in the same strain:

> Property . . . in its particular application means that domination which one man claims and exercises over the external things of the world, in exclusion of every other individual. In its larger and juster meaning, it embraces everything to which a man may . . . have a right; and *which leaves to everyone else a like advantage.* In the former sense, a man's land, or merchandise, or money is called his property. In the latter sense a man has property in his opinions and the free communication of them. He has a property of peculiar value in his religious opinions . . . He has a property very dear to him in the safety and liberty of his person. He has an equal property in the free use of his faculties and free choice of the objects on which to employ them. In a word, as a man is said to have a right to his property, he may equally be said to have a property in his rights.[2]

Chapters 6, 7, and 8 together contain a comprehensive and to my mind totally devastating critique of the theoretical structure presented by John Rawls in *A Theory of Justice.* But that critique is there presented piecemeal and in so far as it is relevant to wider discussions of the particular topics of those several chapters. So bringing the most fundamental objections together here should help to make the critique more effective.

The first step is to object that the title of the book by Rawls is in an important and very relevant way misleading. For his first half dozen pages make it absolutely clear that the book will be concerned exclusively not with old-fashioned, without prefix or suffix, justice, but with *social* justice. It was indeed precisely because so many people had for so long been eager to maintain that their preferred political and social policies constituted the achievement and/ or the maintenance of *social* justice that this book received such an extraordinary welcome on its first appearance and still continues to be more frequently referred to than any other contemporary work of moral and political philosophy.

The main reason why people are eager to describe their favorite policies as productive of a kind of justice is, of course, that this makes them appear to themselves and to others to be in unchallengeable occupation of the moral high ground. Yet Rawls nowhere does anything to warrant claims that social justice actually is a kind of justice—of justice as traditionally conceived and commended, that is. On the contrary: his own uneasiness—for deterministic reasons—about the applicability of the concept of desert and his failure to recognize the possibility of just entitlements which are neither creditably deserved nor discreditably undeserved leave him with no room at all for the idea of doing justice as traditionally conceived.

Most remarkably, and yet in the circumstances all too understandably, Rawls himself offers no definition of the word 'justice.' He must surely be the first author of a substantial treatise pretending to be about justice not to have done so. Instead it is only on his five hundred and seventy ninth page that he explains, without any suggestion of apology, that he was eager "to leave questions of meaning and definition aside and get on with the task of developing a substantive theory [not of 'social' justice but] of justice."[3]

The second necessary step is to recognize that "in the original position" the hypothetical social contractors of Rawls are "for simplicity . . . required to assume that the chief primary goods *at the disposition of society* are rights and liberties, *income and wealth* (ibid., p. 62: emphasis added). The only reason we are given for making this enormous socialist assumption is the commendably frank but otherwise inadequate admission that "We want to define the original position so that we get the desired solution" (ibid., p. 141). This solution, to no one's surprise, is that "the first principle of justice" is "one requiring an equal distribution" (ibid., p. 150-51).

To make this required assumption is in effect to assume that what is customarily called the national income is not, or at any rate ought not to be, what it actually is, namely the sum of all the incomes of all the individuals and all the businesses in the nation. It is instead to assume that it is, or at any rate ought to be, the income of that hypostatized collectivity the nation, or, rather, the state.

Consider, for example, this assumption as it was very clearly made in *An Approach to Social Policy*, an official document of the National Economic and Social Council of the Republic of Ireland, drafted for them by D. V. Donison and first published in 1975 by the Stationery Office in Dublin. From it we learn that that Council is by its terms of reference required to "promote social justice," which for its members apparently involves or simply is "the fair and equitable distribution of the income and wealth of the nation."

This first unargued assumption, that all income and wealth is available for redistribution free of any and all morally valid prior claims to ownership should have astonished anyone with a knowledge of what philosophers typically said about justice in previous centuries. For it is, surely, historically unprecedented. Hume, for instance, in dealing with property in three sections of the part of his *Treatise of Human Nature* which treats 'Of justice and injustice' makes no mention even of the theoretical possibility of the collective ownership of all the wealth in a nation.

The third necessary step is to recognize a second requirement imposed upon the Rawlsian hypothetical social contractors. The first requirement should certainly have astonished anyone with knowledge of what in the past philosophers typically said about justice and property. But readers astonished by that first requirement should be even more flabbergasted by the second. For, in explaining 'The Main Idea of the Theory' Rawls asserts that "Once we decide to look for a conception of Justice that nullifies the accidents of natural endowment and contingencies of social circumstances as counters in the quest for political and economic advantage, we are led to these principles. *They express the result of leaving aside those aspects of the social world that seem arbitrary from a moral point of view*" (ibid., p. 15: emphasis added).

Certainly, if all possible grounds for any differences in deserts and entitlements are thus to be dismissed as morally irrelevant, then, if anyone is to be allowed truly to deserve or to be entitled to anything at all, it does perhaps become obvious that everyone's deserts and entitlements must be equal. For it is precisely and only upon what individuals severally and individually have become and now are, as the result of their different genetic endowments and of their different previous experience and activities, that all their several and often very different present deserts and entitlements cannot but be based.

It is, for instance, only and precisely because one particular individual has justly acquired more property than another that their property rights, their property entitlements, have become unequal. Again it is only and precisely because one individual has committed a crime and another has not that their just deserts necessarily become unequal. It is, therefore, monstrous to dismiss such facts as irrelevant on the grounds that they are "arbitrary from a moral point of view." To seek "a conception of justice" which demands this dismissal is to seek something that is not justice at all. If this is indeed what is required by 'social justice' then 'social justice' is no more justice than People's Democracy is, or was, democracy.

Given the two requirements that Rawls imposes on his social contractors in the original position he cannot but refuse to admit the moral validity of any individual property rights, any individual property entitlements. But now, how is Rawls proposing to justify his own insistence on "the priority of liberty," the insistence that "each person is to have an equal right to the most extensive basic liberty compatible with a similar liberty for others" (ibid., p. 60) and that "each person possesses an inviolability founded on justice that even the welfare of society as a whole cannot override" (ibid., p. 3)?

Far be it from me to deny these claims, whatever I might want to say about their foundation. But for Rawls the insistence on the possession of these inviolable rights constitutes an unwitting admission of the actuality of some most fundamental entitlements which neither are nor could be either creditably deserved nor discreditably undeserved. And, if he were to go on to explore the kind of justifications for claims to the possession of such rights by the Founding Fathers of the American Republic and their contemporaries, then he would find that for them these rights to freedoms were essentially connected with property rights to their persons, to their individual talents, and to the products of the exercise of those individual talents.[4]

My concluding objection to the theory construction of Rawls is that it is based on two monster, not to say monstrous, assumptions. These are said, no doubt truly, to be necessary in order to produce the results that he desires. I am inclined to say that the first is simply unsupported while the second is simply insupportable. Yet without sufficient support for these two fundamental assumptions the whole system must surely collapse.

I am tempted to add, 'And good riddance.' For the unlovely dog-in-the-manger collectivism of Rawls's undertaking "to regard the distribution of natural abilities as a collective asset, so that the more fortunate are to benefit *only* in ways that help those who have lost out" (p. 179: emphasis and a comma added)—is manifestly inconsistent with his initial emphasis upon "the priority of liberty."

There is one recent, most illuminating work of what I should have wished to take account had I been rewriting the present book now. It is Thomas Sowell, *The Quest for Cosmic Justice* (New York: The Free Press, 1999). In it Sowell shows how a great variety of presently popular but ultimately, if not immediately, very damaging policies are products of attempts "to reintroduce concepts of moral responsibility and justice into the cosmos, seeking to rectify the tragic misfortunes of individuals and groups through collective action in the name of 'social justice' . . . this collective action is not limited to correcting the consequences of *social* decisions or other collective action, but extends to mitigating . . . the misfortunes of the physically and mentally disabled . . . In other words to seek to mitigate . . . the undeserved misfortunes arising from the cosmos, as well as from society. It seeks to produce *cosmic* justice . . ." (ibid., p. 5: emphasis original).

But cosmic justice like social justice is quite different from, even if not actually incompatible with, old fashioned, without prefix or suffix, justice. In so far as the former two are falsely assumed to be varieties of the latter the often inordinate costs of their attempted implementation are all too likely to be ignored. As Sowell insists "the question is not what we would do if we were God on the first day of Creation or how we would judge souls if we were God on Judgement Day. The question is: What lies within our knowledge and control, given that we are only human, with all the severe limitations which that implies?" (ibid., p. 21).

He himself proceeds to show in case after case that it is simply not possible for human policymakers to acquire the knowledge needed to do what might seem to be cosmic justice. And, furthermore, attempts to do it usually carry consequent costs which are or ought to be unacceptably heavy. "One of the many differences between human beings and God on Judgement Day is that God does not have to worry about what is going to happen the day after Judgement Day" (ibid., p. 22).

A key phrase in the quest for cosmic justice is "through no fault of their own." Individual human beings and sets of individual human beings have the different natural abilities and deficiencies which they do have, and they have suffered or benefited from the different upbringings which they have had, *through no fault of their own.*[5] But the fact that it is not the fault of the individuals who have been raised in some particular culture that they have been raised in that culture provides no justification either for ignoring the observed differences between the human products of one culture and another or for accepting the cultural relativists' claim that all cultures and all subcultures are equally good. They may all, for whatever that may be worth, be equally *good in themselves.* But it is a known and demonstrable falsehood to assert that they are all equally *good for all purposes.* Cultures, as Sowell has so abundantly demonstrated in his previous publications,[6] have consequences. Ignoring or denying these consequences does nothing to benefit those whose inherited cultures make it difficult to succeed in the societies to which they belong.

General rules, known in advance, are essential to the whole idea of the Rule of Law. But such rules are inherently incompatible with cosmic justice. For the Rule of Law requires that all relevantly like cases should be treated in the same way whereas cosmic justice apparently requires that all persons should be treated in the same way, equally regardless of what might otherwise be thought relevant differences between one individual person and another. Rules applicable to all equally are emphatically not the same as rules having an equal impact on all. Anatole France famously dramatized this distinction in the sarcastic remark that "The law in its majestic equality, forbids the rich as well as the poor to sleep under bridges, to beg in the streets and to steal bread." In today's American legal doctrine that is called 'disparate impact.' Many public and private acts and policies with such 'disparate impacts' on different subcategories of the American population are now banned as constituting hostile discrimination, despite the fact that—as the Rule of Law requires—these acts and policies apply the same procedures and standards to everyone. Sowell himself sadly sees these and other related legal developments as constituting—in the words of the title of his concluding chapter—'The Quiet Repeal of the American Revolution.'

There are, as was remarked earlier, several references in the text below which would have been appreciated by politically well-informed readers in 1989 but which may not be understood by younger readers today. The first is to an address by Janos Kadar in 1957 "one year after the friendly neighborhood tanks of imperial normalization had installed him in office" (p. 21). In 1956 an attempt by a new Communist leadership to emancipate Hungary was bloodily suppressed by the armed forces of the Soviet Union. 'Normalization' was the term introduced by Leonid Brezhnev to describe his military suppression of "the Prague Spring of 1968" (pp. 131-32), in which a new leadership of the Communist Party of Czechoslovakia attempted to introduce 'socialism with a human face.'

Younger readers will probably not be alone in failing to appreciate the claim that it was Lenin's "October Revolution rather than the National Socialist successor lauded by Leni Riefenstahl," which "truly was 'The Triumph of the Will'" (p. 67). For many who have heard of Nazis seem not to be aware that the full name of Adolf Hitler's party was 'The National Socialist German Worker's Party,' and that the achievement of that socialist aim was deferred rather than abandoned when Hitler and his party achieved power. Leni Riefenstahl was the maker of a brilliant film entitled 'The Triumph of the Will' about one of the spectacular annual Nuremberg rallies of that party.7

It may also be helpful to mention that Ernesto Che' Guevara (p. 48) was associated with Fidel Castro (p. 78) in establishing Communist Party rule in Cuba. Later, after his romantic death leading a small band of revolutionary fighters in Bolivia, he became a favorite pinup for leftist students the world over. Ho Chi Minh (p. 78) was the Communist leader of Vietnam. The "Small Helmsman" (p. 78) was the physically diminutive Deng Xiaoping, successor to Mao Tse Tung. Dr. Snezhnevsky (p. 104) was a psychiatrist in the service of the KGB, the secret police of the Soviet Union. A *Day in the Life of Ivan Denisovitch* (p. 107) was the first book about the Gulag

Archipelago—the enormous Soviet system of labor (often to death) camps—to be published by Alexander Solzenitsyn.

The reference to Stalin's Marxist claim that it is "Not abstract justice but socially necessary labor time' which justifies socialism!" (p. 157) has become not less but more topical with the passage of the years since the present book was written. For it was because President Reagan[8] recognized that the productivity of labor in the Union of Soviet Socialist Republics could not even begin to match much less exceed that in the United States of America that he was able, as Sowell reports, to declare:

> that he intended to win the arms race with the Soviet Union, because American resources greatly exceeded those of the USSR, so that Soviet leaders would ultimately be forced to the bargaining table to begin reducing their threatening nuclear arsenal and scale back their international aggressions. To the equal disbelief and disdain of many, he likewise said on more than one occasion that we are seeing the last days of the Soviet Union, which could not take the combined strains of their own counterproductive economic system and foreign military adventures (ibid., p. 111).

Antony Flew
Reading, England
November 1999

Notes

1. Compare, for instance, Tom Bethell, *The Noblest Triumph: Property and Prosperity through the Ages* (New York: St. Martin's Press, 1998), 86-87 and 171-20.

2. Quoted in Richard Pipes, *Property and Freedom* (New York: Kropf, 1999), xii. The same book provides (at pp. 211-13) a concise account of what later came to be described and dismissed as War Communism, an account which shows how right it was to assert that "Lenin in 1917" was "no more in possession of a clear design of the social order" which he wished to establish than "was Marx in the nineteenth century" (p. 87, below).

3. Had he cared to walk from his office across to the library of the Harvard Law School he could have read on its walls the version of the traditional definition given in the *Institutes* of Justinian. See p.120, below.

4. See the paragraph quoted above from James Maddison; also Pipes 1999, passim.

5. Obviously Sowell recognizes the similarity between this insistence and Rawls' insistence on seeking "a conception of justice that nullifies the accidents of natural endowment and the contingencies of social circumstances as counters in the quest for political and economic ad-

vantage." It is through seeking that that we are led to these principles. *"They express the result of leaving aside those aspects of the social world that seem arbitrary from the moral point of view"* (emphasis added).

6. See, for instance, his *Ethnic America: A History* (New York: Basic Books, 1981); and compare his trilogy *Race and Culture: A World View* (New York: Basic Books, 1994), *Migrations and Cultures: A World View* (New York: Basic Books, 1996) and *Conquests and Cultures: An International History* (New York; Basic Books, 1998).

7. Anyone interested in either the philosophy of Arthur Schopenhauer or the ideology of Adolf Hitler would be fascinated by reading Kimberley Cornish, *The Jew of Linz: Wittgenstein, Hitler and their Secret Battle for the Mind* (London: Random House Arrow, 1997), a work which tells of the influence of the former on the latter.

8. I always wanted to ask those outraged by his description of the USSR and its satellites as "the Evil Empire" to which of these two epithets they took exception. But I never received a straight answer. For some it was presumably the first since they were apparently prepared to excuse anything just so long as everything was socialized. (The Labour Party in the UK rescinded Clause IV of its Constitution—the clause stating that its aim was "the public ownership of all the means of production distribution and exchange"—only in 1995). For others it was perhaps the second, because they were unaware that such earlier Empires as the Roman and the British were not entirely ruled directly from the center but in part indirectly through subordinate local rulers. (One of these subordinate rulers in the Roman Empire was the Biblical King Herod).

Part I

Chapter one

The logic of liberty

Our hope that freedom is not going to be ultimately
destroyed by the joint pressure of totalitarianism and the
general bureaucratization of the world, and indeed our very
readiness to defend it, depends crucially on our belief that
the desire for freedom . . . is not an accidental fancy of
history, nor a result of peculiar social conditions or a
temporary by-product of specific economic life
forms . . . but that it is rooted in the very quality of being
human.

Attributed to Leszek Kolakowski
(Sometime Professor of Philosophy
in the University of Warsaw)

Before driving deeply into any intellectual territory it is prudent to
begin by achieving an overview of the main features of what
Gilbert Ryle used to call 'the logical geography'. Less picturesquely,
that is a matter of getting clear about the meanings of the crucial
terms, of learning to eschew the favourite fallacies, and of
emancipating ourselves from at least the commonest confusions.

In the present case this preliminary involves first distinguishing
two quite different yet not unrelated understandings of the words
'liberty' and 'freedom'; differences which can, of course, infect
also any of the many semantic associates of these two words.
Kolakowski's immediate concern was with the first of these two
understandings; with what – so long as we do not forget that
liberties may sometimes be sustained and sometimes restricted by

people and institutions not acting for the state – we can conveniently call political freedom.

In the second sort of understanding the words refer to what is usually dubbed the freedom of the will. It must indeed be very difficult, if not practically impossible, to become or to remain committed to the extension of political liberties and to the defence of political freedom so long as you refuse to recognize that the freedom of the will is indeed 'rooted in the very quality of being human'. I shall try to show that it is in fact so rooted; and, furthermore, that no one could contrive to understand the very words in which any denial of this fact has to be expressed without at the same time being in a position to know that that denial is mistaken. Chapter two will later be going on to argue that, if there is to be any respectable rationale for even the comparatively modest universal human rights claims of the American Declaration of Independence, it will have somehow to ground these claims upon this same fundamental and peculiar fact of our human nature.

The second task in chapter one will be to distinguish three equally different kinds of understanding of the word 'democracy'; and then to say something about the connections and lacks of connection, both necessary and contingent, between, on the one hand, various arrangements describable as democratic and, on the other hand, any particular liberties or sorts of liberties. How far, that is, do any of these sorts of arrangements in fact promote and maintain, and how far must they promote and maintain, any particular liberties or sorts of liberties?

1 Political freedom

In this first understanding, people are correctly described as being free or enjoying liberties inasmuch as and in so far as they are neither confined as prisoners nor constrained by formidable threats. Before proceeding to the freedom of the will it is worth spending a little time on a few of the commonest confusions. For these are often effectively exploited by the ideological enemies of political freedom.

(i)   At one point Hume suggests that a man is free so long as he is not 'a prisoner and in chains' (Hume 1748, VIII (i), p. 95). It would of course be the diametric opposite of the truth to assert of anyone who is 'a prisoner and in chains' that he or she is free and at liberty. But it would also be false to say of people who are not in any way prisoners, much less in chains, that they are free or at liberty to do particular things when the doing of those particular things would incur serious penalties; and this irrespective of whether those penalties would be imposed by law, or non-legally, or even illegally. It is because those who are not prisoners or in chains may still be in many respects unfree, and because too almost everyone is free in at least some respects although in at least some others not free, that it becomes best usually to speak of liberties or of freedoms in the plural, and to begin pedantically to particularize whenever clouds of confusion loom.

Paradoxes arise here because a person or a people may be free from one thing but not another, may enjoy these liberties but not those. Thus, notoriously, the citizens of countries which have achieved freedom from colonial rule may as individuals enjoy fewer legal liberties than they had under the old regimes; while, equally notoriously, the inhabitants of countries in what – because those countries have yet to be conscripted into 'the Socialist Camp' – can properly be called the (still) free world, may nevertheless be subject to other and sometimes comparably burdensome domestic oppressions. Notwithstanding that nowadays such questions seem to be favoured mainly by spokespersons striving to restrict or to devalue existing or expected liberties, it is almost always clarificatory to ask: 'What freedoms, freedom from what, and freedom for whom?'

(ii)   The eighteenth-century French *philosophe* Helvetius wrote: 'The free man is the man who is not in irons nor imprisoned in a gaol'. But he added both a third disjunct, 'not terrorized like a slave by the fear of punishment', and a caveat, 'it is not lack of freedom not to fly like an eagle or swim like a whale' (Berlin 1969, p. 122). A century earlier the most formidable of all English political thinkers, Thomas Hobbes, had produced an even terser epitome: 'A free man is he that . . . is not hindered to do what he hath the will to do' (Hobbes 1651, II (xxi)). It is a pity that he apparently failed to notice both that, always supposing that people would in fact intervene to constrain or coerce someone were some particular action to be performed, then that person must remain in that particular respect unfree; and that this is the case regardless of whether or not 'he hath the will to do' whatever it may be. A prisoner in gaol does not become at liberty to leave just because it so happens that he has no wish to do so. Both the contented and the discontented are, therefore, equally unfree.

The caveat which Helvetius enters is also important. For I may be free to do many things which it is, for various reasons, not in my power to do. The fact that I am incapable of flying like an eagle or even a butterfly may make my freedom to do these things worthless to me. But, since it does not constitute a ban on my doing them if only I could, this limitation is a limitation on my powers, not on my freedom.

Again we may – perhaps we should – sympathize with a scoffing at 'the majestic equality of the law that forbids the rich as well as the poor to sleep under bridges, to beg in the streets and to steal bread' (France 1894, p. 117). But a liberty which some of us or many of us either cannot or do not wish to use remains none the less a liberty. And we reasonably may, and in fact often do, resent the imposition of restrictions upon actions which we ourselves are either unable or else do not wish to take. For instance, resentment against the Group Areas Act in South Africa extends, and not unreasonably, far beyond the comparatively small numbers of those who might be able to afford to buy property in areas in which they are by that Act legally forbidden so to do.

Nor should we overlook the possibility that one set of people, the members of which do not themselves propose to take advantage of certain liberties, may nevertheless stand to gain in less direct ways from the general availability of these liberties. This is most importantly the case with the economic liberties which socialist or merely snobbish intellectuals are so inclined to despise. Like most academics, I myself have never established or engaged in any banausic commercial enterprise, and never shall. But I have benefited, and continue to benefit, from the facts: that there are already in most directions several suppliers competing for my custom – because it pays them to get it; and that my present suppliers are always, lest they become complacent or exploitative, under threat from the possible entry of further competition. A sovereign cure for the contempt of those minimizing the merits of markets and competition is a shopping expedition in People's Poland, preferably conducted after some instructive preliminary inquiry into the salaries paid to one's opposite numbers in that sadly impoverished country. (The reason for introducing the word 'set' in the previous paragraph was to avoid the different but uniformly unwanted implications of such terms as 'race', 'class', 'community', or 'group': by Cantor's Axiom for Sets the sole essential feature of a set is that its members have at least one common characteristic, any kind of characteristic.)

(iii)   Another rich source of confusion lies in the fact that there are those who want to restrict the word 'liberty' to those freedoms alone which they think that we ought to have; and which, if available, they think that we are morally required or at least entitled to exercise. Thus, in his essay on the *Tenure of Kings and Magistrates*, the poet and champion of the liberty of unlicensed printing John Milton wrote: 'None can love freedom but good men; the rest love not freedom but license' (Milton 1649). At the end of the following century men of quite another stamp, proto-Leninists of the French Jacobin clubs, used to say: 'No man is free in doing evil. To prevent him is to set him free.'

Any such recommendation for a change in our verbal usage should be rejected without hesitation. For it conceals the essential truth: even liberties which it was agreed that we ought not to have at all, or which no one, though having, ought to exercise, still remain, like any other liberties, absences of external coercion or constraint.

In the present context it is essential to insist upon that qualification 'external'. It is correct English, and often true, to say such things as: 'I was forced to do it, I had promised'; or 'I could not help myself, I felt so ashamed'. But these are constraints of a very different kind from the obstacles put in our way by other people. It is those last, and only those last, with which we are concerned here.

It may sometimes and for some people be the course of prudence to recognize that some kinds of external coercion or constraint may be irremovable, at least by them; and hence that, at least for them, it may be realistic to react by somehow abandoning or disengaging all those desires to the satisfaction of which the irremovable kinds of coercion or constraint constitute an obstacle. But what you become, by thus 'emancipating yourself from enslavement' to those unsatisfiable desires is most emphatically not, in the relevant respects and the relevant understanding, free or at liberty.

Certainly there was something magnificent in the deathbed

response of the Stoic sage Posidonius. Suffering agonies he insisted, as his philosophy required, that these, like everything else, were expressions of the Cosmic Reason; and therefore welcome: 'Do your worst, pain; no matter what you do, you cannot make me hate you.' (A good secondary account of Posidonius can be found in J. B. Bury's *Ancient Greek Historians* 1909.) Yet, whether or not this response is to be accounted a manifestation of the spiritual freedom of Posidonius, freedom in the political understanding neither is nor can be any kind of recognition of necessity. It is, rather, the opening of alternatives; whether these be good or bad, desired or undesired.

(iv) Liberties, though they can be secured only by powerful positive measures, are in themselves – like peace and health – essentially negative. In all three cases there is a temptation to argue that nothing so important and so good as freedom, or peace, or health, can in truth be merely negative. These misconceptions are then gleefully seized upon as offering opportunities for the misconceivers to commend their personal agenda as constituting the elements of *true*, *positive*, whichever it may be. It then emerges, in the present case, that a man is endowed with *positive* freedom not in so far as he 'is not hindered to do what he hath the will to do'; but inasmuch as he is in fact – perhaps more nilly than willy – behaving in some approved way.

Programmes for the promotion of particular sorts of behaviour – often programmes proposing the employment of every means of compulsion – can thus be commended as promising the realization of an alternative conception of *freedom*; an alternative supposedly superior, and hence referring to what alone is truly so describable. Gullible or sometimes perhaps themselves intentionally gulling interpreters are then all too ready to respond by misrepresenting thinkers who were in fact pursuing altogether different or actually incompatible ends as if these thinkers had been close political associates of the author of *On Liberty* (Mill 1859; cf., for instance, Singer 1980 and ch. four, below).

The truth is that 'positive' in the expression 'positive freedom' is what the Scholastics used to call an *alienans* adjective. Positive freedom is thus no more a kind of freedom than imaginary horses or incorporeal substances are sorts of horses or sorts of substances. Certainly it appears to be almost irresistibly tempting to assume that it is the positive-sounding terms 'liberty', 'peace', or 'health' rather than 'unfreedom', 'war', or 'disease' which are, so to speak, logically dominant. But again the truth is that here it is the seemingly negative notion rather than the apparently positive which – in J. L. Austin's memorably inelegant phrase – 'wears the trousers'. For, as the same sage continued, 'commonly enough the "negative" (looking) word marks the (positive) abnormality, while the "positive" word . . . merely serves to rule out the suggestion of that abnormality' (Austin 1970, p. 192; and, for applications of this contention to the other two cases cited, cf. Flew 1973a, *passim* and Flew 1987a, ch. 6).

Accepting such false assumptions, people will argue that their entire political and social agenda should be subsumed under what is presented as a properly positive conception of health, or peace, or liberty. Against this we have stubbornly to insist that 'Everything is what it is: liberty is liberty, not equality or fairness or justice or culture, or human happiness or a quiet conscience.' So, suppose that some of the other things commended in its name sometimes are, and perhaps even ought to be, bought at the price of less liberty. Then still 'the loss remains, and it is a confusion of values to say that although my "liberal" individual freedom may go by the board, some other kind . . . is increased' (Berlin 1969, pp. 125–6).

2 Freedom of the will

Turning now to the second sort of understanding of our two key terms, we may truly be said to be endowed with freewill when and in so far as – in a strong sense soon to be elucidated – we could do or could have done other than we do do or did do. The intended reference is to the familiar fact that, always throughout our waking lives, we are all of us agents; although the scope of that agency varies not only from one individual to another, but also, from time to time, in one and the same individual – whether in sickness or in health, whether in maturity or in senility. Necessarily, as agents, we can and cannot but make choices. Equally necessarily as agents, in a sense shortly to be elucidated, we always could do or could have done other than we do do or did do (Flew and Vesey 1987).

(i) What makes the use of the words 'free' and 'freewill' misleading here is the logical fact that all agency is not, as such and necessarily, free agency. For the man who receives from *The Godfather* 'an offer which he cannot refuse' is in a crucially different case from the errant mafioso who is without warning gunned down from behind. As the latter collapses into a pool of his own blood he simultaneously ceases both to live and to act. In that very collapse he is no longer an agent at all, but purely a patient. Contrast with him the unfortunate who is told that within thirty seconds either his signature or his brains will be on the document surrendering his property: 'Now choose!' Although in this transaction far from a free agent, he nevertheless remains an agent still.

He remains still an agent because, although the signing is most certainly not done of his own freewill, he did – in the more fundamental senses still to be elucidated – have a choice, and he could have done other than he did. Certainly, in the less fundamental but more common senses of these expressions, we do correctly say that people really had no choice or that they could not have done other than they did; when, although it is our belief that in those more fundamental senses they did or they could, nevertheless there were in fact no alternative courses of action open to them which – in either the descriptive or the prescriptive interpretations of 'expect' (Flew 1975, sections 5.9 and 6.11) – they could reasonably have been expected to adopt. These correct and idiomatic usages, like the philosophical abuses of the terms 'free' and 'freewill', are seriously misleading. For they draw our attention away from the essentials of agency.

(ii)   The better to appreciate what these essentials are, we need now to consult the great chapter 'Of power' in *An Essay concerning Human Understanding* (Locke 1690a, II (xxi)). It is as certain as without direct testimonial evidence this sort of thing can be that Hume had this chapter most in mind, perhaps even open before him, when in both the *Treatise* and the first *Enquiry*, he composed his enormously yet not always happily influential sections, 'Of the idea of necessary connexion' and 'Of liberty and necessity' (Hume 1739–40, I (iii) 14 and II (iii) 1–2, and Hume 1748, VII and VIII; also compare Flew 1986a, chs 5 and 8). A critical examination of this seminal chapter in Locke's *Essay*, together with an equally critical examination of the results of Hume's consequent meditations, can yield two very valuable trophies.

(a)   First, our study of these classical sources should in the end be sufficient to show us that we all have the most direct and the most inexpugnably certain experience: not only both of physical (as opposed to logical) necessity and of physical (as opposed to logical) impossibility; but also both of being, on some occasions, able to do other than we do do and of being, on other occasions, unable to behave in any other way than that in which we are behaving. Logical necessity and logical impossibility – with which physical necessity and physical impossibility are always implicitly or explicitly contrasted – are, of course, definable without direct reference to the non-linguistic world: one proposition follows from another with logical necessity if and only if to deny the one while asserting the other would be to contradict yourself; whereas a proposed project, or a supposed situation, is to be dismissed as logically impossible if and only if that very proposal, or that very supposition, is self-contradictory.

(b)   Second, once we are seized of these insights, we should be ready to recognize that there is no way in which creatures neither enjoying nor suffering experiences of both these two contrasting kinds could either acquire for themselves, or explicate to others, any of the corresponding notions. If this contention is indeed correct, then it must constitute an objection of overwhelming and decisive force against any doctrine of universal, physically necessitating, determinism. If it really is right, then no one could ever be in a position to assert that the entire universe is subject to universal and inexorable physical necessitation, without at the same time being in a position to know that any such assertion cannot but be false. For if the very ideas both of physical necessity, and of the ability to do other than we do do, both are, and can only be, acquired by references to our abundant experience of the two contrasting kinds of reality to which these ideas refer; then who but the most bigoted of behaviouristic psychologists could continue to insist that, *really*, even paradigm instances of the latter are covert cases of the former?

(iii)   Anyone inclined to doubt either the first or especially the second of these two findings should be challenged to excogitate their own explications of all the various notions in the kinds distinguished – including the intellectually indispensable concept, not so far explicitly mentioned, of the contrary-to-fact conditional.

A contrary-to-fact conditional is a proposition of the form: 'If this were to have happened (which, as a matter of fact, it did not), then that would have occurred.' Such propositions are relevant and of great importance because nomologicals (propositions stating what are thought to constitute laws of nature) can only be distinguished from merely material implications (propositions stating – without any implications about what might have been but in fact was not – only not-as-a-matter-of-fact-this-and-not-that) by the logical fact that they entail contrary-to-fact conditionals. Also implicit in the notion of nomological is the idea of physical necessity: it is precisely and only because to assert a nomological is to assert that certain relationships between sorts of logically possible events hold with physical necessity that we become licensed to infer contrary-to-fact conditionals from nomologicals.

Perhaps the challenge put at the beginning of the previous paragraph can, after all, be met. But, until and unless it is met, and met convincingly, the prudent philosopher is bound to adopt the archetypical attitude of the man from Missouri, who, notoriously, has to be shown! Our own assurance that these things just cannot be shown should be strengthened by considering why Hume failed to locate any suitable sort of parent experiences ('impressions') by reference to which the concepts ('ideas') of physical necessity and physical impossibility could have been legitimated.

This failure, like so much else which is most characteristic of Hume, is to be attributed to his misguided Cartesian insistence upon starting all his philosophical thinking from the position which Descartes reached at the end of the second paragraph of Part IV of the *Discourse on the Method*. Hume insisted, that is to say, upon thinking of himself as an essentially incorporeal and impotent subject of (always private) experience – as solely a bodiless observer, rather than as the flesh-and-blood observer-cum-agent which he was, and all of us are (Flew 1986a, *passim*). It is no wonder that such a pure observer was unable to detect in causation anything more than a relationship definable entirely in terms of exclusively material implications; a relationship involving no physical necessities, and carrying no consequences about the contrary-to-fact.

(iv) Locke, in the chapter 'Of power' was concerned solely with the sort of power which can be predicated only of people – or of such other putative, quasi-personal beings as the theist God, the Olympian gods, archangels, angels, devils, and other assorted disembodied or ever-bodiless spirits. Let us, therefore, attach to this first sort of power the label 'power (personal)'. In another sense, which is the only sense in which the word can be applied to inanimate objects and to most of animate nature, a power simply is a disposition to behave in such and such a way, given that such and such preconditions are satisfied. Thus we might say that the 'nuclear device' dropped at Nagasaki possessed an explosive power equivalent to that of so many tons of TNT, or that full-weight nylon climbing rope has a breaking strain of (a power to hold up to) 4,500 lb. Let us label this second sort of power 'power (physical)'.

A power (personal) is an ability at will either to do or to abstain from doing whatever it may be. Thus we might say that in his heyday J. V. Stalin had the power of life and death over every subject of the Soviet Empire, or that a fertile pair of people of opposite sexes have the power to start a baby. Locke, in three characteristically vivid passages, not only explicates both this idea and the contrasting concepts of physical necessity and physical impossibility, but also demonstrates that there can be no question but that all these ideas have abundant application. It is regrettable that Locke, in the third of the passages following, mistakes it that he is explaining what is meant not by 'an agent' but by 'a free agent':

> This at least I think evident, that we find in ourselves a Power to begin or forbear, continue or end several actions of our minds, and motions of our Bodies. . . . This Power . . . thus to order the consideration of any idea, or the forbearing to consider it; or to prefer the motion of any part of the body to its rest, and *vice versa* in any particular instance, is that which we call the Will.
>
> (Locke 1690a, II (xxi) 5, p. 236)

> Everyone, I think, finds in himself a Power to begin or forbear, continue or put an end to several Actions in himself. From the consideration of the extent of this power over the actions of the Man, which everyone finds in himself, arise the Ideas of Liberty and Necessity.
>
> (ibid., II (xxi) 7, p. 237)

> We have instances enough, and often more than enough in our own bodies. A Man's Heart beats, and the Blood circulates,

which 'tis not in his Power . . . to stop; and therefore in respect
of these Motions, where rest depends not on his choice . . . he is
not a free agent. Convulsive Motions agitate his legs, so that
though he wills it never so much, he cannot . . . stop their
motion (as in that odd disease called *chorea Sancti Viti*), but he
is perpetually dancing: He is . . . under as much Necessity of
moving, as a Stone that falls or a Tennis-ball struck with a
Racket.

    (ibid., II (xxi) 11, p. 239: the Latin means 'St Vitus' dance')

3 Deny freewill and disdain political liberty

If once we have recognized that we are indeed agents, who as such
can and cannot but make choices between alternative physically
possible courses of action or inaction, and who, also as such,
possess various kinds and amounts of power (personal); then it
becomes obvious, both that this complex fact is of enormous and
quite fundamental importance for our understanding of the nature
of man, and that it must have substantial bearing upon consequent
questions about which of our choices ought properly to be subject
to some external coercion or constraint, and how much and of
what kinds. Some years ago now, under the sinister yet altogether
fitting title *Beyond Freedom and Dignity*, the doyen of behaviouristic psychology, B. F. Skinner, made what his publishers
described as his 'definitive statement about man and society'. This
'definitive statement' provides abundant illustrative material under
both heads.

    (i)   Skinner's catastrophic, misguiding principle is that, to be
genuinely scientific, any study of man must eschew all anthropomorphic notions. The explicit and authoritative statement of this
grotesque general assumption is possibly more important than
anything else in the entire book. For Skinner is saying outright
what others more cautious leave implicit. He begins: 'We have
used the instruments of science; we have counted and measured
and compared; but something essential to scientific practice is
missing in almost all current discussions of human behaviour'
(Skinner 1971, p. 7).

    It appears that what is missing is, awkwardly, the absence of
certain notions which Skinner insists can have no place in any truly

scientific discourse. For, he continues; 'Although physics soon stopped personifying things . . . it continued for a long time to speak as if they had wills, impulses, feelings, purposes and other fragmentary attributes of an indwelling agent. . . . All this was eventually abandoned, and to good effect.' Nevertheless, deplorably, what should be 'the behavioural sciences still appeal to comparable internal states' (ibid., p. 8).

We are, therefore, supposed to regret that 'Almost everyone who is concerned with human affairs – as political scientist, philosopher, man of letters, economist, psychologist, linguist, sociologist, theologian, educator, or psychotherapist – continues to talk about human behaviour in this prescientific way' (ibid., p. 9). We all of us, that is to say, continue to ask for and to offer explanations of the conduct of agents in terms of the plans and the purposes, the desires and decisions, of those agents themselves. But 'A scientific analysis', we are told, 'shifts both the responsibility and the achievement to the environment' (ibid., p. 25).

So it is, it seems, unscientific to claim that anyone ever effected anything. Hence certain unnamed Freudians are rebuked for recklessly 'assuring their patients that they are free to choose among different courses of action and are in the long run the architects of their own destinies' (ibid., pp. 20–1). For Skinner as a psychological scientist the true causes of all human behaviour are, and can only be, both environmental and necessitating.

Certainly all such everyday discourse about the conduct of agents has to be prescientific in the obvious, purely temporal, sense that it was going on long before there was anything which deserved to be called science. Yet Skinner clearly takes it to be not only, innocuously, prescientific, but also, damagingly, unscientific. He takes it that it must be just as much a superstitious mistake thus to try to explain the actions of an actual person by reference to his will, impulses, feelings, and purposes as it undoubtedly would be first to personify some inanimate object, and then to undertake to explain its movements in the same sort of way. However, the reason why the latter enterprise would be superstitious and a mistake is, of course, that inanimate objects are not people or even brutes; and hence do not and cannot have wills, impulses, purposes, or any other such anthropomorphic attributes. But the former undertaking is, by the same token, neither superstitious nor a mistake. So any psychological programme committed to maintaining the contrary is, by that preposterous commitment alone, sufficiently discredited.

The first reason why Skinner believes that he has to embrace this absurdity is, as we have just seen, that he misconstrues the expulsion of such notions from physics as the repudiation of essentially superstitious ideas, rather than as the rejection of misapplications of ideas in themselves entirely proper, indeed indispensable. The second reason is more particular. He sees all these ideas as involving and involved in what is for him an utterly unacceptable concept, 'autonomous man'. This is something of which he has much to say in *Beyond Freedom and Dignity*. But the most revealing statement is put into the mouth of Frazier in chapter 29 of Skinner's earlier utopian novel *Walden Two*: ' "I deny that freedom exists at all. I must deny it or my programme would be absurd. You can't have a science about a subject matter which hops capriciously about." '

On the contrary: it is Skinner's actual programme which truly is absurd; a programme for erecting a science of human behaviour upon the false and perversely factitious assumption that all behaviour is physically necessitated, and none of it the conduct of agents who always as such could do other than they in fact do do. Skinner is wrong too in insisting that to admit the reality of agency must be to foreclose on the possibility of discovering causes and developing a science.

The first essential here is to distinguish two crucially different senses of the word 'cause'. Such a distinction was suggested by Hume. But, having earlier denied the legitimacy of any conception of physical necessity, he had disqualified himself from admitting what is for us the crux. In his essay 'Of national characters' he wrote: 'By *moral* causes I mean all circumstances, which are fitted to work on the mind as motives or reasons. . . . By *physical* causes I mean those qualities of the air and climate, which are supposed to work insensibly on the temper, by altering the tone and habit of the body' (Hume 1741–77, p. 198).

This distinction between two senses of the word 'cause' is at the same time a distinction between the different subject materials of the physical and the human sciences – what Hume would have called the moral sciences (Flew 1986a, chs 5 and 8; and compare Flew 1985, *passim*). For there is an absolutely fundamental difference between, on the one hand, ensuring that some person will act in one particular way by providing them with some overwhelmingly strong reason so to do; and, on the other hand, making some purely physical phenomenon happen by bringing about the causally sufficient conditions of its occurrence. That absolutely fundamental difference is that, whereas such sufficient physical causes necessarily necessitate the occurrence of their effects, correspondingly sufficient moral causes do not. If, for instance, I convey to you some splendid news – news which, if you decided to celebrate, you and everyone else would point to as the cause of that celebration – then I do not by so doing ensure that you must, willy-nilly, make whoopee. Actions which are thus caused by moral causes are neither uncaused nor necessarily capricious and inexplicable; although, inasmuch as they are indeed actions, it is impossible for them to be physically necessitated. It is equally mistaken to assume – as most professing social scientists, apparently, do assume – that all environmental causes are, in the sense explained, physical, and therefore physically necessitating.

(ii)   Since he outright denies the reality of agency and choice, Skinner is bound to make a shambles of all the crucial distinctions. And so he does. In subsection (i) of this section 3 we attended to what he insisted must be the necessary presuppositions of a science of psychology. But his chief concern, not only in *Walden Two* but also in *Beyond Freedom and Dignity*, is with the application of that science; which nowadays he writes as if we already have – or, at any rate, as if he already has. Thus the later book begins with a review of 'the terrifying problems that face us in the world today'. It then proceeds to argue that to solve these 'we need to make vast changes in human behaviour'; so that 'what we need is a technology of behaviour'. He eventually concludes: 'A scientific view of man offers exciting possibilities. We have not yet seen what man can make of man' (Skinner 1971, pp. 3, 4, 5, and 215).

We have to recognize, what is not immediately obvious from this latest statement, that Skinner's political programme is both authoritarian and elitist (Flew 1987b, ch. 3.3); although it is in our time unusual among such programmes in owing nothing to Lenin. The crux is to appreciate that the words 'we' and 'man', upon which so much depends, are not always used to refer to exactly the same sets. Earlier, in chapter 31 of *Walden Two*, Frazier made exactly this point, with characteristic frankness: ' "When we ask what Man can make of Man, we don't mean the same thing by

"Man" in both instances. We mean to ask what a few men can make of mankind. And that's the all-absorbing question of the twentieth century. What kind of world can we build – those of us who understand the science of behaviour?" '

(a)   Several elements in the answer to this key question are revealed in *Beyond Freedom and Dignity*. First, Skinner refuses to recognize any real difference between a set-up in which abortion is illegal and one in which it is not. In the latter case, 'The individual is "permitted" to decide the issue for himself [*sic*], simply in the sense that he [*sic*] will act because of consequences to which legal punishment is no longer to be added' (Skinner 1971, p. 97). It is, of course, about precisely this, to Skinner, entirely insubstantial difference that the legalization versus criminalization battles rage.

(b)   Second, he considers 'the practice of inviting prisoners to volunteer for possibly dangerous experiments – for example, on new drugs – in return for better living conditions or shorter sentences'. He asks, rhetorically, 'but are they really free when positively reinforced?' (ibid., p. 39). Since positive reinforcement is Skinner's technical way of talking about the promised rewards the correct answer is, clearly, 'Yes.' The contrast is, for instance, with those prisoners in Belsen and Dachau who were forced to become subjects for medical experimentation; with no alternative choice, and without promise of reward.

(c)   Third; 'A person never becomes truly self-reliant. Even though he deals effectively with things, he is necessarily dependent upon those who have taught him to do so' (ibid., p. 91). But what self-reliance excludes is present dependence, not having been so educated in the past that you have now become self-reliant.

(d)   Fourth, and finally, Skinner refuses to allow any important difference between persuasion by the giving of reasons and 'persuasion' by forcible methods of mind-bending: ' "Brain-washing" is proscribed by those who otherwise condone the changing of minds, simply because the control is obvious' (ibid., p. 96). But the issue – examined in chapter five, below – does not concern what is overt as opposed to what is covert. It is, rather, a matter of giving or not giving what are, or are thought to be, good reasons; as well as of employing or not employing force and the threat of force. (No doubt the whole business of giving and considering reasons is out of place and unfamiliar in and around the rat cages and pigeon lofts of a Skinnerian psychology laboratory.)

Politically libertarian hopes perhaps rise a little when we read: 'Permissive practices have many advantages.' Any such hopes are soon dashed: 'Permissiveness is not, however, a policy; it is the abandonment of policy, and its apparent advantages are illusory. To refuse to control is to leave control not to the person himself, but to other parts of the social and non-social environments' (ibid., p. 84).

This statement is on two counts obnoxious. First, even if I have got to be controlled either by a person or by impersonal forces, still the difference between these alternatives matters enormously. If, for instance, I suffer something painful I am much less upset if I believe this to be the result of blind forces than if I believe it to be someone's malign intention. (This is one reason why a moment's thought makes the ideal of a totally planned society so repellent to all but those who see themselves as the total planners; and, correspondingly, so endlessly enchanting to actual or aspiring members of such power elites.)

Second, Skinner's contention that leaving control to the person himself is an illusion is supported only by his insistence that the true and always necessitating causes of human behaviour are, and can only be, environmental. This popular misconception has been demolished already. Furthermore, it is a misconception peculiarly incongruous with the present proposal; the proposal, that is, that the unenlightened laity should be controlled by the psychologically illuminated elite. For how, upon Skinnerian principles, can it be right to say that in Skinner's utopia it would be Skinner's Controllers who would be controlling the lesser breeds; rather than the environment of the Controllers which would be ultimately controlling everybody?

4 Liberties and democracies

Most of us associate democracy very closely with liberty; we are even inclined to employ expressions like 'a free society' or 'a democratic society' almost interchangeably. It is right to be curious about the nature of any connections between the two. Having become rather clearer about liberty the next step must be to examine ideas of democracy.

(i) In his wittily entitled *Sense and Sensibilia* 'the implacable Professor' J. L. Austin picked out 'democracy' as an example of 'a notoriously useless word' (Austin 1962, p. 144). In this he was, for once, quite ruinously wrong: persistently and systematically abused, yes; useless, most emphatically not. For it is the only or the best available word for saying various very important things. We need to discover what these things are by distinguishing, if not three precise senses, at any rate three areas of meaning. We can find mnemonic labels for these in the concluding resolution of Abraham Lincoln's Gettysburg Address: 'that governments of the people, by the people, for the people, shall not perish from the earth'.

(a) First in that order is the understanding in which the word has no essential reference to anything political. The big *Oxford English Dictionary* glosses this, with little enthusiasm: 'In modern use often more vaguely, denoting a social state in which all have equal rights, without hereditary, or arbitrary, differences of rank or privilege.' It is with this sort of concern, usually, that people speak of democratizing an educational institution or a department of state. So democracy here is, in a sense, 'of the people', but in this understanding it has few, if any, necessary connections with the government of anything.

(b) Next in the present ordering, although in every other way primary, there come the applications to methods of making state or, more generally, group decisions. If some group as a whole takes decisions by majority vote, then that is democratic. So, too, are institutions under which decisions are made by delegates, representatives, or officers who can all in due course be voted out.

Two points require immediate further attention. First, notice the heavy non-paternalist emphasis upon what the voters themselves decide as opposed to what they might, by others, be supposed to need or what it may or may not be in their interests to have. Second, notice the emphasis upon voting out, not voting in. It is sometimes urged as a paradox of democracy that an electorate may give a majority to a party intending to make that the final free election. It is remarked much less often that there are parallel paradoxical possibilities with every other form of government: an oligarchy might conceivably decide to hand over the sovereignty either to a dictator or to the populace, and so on. However, if, as I suggest, we adopt as part of our criterion of democratic legitimacy the possibility of – in a good old phrase – 'voting the scoundrels out' then we shall not be committing ourselves to accepting, as democrats, the verdict of what was intended to be the final free election. In this more sophisticated understanding the guarantee of future free elections, and hence the permanent possibility of reversals, are elements of the essence of democracy.

It is, therefore, an affront to democracy for any party to threaten irreversible changes, as in the 1970s and 1980s one of Britain's two parties of government has taken to doing. The democratic alternative is to promise measures which, once implemented, you hope and expect that almost no one will want to undo. In an earlier and happier period it was the sometime Labour Prime Minister, Lord Attlee, who therefore insisted: 'Democracy is not a one-way street.'

(c) The importance of the earlier emphasis upon what the voters themselves decide emerges most fully when we enter the third area of meaning: not 'of the people'; nor 'by the people'; but 'for the people'. Labels like 'German Democratic Republic' or 'People's Democratic Republic of the Yemen' become ever more common. Those devoted to democracy in our second understanding may too quickly put down these employments of the term as just so much flagrantly mendacious propaganda. But that is not the whole story, and for us now the other part is the more important.

Consider two revealing and authoritative statements. The first was made by Janos Kadar, addressing the Hungarian National Assembly on 11 May 1957, one year after the friendly neighbourhood tanks of imperial normalization had installed him in office. The second comes from Abdul Kharume, First Vice-President of Tanzania, and it was made on 7 July 1967 at the anniversary celebrations of the ruling and, of course, only legal party on the Tanzanian mainland. Abdul Kharume, who has since been assassinated, was, as his Afro-Shirazi party in Zanzibar still is, strongly influenced by advisers from Soviet Germany. The Tanzanian government had recently rounded up everyone in Dar-es-Salaam without visible means of support and driven them out into the countryside. The two statements ran:

The task of the leaders is not to put into effect the wishes and will of the masses. . . . The task of the leaders is to accomplish the interests of the masses. Why do I differentiate between the will and the interests of the masses? In the recent past we have encountered the phenomenon of certain categories of workers acting against their interests.

Our government is democratic because it makes decisions in the interests of, and for the benefit of, the people. I wonder why men who are unemployed are surprised and resentful at the Government . . . sending them back to the land for their own advantage.

It is evident that Comrade Kadar and Comrade Kharume were not even pretending to be democrats in any sense of our second sort. On the contrary: they made it utterly clear that for them the crux was, not what some popular electorate actually has decided or will decide, but what satisfies the needs or serves the interests or expresses the real will of the people; while for them too what so satisfies or serves or expresses, and who is to count as truly of the people, is for the party elite to decide. We shall in chapter three, below, be scrutinizing a sophisticated classical source for ideas of this sort.

Some of the modern expressions can provide a moment of wry comic relief. Thus Noam Chomsky – not only famous for his contributions to Lingustics but also notorious for the furies of his Leninism – did not scruple to write, 'the people of Vietnam (the Communists, that is)' (Chomsky 1969, p. 14). Again, during the rule of President Allende, the pro-Communist and hence then the pro-government daily *Puro Chile* announced what it found the disappointing results of inadequately rigged legislative elections under a memorable heading: 'The People: 43%. The Reactionaries: 55%' (Moss 1973, p. 23).

(ii) It would seem that, when the word 'democracy' is understood in either the first or the third of the three sorts of ways distinguished in the previous subsection, there are no connections, either logically necessary or logically contingent, between liberties for individuals and arrangements thus describable as democratic. It is in the second sort of understanding that there are connections of both kinds.

(a) First, it is obvious that there is a logically necessary connection between democracy in an understanding of this second sort and certain minimum individual political liberties. These are the liberties which are the conditions of its being truly said that citizens make and implement their voting decisions freely. They must include, for a start, obviously, guarantees against intimidation. Again, it must be possible to get and to spread relevant information, to discuss issues with other people, and to organize opposition. Exactly what and how much should be included under this head it is here neither necessary nor possible to decide. But that quite a lot is essential can be appreciated by reflecting on how in many countries, which do regularly conduct what they call elections, these proceedings are rendered altogether empty by the lack of such guarantees and such possibilities. What sort of electoral decision can a voter be making when, for instance, every channel of information is controlled by the monopoly governing party; and when there can be – as under full socialism – no unofficial and privately owned presses, or even duplicators?

(b) Second, there is a very strong case for thinking that a generally pluralist economic foundation, and the various economic liberties which this requires, is, while certainly not sufficient, a contingently necessary condition for democratic politics. The theoretical case has been made by Hayek (1944) and Friedman (1962), while during the late seventies it constituted the main message in Sir Keith Joseph's mission to the universities. Can it really be nothing but a chance quirk of history that, among all the now numerous countries which have become as near as makes no matter fully socialist, there is no case of any opposition party being allowed even to organize and contest a general election, much less to take office as a result of winning?

Certainly the Institute of Marxism–Leninism in Moscow is happy to recognize that, in a favourite Soviet phrase, 'it is no accident'. In 1971, with their eyes most immediately upon Chile and France, they sketched a programme for achieving, through 'United Front' or 'Broad Left' tactics, irreversible Communist domination: 'Having once acquired political power, the working class implements the liquidation of the private ownership of the means of production. . . . As a result, under socialism, there remains no ground for the existence of any opposition parties counter-balancing the Communist Party' (quoted, with full reference supplied, in Flew 1981, pp. 44–5 and 189).

(c) Certainly democracy in any understanding of our second sort logically presupposes fairly extensive political liberties. There also seems to be good reason for believing that it is in practice incompatible with the maintenance of a fully socialist command economy. But it is important to recognize that decisions democratically reached, and democratically reversible, may grossly restrict both the liberties and the powers of individuals.

It is manifest that this applies to the UK today, under a system described by one former Lord Chancellor as 'elective dictatorship'; a system in which nowadays parties winning a little less or a little more than 40 per cent of the votes cast in the last general election, and hence a very much smaller proportion of the votes of the qualified electorate, boast that they have mandates to force through every policy proposed in their extensive election manifestos. (The 1935 General Election was the most recent to give the incoming administration a majority, however narrow, of all the votes cast.)

But the possibility of such gross legal restrictions of the liberties and powers of individuals would still remain, although it would no doubt be realized much less often, under a different, fairer, and indeed more democratic system: a system, that is, with electoral laws ensuring that no government could attain office without actual majority support; and perhaps providing also that referenda must be held on particular legislative proposals against which some specified large number of electors chooses to petition. Dedicated as they were to securing liberties demanded in the Declaration of Independence, the Founding Fathers of the USA became almost obsessively aware of the danger that majorities in sovereign assemblies will exploit and oppress minorities, and will restrict liberties (Vieira 1979). That is why they created, as American conservatives love to say, not a democracy but a republic. That is the reason too for most of the entrenchments, above all the entrenchment of the amendments known collectively as the Bill of Rights. It is also the reason why many in Britain who hold to similar ideals of liberty have recently begun to worry the ideas of writing the previously unwritten constitution, and of entrenching into that new written and justiciable constitution a new British Bill of Rights.

However fully democratic a system is, and however fully everyone is able to and does participate, it remains true that, if a majority does not want anyone to be free in certain respects, or wants some practically incompatible something else more, then decisions can be taken and laws passed which will restrict everyone's liberty in that direction; and this without any compensating gain of more liberty for all in some other direction. Consider, for example, those who want to impose a uniform regimen of universal, compulsory – maybe also unstreamed and unsetted – comprehensive education; and/or those who want to take legislative or fiscal steps to destroy all the remaining private schools.

That places in these are not available to all but only the children of that minute minority of parents able and willing to pay twice for their children's education – once through general taxation and then again in particular school fees – is seen as intolerable and 'divisive' privilege. It is revealing that this is taken as a reason, not for trying to ensure that all parents get their equal chances to choose – perhaps by developing an educational voucher system – but rather for insisting that no one at all should ever again enjoy such a liberty, much less possess the power to make use of it. It is also significant that, while those who think only of defending the existing independent schools see themselves as simply defending an existing liberty, those who want also to extend to all parents the possibility of choosing an independent education for their children have adopted the slogan: 'Power to the parents!' (Flew 1987a).

Although the Labour Party has for several years been most categorically committed to the socialist policy of establishing a total state monopoly in the supply of primary and secondary educational services, there is excellent reason to believe that this particular policy is not at present supported by a majority even of those who in general elections vote for the candidates of that party. But this, for reasons indicated already, provides no guarantee that such policies will not be intolerantly implemented by some future administration claiming to have a popular mandate, and perhaps eventually enjoying majority support for that implementation. We have therefore one more occasion for pondering two wise warnings, the first from *The Rights of Man*, and the second from *On Liberty*:

It is not because a part of the government is elective that makes it less a despotism, if the persons so elected possess afterwards, as a parliament, unlimited powers. Election, in this case, becomes separated from representation, and the candidates are candidates for despotism.

(Paine 1791–2, IV, p. 281)

The 'people' who exercise the power are not always the same people with those over whom it is exercised; and the self-government spoken of is not the government of each by himself, but of each by all the rest.

(Mill 1859, p. 67)

Chapter two

Could there be universal natural rights?

The State of Nature has a Law of Nature to govern it, which obliges every one: And Reason, which is that Law, teaches all Mankind, who will but consult it, that being all equal and independent, no one ought to harm another in his Life, Health, Liberty, or Possessions.

John Locke, (1690b)
The Second Treatise of Government, Section 6

We hold these truths to be self-evident, that all men are created equal, that they are endowed by their Creator with certain unalienable Rights, that among these are Life, Liberty and the pursuit of Happiness.

The American Declaration of Independence

Right is the child of law; from real laws come real rights, but from imaginary law, from 'laws of nature', come imaginary rights. Natural rights is simple nonsense, natural and imprescriptable rights, rhetorical nonsense, – nonsense upon stilts.

Jeremy Bentham,
Anarchical Fallacies (II, p. 501)

The concern of the present chapter is precisely and only with what the American Declaration of Independence held to be self-evident, and what Jeremy Bentham put down as 'rhetorical nonsense, nonsense upon stilts'. It is not with those rights which are in fact realized or recognized, endorsed or created, by various systems of positive law. It is instead with natural rights, and then only with such of these as may or might be universal. It is with rights, that is, inasmuch and in so far as these either do serve or could serve as a basis for criticizing, both types or tokens of individual conduct, and general principles or particular prescriptions of positive law. Such moral criticism must result in commending whatever respects, and condemning whatever violates, whatever natural and universal rights there are.

The modal form of the title question is also significant. For the answer to be given in the end is not an unqualified and categorical affirmation that there actually are any such universal natural rights. Instead the present chapter, by indicating the lines on which we might develop a rationale for the particular conclusions which the Signers asserted to be self-evident, will be making a case for saying only that there could be. The least qualified and most categorical contention of the whole chapter will be that, whereas this development may be and hopefully is possible, what must remain out of the question is the erection of a similarly systematic rationale for any of the miscellanies of additional rights proclaimed by the UN and other organizations since the Second World War.

1 The objectivity of natural rights

The first point to seize about natural rights is that they are always thought of, and appealed to, as being both universal and somehow objective: universal inasmuch as they are supposed to be the rights of all, at all times, and in all places; and objective in the somewhat artificial sense of being altogether independent of all particular individual or collective wishes, interests or decisions. This last is the reason why so many modern-minded people are inclined to follow Bentham in dismissing the whole business. The point has been well put by one who claims to be himself *Taking Rights Seriously*: 'A great many lawyers are wary of talking of moral rights, even though they find it easy to talk about what it is right or wrong for governments to do, because they suppose that rights, if they exist at all, are spooky sorts of things that men have in much the same sort of way that they have non-spooky things like tonsils' (Dworkin 1977, p. 139).

No doubt there is room for discussion about exactly how far and in what ways having a natural right is, or would be, like having tonsils. But the wary lawyers of whom Dworkin speaks are not wrong in thinking that an affirmation of such rights is an affirmation that there are certain entitlements which are endowed with a peculiar kind of objectivity; a kind certainly not possessed of necessity by any particular prescriptions of merely human, and hence limited and always more or less ephemeral, positive law. This idea of a peculiar kind of objectivity is, surely, implicit both in Locke's contention that certain fundamental negative norms are revealed by Reason and in the later, American, claim that what is thus revealed is self-evident truth. Exactly, or even roughly, how such things can be is no doubt obscure. It is also for present purposes unfortunate that the Declaration of Independence speaks of its natural rights as an endowment from the Creator, thus suggesting that these moral rights must be, if only under the Divine Law, legal also. But what does come out with total clarity is that the Founding Fathers here saw themselves as asserting general truths rather than making particular demands, as reporting revelations of the natural light rather than announcing decisions of revolutionary policy.

(i)   It seems, therefore, that the first essential of any natural right is that it must possess this special kind of objectivity. Hence, if anyone is going to maintain, against Bentham and so many others, that there are such rights, then they have somehow got to show both how this can be possible, and that it is the case. It appears that in the past these were often not seen to be problems or, if they were so seen, they were considered to be soluble – as the Signers thought to solve them – by some reference to the Creator. In the Declaration itself the reference is perfunctory. But in that same year 1776 John Adams was speaking of 'Rights antecedent to all earthly government – Rights that cannot be repealed or restrained by human laws – Rights derived from the great Legislator of the universe' (quoted Corwin 1955, p. 79). Our natural and unalienable rights are thus endowments from God, and their objectivity is taken to be the objectivity of a prime theological fact.

That is a kind of fact, or a putative kind of fact, which Dworkin's wary lawyers might perhaps be pardoned for eschewing as 'spooky'. But we have to object to this move here on a quite different ground: neither maintaining, as atheists, that there are no positive theological facts, nor, as agnostics, contending that, even if such there be, it is impossible for us to know what they are. Our present objection has to be that rights originally conferred under God's prescriptive and positive law would not be rights of the kind presently under discussion. They could not, that is to say, be rights by reference to which all prescriptions of positive law – repeat, all – might in principle be criticized.

The heart of this particular matter of logic was first laid bare in Plato's *Euthyphro*. If you define a word such as 'good' in terms of the will of God, then you thereby disclaim all possibility of praising that will as itself good. So the words 'God is good' become on your lips the expression of only the most empty and formal of made-to-measure or, as North Americans say, custom-built necessary truths (Flew 1971, pp. 26–33). The classic treatise on *The Law of War and Peace* makes it clear that Grotius was master of the crucial points. He was of course writing in general about the law of nature, not particularly about rights arising either under that law or independently of it. He stresses what he sees as its necessary objectivity: its principles, 'if only you pay strict heed to them, are in themselves manifest and clear, almost as evident as the things we perceive by the external senses; and the senses do not err if the organs of perception are properly formed and if the other conditions requisite to perception are present' (Grotius 1625, p. 23).

He then goes on to insist that this objective law is no sort of function or creature of the will of God:

> The law of nature is a dictate of right reason, which points out that an act, according as it is or is not in conformity with rational nature, has in it a quality of moral baseness or moral necessity; and that, in consequence, such an act is either forbidden or enjoined by the author of nature, God. The acts in regard to which such a dictate exists are, in themselves, either obligatory or not permissible, and so it is understood that necessarily they are enjoined or forbidden by God.
>
> (ibid., pp. 38–9)

The last and most emphatic words, insisting both on the objectivity of the law of nature and on its original independence from the will of the Creator, draw a comparison with the truths of logic and pure mathematics: 'The law of nature, again, is unchangeable – even in the sense that it cannot be changed by God. . . . Just as even God . . . cannot cause that two times two should not make four, so

He cannot cause that that which is intrinsically evil be not evil' (ibid., p. 40).

Before leaving both Grotius and the rejected suggestion that moral rights could be creatures of the Creator's will, there are two things to underline: one encouraging, and the other discouraging. First, both in identifying prescriptive laws of nature as dictates of right reason and in comparing them with the truths of pure mathematics Grotius can be seen as indicating – a century before Kant was born – a Kantian route towards the solution of our objectivity problem. That problem, in correspondingly Kantian terms, is to show how universal natural rights are possible – how there can be such Popperian Third World entities as objective entitlements (Popper 1979). Second, in insisting that actions have in them 'a quality of moral baseness or moral necessity', that they are, in themselves, either not permissible or obligatory, Grotius can be seen as signposting, before the birth of G. E. Moore – this time not one but two and a half centuries before – what we must surely recognize to have been a blind alley. For what are these intrinsic characteristics if not the simple, non-natural qualities of *Principia Ethica* – qualities which must as 'non-natural' be paradigmatically 'spooky' (Moore 1903).

(ii)   The enormous obstacle obstructing any attempt to show how (moral) rights can possess the required kind of objectivity, and to show that and what these rights are, is the whole great Humean tradition of philosophy and social science. Epitomized in the proverbial nutshell, it is the glory of Hume to have developed a world-outlook through and through secular, this-worldly, and man-centred. To us the most relevant aspect of all this is Hume's anti-Copernican counter-revolution. Copernicus was said to have knocked man and his earth from the centre of the universe by revealing that what appears to be the diurnal circulation of the heavens above us and around us really is a movement of our own peripheral planet. Hume took as his model a supposed discovery of the new science of Galileo and Newton, the supposed discovery that secondary qualities are not really qualities of things in themselves, but are instead reactions in our own minds, reactions which, by a false projection, we commonly but mistakenly attribute to those things. Guided or misguided by this seductive model Hume hoped to demonstrate that the same applies to much else which we might uninstructedly have believed to be characteristic of the Cartesian external world; namely, causal connection; the necessity of descriptive laws of nature; and moral and aesthetic values (Flew 1986a, chs 8–10).

In this Humean perspective it becomes almost impossible to admit as objective anything but straightforward, unspooky matters of natural fact about that external world; while the norms and values which are somehow projected functions of individual or collective human desire appear as correspondingly subjective. It is easy then to proceed, although Hume himself would never have dreamed of so proceeding, to the demoralizing conclusion that the are as such to be despised and dismissed as *merely* human creations (Flew 1971, pp. 81–5). It is upon philosophical assumptions of this kind, and in the same sort of understanding of the findings of the social sciences, that today so many of the young, and of the not so young, believe that the slightest tincture of anthropology or sociology is enough to expose all value judgement as inherently and essentially arbitrary, relative, and subjective (ibid., ch. 4).

If we are to succeed in showing how natural rights are possible, by providing for them the required kind of objectivity, then we have either to circumvent or to overcome the particular subjective/objective dichotomy which is the form of representation in the previous paragraph. We have to find a way in which something can be objective, in the relevant though artificial sense of being independent of our self-interested and capricious wills, while at the same time in some way authoritative over those wills; and all this without simply being just one more brute fact about the material universe.

Here it should be instructive to ponder again the last words quoted earlier from Grotius. For logically necessary truths are objective in precisely the sense just explained, and they neither are nor state facts about either human or non-human nature. Yet this is notwithstanding that it is a matter of individual or collective human choice what concepts we use, and what words we employ to express those concepts. But what is not a matter of choice, whether human or Divine, is what does or does not follow necessarily from propositions embracing the concepts chosen. We have here, therefore, truths which are in the required sense objective. For, if the conclusion does follow necessarily, then the proposition stating that this is so is itself a logically necessary truth.

Of course the general claim that there are natural rights, as well as less general claims about the subsistence of this or that particular right, seem to be far removed from the abstract truths of logic and mathematics. Nevertheless, and without aspiring to produce the sort of system of casuistical moral geometry once envisioned by Locke (Locke 1690a, II (iii) 18–19), it may begin to look as if, given the basic concepts of morality, it might be possible to deduce some conclusions about universal natural rights. Let this reference to these other examples of the sort of objectivity which we are seeking serve to encourage our philosophical investigations.

The suggestion is not so much that claims to universal natural rights constitute logically necessary truths – QED; but rather that logically necessary truths do at least have the right sort of objectivity, something which might eventually be shown to characterize those claims also. This suggestion, for better or for worse, parallels that which inspired Plato, once he had persuaded himself that his Forms or Ideas must constitute one class of eternal and immaterial substances, to wonder whether individual human souls might not constitute another such class (Flew 1987b, ch. 3 section 4).

2 The groundedness of all rights

The first conceptual truth about possible natural rights is that they must be entitlements possessing a certain kind of objectivity. The second, and this is a truth about all rights, is that they must be entitlements grounded in – which is not to say deduced from – some fact or facts about their bearers. Suppose that two bearers of rights are to be said to have different rights. Then this difference has to be justified by reference to some dissimilarity between what each has done, or suffered, or is. Suppose, on the other hand, that two bearers of rights are to be said to have the same right. Then there is no parallel necessity requiring that in both cases these be identically grounded. The rule 'Treat like cases alike' does not entail 'Treat unlike cases unlike' (Honoré 1968). Two or more different foundations might conceivably give rise to one and the same right; a particular sum, for instance, might have been promised as the reward for two quite disparate performances; indeed in one or other case it might have been promised unconditionally.

That all this is so – if indeed it is all so – is a purely formal truth. It places no substantial restriction on the respects in which bearers of rights, if they are correctly to be said to have the same or different rights, must themselves either be or have been similar or different. It is also a formal truth about all rights, and not only about those which may be both universal and natural. Thus it is perfectly proper to say that we all have acquired moral rights to the fulfilment of any promises made to us; notwithstanding that the only facts about us on which these particular rights have to be grounded are the facts that we are the people to whom these promises were in fact made; and notwithstanding that the original selection by the promisors of us as the promisees could conceivably have been wholly random and gratuitous. A right of any kind, as has been nicely said, 'is a normative resource' (Benn 1978, p. 64), and I may acquire such a resource without any antecedent desert or entitlement to warrant this acquisition. Indeed, since the notion of desert surely presupposes that of entitlement – entitlement, that is, to whatever personal factors are exercised in the conduct producing that desert – there could be no entitlements at all unless some of these were themselves unwarranted by desert. (cf. ch. seven, below.)

It needs to be emphasized also that this grounding of rights upon facts about the bearers of those rights involves no violation of Hume's Law (Hume 1739–40, III (i) 1; and compare Flew 1986a, pp. 45 and 144–9). Conclusions about what ought to be are not being deduced – nor could they validly be so deduced – from premises themselves purely neutral and detached, premises stating non-committally only what is the case. It may appear that this impossibility is being actualized, especially if we continue to attend to the example of promising (Searle 1969; and compare Flew 1969). Can we not, it may be asked, more or less brashly, deduce 'Brenda has a right to receive £100 from Bill' from 'Bill promised Brenda to give her £100'?

Yes, indeed we can. But the premise in this valid deduction is no more purely neutral and detached than the conclusion. Both express commitment to the institution of promising. What would not legitimate the move to 'Brenda has a right to receive £100 from Bill' would be any one of the corresponding reports by some truly non-participant social observer, such as the report: 'Bill said to

Brenda, "I promise to give you £100".' (Compare, and perhaps contrast too, the way in which the truth of that dull philosopher's proposition p can be deduced from the truth of the proposition 'Letitia knows p'; whereas from the truth of the likes of the very different proposition, 'Letitia said, "I know p",' it cannot.)

This second conceptual truth about rights is one particular case of much more general truth about all appraisal and valuation. So in making both the particular and the general point we are 'looking not *merely* at words . . . but also at the realities we use words to talk about; we are using a sharpened awareness of words to sharpen our perception of the phenomena' (Austin 1970, p. 182).

The general truth is that in appraising and valuing – as opposed to either stating our likes and dislikes or simply reacting with squeals of delight or howls of anger – we are engaged in an essentially rational activity; albeit an activity which is, as far as the present point is concerned, essentially rational only in the thin sense that in it we necessarily commit ourselves to returning the same verdicts in all relevantly similar cases. Even this is by itself sufficient to rule out all analyses of, for instance, 'She is a good woman' or 'He is an unjust man' in terms of anyone's likes or dislikes, advantages or interests; to say nothing of the still more implausible suggestions that these utterances mean instead something like 'She is a woman: hooray!' or 'He is a man: boo!' However, for a fuller discussion, compare chapter six, section 1, below.

Another corollary of the same general truth is the elimination of Moore's account of moral value in *Principia Ethica*, at least in its most famous formulation. Whatever we conclude about Hume's contention that value characteristics are really reactions in our minds, falsely projected out onto their provocations, we still cannot allow that they are like colours. For two objects may be for all practical purposes identical, save that one is yellow while the other is not: it happens all the time. Yet it cannot happen that two objects are similarly identical, save that one is a good one and the other is not. It must, therefore, be by the same token incoherent to maintain that, of two people who are the same in respect of whatever may be allowed to constitute the grounds of some right, one is, and the other is not, endowed with that normative resource.

3 The reciprocities of rights

In a methodological manifesto which was at the same time an exquisite philosophical masterpiece J. L. Austin concluded a paragraph on 'the Last Word' with the eager concession: 'Certainly, then, ordinary language is *not* the last word: in principle it can everywhere be supplemented and improved upon and superseded. Only remember, it *is* the *first* word' (Austin 1970, p. 185). The conceptual truths about rights presented in the two previous sections are firmly grounded upon established usage of the word 'right'. But some points in this third section do apparently involve some supplementing, improving, and superseding.

(i) This seems to be true of the proposal that rights be attributed only to those capable of – or, to allow for infants, capable of becoming capable of – themselves claiming rights for themselves; and, in and by that claim, undertaking the reciprocal obligation to respect the rights of others. No doubt Cicero was right about his own contemporaries when he wrote, 'We do not speak of justice in the cases of horses or lions' (quoted Grotius 1625, p. 41). But times change, and today some people do in fact speak about the rights of the brutes, and even of trees; and any deficiency which they display in so doing is not one of basic word-training. In the late 1970s, for instance, UNESCO adopted, with all the customary brouhaha, a Universal Declaration of the Rights of Animals.

This new declaration, supposedly set to become UN 'law' by 1980, begins by asserting 'that all animals are born with an equal claim on life and the same rights to existence'. It then proceeds to spell out the human duties implied by these brute rights: 'No animal shall be exploited for the amusement of man', for one; and, for another, 'scenes of violence involving animals shall be banned from cinema and television'. To no one's surprise the charter skirts the awkward issue of killing animals for food. Yet it makes up for this with a bold declaration that 'any act involving mass killing of wild animals is genocide'.

The proposal that rights should be ascribed only to potential claimers and protectors of rights does not, of course, foreclose on the possibility of insisting that all callousness and cruelty is wrong. Here the question is indeed, as Bentham urged, not ' "Can

they *reason*?" nor "Can they *talk*?" but, "Can they *suffer*?" '
(Bentham 1789, XVII section 4, p. 283n: in the same note, and on
the same basis, he disposes in short order of any principled
vegetarianism). So it could be, as I myself should with Bentham
wish to insist that it is, that we ought to treat the brutes with a
kindness and restraint which they have no right to demand; just
as, as we shall shortly be reminding ourselves, we have some
duties to persons the performance of which those persons have no
right to demand.

(ii) Section (i) suggested that a certain sort of reciprocity
should be made essential to the idea of rights: that is, that rights
should be ascribed only to those capable of themselves claiming
some rights for themselves; and, in and by that claim, undertaking
the reciprocal obligation to respect any rights with which others
might be endowed. The present subsection brings out that and
how it might be a good thing that someone should have something,
or should be treated in some way, even that it might be someone's
duty to secure these objectives, without its being the case that the
beneficiary has any kind of right to be provided with that
something, or to be treated in that way. The most obvious, least
controversial, yet by itself decisive example is that of my promising
you to give that, or to do that, to him. My promise creates your
(artificial) rights to fulfilment, but, at least until it is fulfilled, it
gives him no new rights or duties. Another favourable and scarcely
controversial example is that of the person drowning. It may be my
duty as a chance passerby to effect a rescue. But it is not the
drowner's right that I should. The upshot is that, whereas all rights
generate some corresponding duties – the duties, namely, of
respecting those rights – it is not inconsistent to speak of particular
duties without any corresponding particular rights. The chairman
of the perversely misnamed Human Rights Society was not,
therefore, formally contradicting himself when – as we learned
from the (London) *General Practitioner* for 26 November 1976 –
he announced: 'There are no such things as rights. You are not
entitled to anything in this Universe. The function of the Human
Rights Society is to tell men their duties.'

(iii) In our century, but especially since the end of the Second
World War, people have become increasingly inclined to affirm
that we all have presumably natural rights to whatever it is thought
that it would be good for everyone to have. It is significant that

modern declarations are much longer than those adopted in the American and French Revolutions of the eighteenth century – as well as being far less well written. The most notorious, that adopted by the General Assembly of the United Nations in December 1948, covers in my text six printed pages. Among many other things, it tells us that 'Everyone, as a member of society, has a right to social security' (Article 22); that 'everyone has the right to . . . periodic holidays with pay' (Article 24); and that 'everyone has the right to a standard of living adequate for the health and well-being of himself and of his family . . . and the right to security in the event of unemployment, sickness, disability, widowhood, old age or other lack of livelihood in circumstances beyond his control' (Article 25). Oh yes, and be sure not to miss Article 26: 'Everyone has the right to education. Education shall be free, at least in the elementary and fundamental stages. Elementary education shall be compulsory'; and so on, through a clause specifying that it must 'further the activities of the United Nations', to the slightly incongruous afterthought conclusion that 'Parents have a prior right to choose the kind of education that shall be given to their children.'

To someone detecting, and objecting to, a note of reactionary ridicule in the previous paragraph, the reply must be that any formulation of such claims, and any reporting of them, is bound to sound absurd. This is so for the excellent Groucho Marxist reason that they are absurd. The absurdity derives from three connected causes. First, no even halfway systematic rationale is or, it seems, could be offered to justify the inclusion of all and only those members actually admitted into this particular miscellany of claims. Second, they are put forward as universal and natural notwithstanding that many if not most are demands which it would not be sensible to make against anything but a modern industrial state, and that – incidentally – one in which there is no self-employment. (For it is, we must presume, employers who are expected to provide both paid employment and holidays with pay.) Third, nearly all the items on the UN list are welfare rather than option rights; claims, that is, that everyone must be supplied with some good – educational services, perhaps, or paid employment and holidays with pay – rather than claims that in some directions everyone must be left to their own devices.

The three famous option rights of the American Declaration of

Independence are rights only to non-interference. As such they must be and are rights against all comers, everywhere, and at all times; rights which everyone else has corresponding and completely reciprocal duties to respect. My rights to do whatever I wish, provided only that I harm no one else, become the grounds for everyone else's rights to do the same; and the other way about. It was because reciprocity of this second and much more closely corresponding kind is and has to be the secret of any systematic rationalization of universal natural rights that we were so reluctant to talk of the rights of brutes or trees. We should here take both to heart and to head one most excellent saying of a sage now again, it seems, to be honoured in his own country. A pupil once asked Confucius whether his rule of conduct might not perhaps be epitomized in a single word: 'The Master replied, "Is not 'reciprocity' the word?"' (*Analects* XV, section 23).

But the welfare rights proposed by the UN are rights to provision, and for these there surely cannot be corresponding and closely reciprocal moral duties. A question characteristic of a very different guru was: '*Kto-kogo?*' ['Who whom?'] In its present application this becomes: 'Who in particular is supposed to be morally obliged to provide which of all these various welfare goods to which other particular people; and what are the grounds of all these putative obligations to provide?'

It is, perhaps, all very well to maintain that all states ideally ought to be or to become welfare states; and hence that all these welfare rights ought to be legally established whenever and wherever it becomes practically possible to guarantee so ambitious a tax-financed (re)distribution. But if we are going to say that everyone, always, and everywhere, has a moral right to these welfare goods, then we have to meet and to overcome the challenge of that 'Who whom?' question. Since there is, surely, in fact no possibility of excogitating a response which would be in any degree plausible and precise, we have to conclude that any natural and universal rights must be option rather than welfare rights.

4 Rights and compulsions

It has been claimed that the notion of a right is 'peculiarly connected with the distribution of freedom of choice' (Hart 1955, p. 184). Yet this is not necessarily true of welfare rights. For there would, surely, be neither contradiction nor even paradox in the complex contention that every child of school age has a right to attend some educational institution; and, furthermore, that they should all be effectively compelled so to do.

But of option rights Hart's thesis is both true and necessarily true. There are, however, many whom this necessary truth has escaped, and still does escape. This is in part because the practical implications are in some cases both very important and to many people uncongenial, and in part because the basic distinction between two possible kinds of rights has not been taken. The two cases to be considered are complementary in a salutary and instructive way. Many of those sympathetic with one will be unsympathetic with the other. Yet, if either of these two possible option rights is conceded, then there is no escape from admitting, in both cases, those widely unwelcome implications.

(i) First, in Britain both the industrial Trades Union Congress and its political creature, the Labour Party, lose no opportunity of insisting upon the workers' unalienable rights to form and to join labour unions. Yet traditionally they have also demanded and, so far as they could, enforced closed shops. These demands have been muted, and the possibilities of enforcement substantially limited, under successive administrations headed by Prime Minister Thatcher. There is, nevertheless, every reason to expect that the demands will become louder and the possibilities will be greatly increased under a future Labour administration sustained by a parliamentary majority. In the later 1970s, under previous Labour administrations, British Rail and other state monopolies – with the full support of the TUC, the Parliamentary Labour Party, and the Cabinet, indeed at their behest – dismissed many employees with records of long and impeccable service on the sole grounds that they were so cross-grained, or so principled, as to refuse to join the approved (and, of course, Labour Party affiliated) trades union.

In proclaiming the general right of association both the UN Universal Declaration of Human Rights and the later specifically European version make it quite clear that this right is the right to join or not to join, at will. Carping critics have even suggested that this is one reason why the TUC and the Labour Party have been so hostile to supra-governmental European institutions. Certainly it was a judgment handed down by the European Court of Justice at The Hague, in a case supported by the 'ultra right-wing' Freedom

Association, which constituted the first step on the road to some still insufficient redress for the victims of such socialist tyranny. The same carping critics would explain the failure to extend the hostility to the UN and its Declaration (1948) by pointing out that, while Article 23(4) reads specifically, 'Everyone has the right to form and to join trades unions for the protection of his interests', it is only elsewhere, in Article 20(2), that the correlative general freedom not to join gets a mention: 'No one may be compelled to belong to an association.'

(ii) Our second, equally contentious, case is provided by what the Founding Fathers put first, namely, the right to life. If this is, as it surely is, an option rather than a welfare right, then it must embrace a complementary right to death. For what is the right to life if it is not the right, so long as nature permits, to go on living, or not, as I choose? Certainly it is at least the right not to be killed by anyone else; unless and until I forfeit that right by, for instance, committing murder.

(a) That the rights of the Declaration of Independence are indeed option rights becomes clear once we consider how, with that 'peculiar felicity of expression' that led to his being given the drafting job, young Mr Jefferson wrote, not about rights to health, education, and welfare – and whatever else might be thought necessary to the *achievement* of happiness – but about rights to life, liberty, and the *pursuit* of happiness; it being up to you whether you do in fact pursue (and to the gods whether, if so, you capture) that prey.

As an option right the right to life must also and necessarily keep open the alternative of suicide, and even of the assisted suicide that is voluntary euthanasia. Nor is it to the point to insist that few if any of the Signers thought that they were putting their names to a demand for the decriminalization of suicide and of assistance to suicide. Maybe they did not, any more than many of them saw that their demands must apply also to women and to Blacks. But what these or any other utterances actually imply is determined by their conventional meanings rather than by the fleeting intentions of particular utterers.

The refusal to recognize that the option right to life entails a complementary option right to death has been and still is encouraged by appeals to theological considerations. As creatures of a Divine Creator, it might be argued, we have only a leasehold and not a freehold on our lives. Therefore, inasmuch as it is God who has endowed us with a right to life, that right is only a right against other people and not against God. They are not entitled to destroy my life. But then neither am I. For that is the exclusive prerogative of its true owner, God. Thus in his description of the supposed original State of Nature, in the sentence immediately preceding the one quoted as the first epigraph of this chapter, Locke wrote: 'But though this be *a State of Liberty*, yet it is *not a State of License*, though Man in that State have an uncontroleable Liberty, to dispose of his Person or Possessions, yet he has not Liberty to destroy himself' (Locke 1690b). (God's putative proscription of suicide was, of course, of special importance to Locke: it provided the premise of his own main argument against consent to despotism.)

(b)   In the lower court decision in the now famous case of Karen Ann Quinlan, Judge Muir denied the plaintiff's request to have the life-sustaining apparatus switched off, indicating that he did not find grounds in the Constitution for any right to die. In so far as the Declaration is not part of the Constitution we might give him the point; while perhaps noting parenthetically, with a smile or a sigh, that so unfashionable a concern for the actual content of the Constitution would nowadays be seen by the dominant 'liberal' establishment as an indefeasible disqualification for appointment to the Supreme Court.

Judge Muir, however, went on to say that if he were to grant the request of the plaintiff, then 'such authorization would be homicide and a violation of the *right to life*' (Muir 1975: emphasis added). Since it was not disputed that on at least three occasions Karen Quinlan had insisted that, should this sort of situation arise, she would not wish to be maintained in the condition in which she then was – and for many years was to remain – it becomes difficult to reconstruct his argument. But consider, as an example of a similar confusion, a passage from the September 1978 issue of the magazine *Reason*:

> Our second Doublespeak Award goes to Mr James Loucks, President of Crozer Chester Medical Center . . . Loucks got a court order allowing his hospital to give a Jehovah's Witness a blood transfusion. The woman had requested in writing that the hospital respect her religious beliefs and not give her a

transfusion under any circumstances, but Loucks says he ignored her wishes 'out of respect for her rights'.

Here the confusion leads to the confident offering of a rights justification for committing what, as a physical assault upon an unconsenting patient, surely ought to have been a criminal offence. Certainly, if the amendment upon which *Roe v. Wade* was decided really does warrant what the Supreme Court ruled that it did warrant, then it must also warrant both suicide and assisting suicide. For in abortion what the pregnant woman is killing, or getting her doctor to kill for her, is arguably although by no means unquestionably another person with his or her right to life. So, if it would be a constitutionally unacceptable invasion of privacy to prevent a pregnant woman from killing the foetus, or from getting someone else to kill it for her, then it must be a far more unacceptable incursion to prevent women, or for that matter men, from either killing themselves or getting someone else to kill them; if that is what they want either to do or to have done for them. For, in all those secular systems of law in which suicide remains a crime, it is always allowed to be a much less serious crime than murder.

5 The road to a rationale

Since, as was argued in section 2, every right must be grounded upon some fact about its bearer, any universal natural rights will have to be grounded upon some characteristic or characteristics common to all humankind. For a first hint as to what that or they might be let us look at Blackstone's *Commentaries on the Laws of England*. This book had a profound influence on all Common Law jurisdictions, an influence which in the USA continued well into the Federal period:

> The absolute rights of man, considered as a free agent, endowed with discernment to know good from evil, and with the power of choosing those measures which appear to him to be most desirable, are usually summed up in one general appellation, and denominated the natural liberty of mankind. . . . The rights themselves . . . will appear from what has been premised, to be no other, than that *residuum* of natural liberty, which is not required by the laws of society to be sacrificed to the public convenience; or else those civil privileges, which society has

engaged to provide in lieu of the natural liberties so given up by individuals.

(Blackstone 1765, pp. 125 and 128)

The absolute rights of man – rights to liberties in the first sense distinguished in section 1 of chapter one – are thus to be grounded upon that most distinctive fact about our human nature – our unalienable freedom in the second and more fundamental sense there distinguished. Immanuel Kant too was, twenty years later, feeling his way towards similar conclusions when he offered 'The Formula of the End in Itself'. For, after accepting 'rational nature' as 'something *whose existence* has *in itself* an absolute value', his Categorical Imperative became: '*Act in such a way that you always treat humanity, whether in your own person or in the person of any other, never simply as a means, but always at the same time as an end*' (Kant 1785, pp. 90 and 91).

In this dress these formulations will not do. For, as one of Kant's most respectful critics objected, it is, strictly, incoherent to speak of 'ends in themselves'. There can be no more 'ends in themselves' unrelated to the persons whose ends they are, than there can be sisters in themselves, unrelated to any siblings of whom they are the sisters (Schopenhauer 1841, p. 45). Again, having insisted so strongly in the previous section 4 that the right to life entails a complementary right to death, we must at least mention that Kant was mistaken when, later in the same book, he went on to contend that respect for persons as self-legislating choosers of ends for themselves required that they never choose as the last of those ends for themselves the final end of themselves through self-accelerated death.

For our purposes it is most important to get straight about our 'rational nature' as 'something *whose existence* has *in itself* an absolute value'. Especially when this is accompanied – as in Kantian contexts it usually is – by some sort of genuflexion, talk of rational beings may suggest: either creatures who are rational as opposed to irrational; or inert and detached intellectuals as opposed to lowbrow activists. Both suggestions are out of place. For we have to distinguish both two different senses in which we can all of us be truly said to be already rational beings; and both commendatory and non-commendatory understandings of the term 'rational'.

In one of the two senses of 'rational being', a rational being is an exclusively intellectual creature; a creature forever occupied in examining evidence, discerning inconsistencies, and drawing conclusions. In the other sense, the sense which is the more relevant to us now, rational beings are agents capable of having and of giving their own reasons for choosing to act however they do choose to act. They are not, and so we are not, what nothing could be, ends in themselves or ends in ourselves. What they and therefore we are is creatures who can, and cannot but, form ends for themselves. The ends once chosen it becomes time for a rational being in the exclusively intellectual sense to take over, working out what in fact will be the most effective and acceptable means for achieving those ends.

We are all of us rational beings in both of these two detached and purely descriptive understandings; while in both cases a being has at least to be rational, in the sense of capable of the relevant kind of rationality or irrationality, before any question can arise of either commending its actual rationality or condemning its actual irrationality.

From these familiar if somewhat stylized non-moral truths about our human nature nothing can immediately be deduced about either any rights which must be possessed by, or any obligations which must be incumbent upon, beings such as we. To attempt any deduction of this form would be flagrantly to violate Hume's Law. This, as we have noticed already, forbids us to attempt to deduce prescriptive conclusions about what ideally *ought* to be from premises stating, or purporting to state, quite neutrally and non-committally, only what actually *is* the case. However, to borrow another characteristic concept from Kant, 'as legislating members of the Kingdom of Ends', as creatures, that is, prescribing laws to apply to all creatures adopting and pursuing ends for themselves, we ourselves can lay it down that all rational agents are to be respected in their pursuit of their own chosen ends; or, in the favourite words of a more recent generation, their doings of their own things (Gewirth 1978).

In so far as we all want to claim such rights, such liberties, for ourselves – and that, presumably, we all do – we are, by the very logic of the term 'right', bound to claim them equally for everyone else as well. The content of such rights cannot but in consequence be the same for all. A still agreeably unhackneyed statement is to be found in the 1945 Constitution of Kemalist Turkey: 'Every Turk is born free and lives free. He has liberty to do anything which does not harm other persons. The natural right of the individual to liberty is limited only by the liberties enjoyed by his fellow citizens.' The practice presents every kind of problem. The principle is luminous.

The notion of equality is here inescapable. It has to come in because we are all necessarily equal in the essentials of our common humanity: 'All citizens' – as we may read in Article 40 of the 1937 Constitution of the Republic of Ireland – 'are, as human beings, equal in the eyes of the law.' Precisely this must be the necessary ground of any universal natural rights. In discussing the Declaration of Independence Abraham Lincoln once wrote, with his usual shrewd grasp of fundamentals:

> The authors of that notable instrument . . . did not intend to declare all men equal in all respects. They did not mean that all men were equal in color, size, intellect, moral developments, or social capacity. They defined with tolerable directness in what respects they did consider all men created equal – equal in certain 'unalienable rights, among which are life, liberty, and the pursuit of happiness'.

Chapter three

Social Contract or General Will?

Jean-Jacques Rousseau . . . is the father of the romantic movement, the initiator of systems of thought which infer non-human facts from human emotions, and the inventor of the political philosophy of pseudo-democratic dictatorships as opposed to traditional absolute monarchies. Ever since his time, those who considered themselves reformers have been divided into two groups, those who followed him and those who followed Locke. Sometimes they cooperated, and many individuals saw no incompatibility. But gradually the incompatibility has become increasingly evident. At the present time, Hitler is an outcome of Rousseau; Roosevelt and Churchill, of Locke.

Bertrand Russell,
A History of Western Philosophy (pp. 684–5)

Here lies your secret O Lenin, – yours and ours
No' in the majority will that accepts the result
But in the real will that bides its time and kens
The benmaist [inmost] resolve, is the poo'er in which we exult
Since nobody's willingly deprived o' the good;
And, least o' a', the crood!

Hugh Macdiarmid,
'First hymn to Lenin', *Selected Poems*

It can be illuminating, as Russell suggested, to see Locke and Rousseau as each providing the main intellectual inspiration for two antithetical political traditions. Russell was right, too, to emphasize that many people fail to recognize their incompatibility.

He went wrong only – albeit, in the circumstances of the time in which he was writing his *History*, very understandably – in picking out Hitler rather than Lenin as by far the most important twentieth-century figure in the anti-Lockian, anti-liberal tradition.

The true implications of Rousseau's political thought, and in particular the despotic justificatory possibilities of its most original and distinctive idea, emerged only slowly. *The Social Contract*, the fullest and final expression of that thought, was first published in 1792. But from then until the beginnings of the great French Revolution in 1789 this seems to have been the least read of all his works. And, although the entire revolutionary generation practised a cult of Rousseau, at least in the earlier years this devotion rarely if ever involved either acceptance or even much knowledge of his explicitly political ideas (McDonald 1965, ch. 5 and *passim*).

It was only with the rise of the Jacobins that would-be despots and apologists for despotism began to recognize the conveniences of a national and inherently all-overriding collective general will, the particular sense of which might from time to time be discovered and revealed without reference to – or even contrary to – the vulgar and pedestrian countings of actual individual votes; thus, to put it in the words of Ernesto Che' Guevara, 'avoiding the commonplaces of bourgeois democracy' (quoted Hook 1975, pp. 162–3).

This authoritarian progress is the subject of J. L. Talmon's classic study, *The Origins of Totalitarian Democracy* (1952). Whereas there is no evidence that Hitler ever identified himself and his National Socialist German Workers' Party with the Jacobins, Lenin most certainly did pick them out for commendation as the first true Bolsheviks. (See, for instance, his article, 'Enemies of the people', originally published in *Pravda* in June 1917 and reprinted in, for instance, Tucker 1975, pp. 305–6.) Again, whereas there was no significant Jacobin tradition in Germany before the formation of the local section of the Third International, Lenin could, and did, look back towards the quintessentially Russian *Narodnaya Volya* (People's Will) movement. He deliberately borrowed Chernyshevsky's title *What is to be done?* for the foundation document of Bolshevism (see, for instance, Wolfe 1984). Wolfe also points out, what we shall soon come to see as significant, that the Russian word '*Volya*' means both will and freedom.

1 Sources of misunderstanding

Turning to *The Social Contract*, it is easy to be misled, either by studying the work out of context, or by its stylistic adornments, or even by its title. Let us consider these three sources of easy error in turn, taking them in reverse order.

(i) First, the book should surely have been called, after its most original and distinctive idea, *The General Will*. The actual title is bound to suggest, what Rousseau's work emphatically was not, but what Locke's *Two Treatises of Government* most famously were, a plea for limited government. It is significant that those *Treatises* were first drafted for possible pamphlet publication during the struggle to exclude the Roman Catholic Duke of York from succeeding his elder brother King Charles II. Locke then had been serving as one-man brains trust to his patron and friend, Anthony Ashley Cooper, the First Earl of Shaftesbury and founder of the Whig Party. The *Two Treatises* eventually appeared only after the Glorious Revolution of 1688–9. They were then intended to justify and to confirm the consequent constitutional settlement; after the final defeat of the long-feared attempt of James II to establish a French-style and French-supported Roman Catholic despotism.

In the *Two Treatises* Locke started from the traditional idea of a pre-political state of nature, traditionally conceived as the actual and universal past condition of all mankind. In that state our ancestors were subject, as we all are always, to the universal prescriptive law of nature. Although Locke had no nightmare Hobbist vision of a war of all against all, he did insist that this state of nature must have its 'inconveniences'. It was in order to escape these, Locke inferred, that our pre-political ancestors would, and did, make, even if they could not yet literally sign, a social contract:

> And thus that, which begins and actually constitutes any
> political society, is nothing but the consent of any number of
> freemen capable of a majority to unite and incorporate into such
> a society. And this is that, and that only, which did, or could
> give beginning to any lawful government in the world.
>
> (Locke 1690b, II (viii) 99)

Locke then proceeded to derive from his fundamental notions of

a social contract and of the rights of the contracting parties in a
state of nature all the guiding principles of the Glorious Revolution –
limited and constitutional government, the rule of law as opposed
to arbitrary power, no taxation without consent through representatives, and so on. Reinforced by the thought of the
Frenchman Montesquieu and the Scot Hume, these were to
become in the following century the principles of the Founding
Fathers of the American Republic. (It was because the American
colonists were clearly within the Lockian, Whig tradition, whereas
the ultras of the great French Revolution were equally clearly not,
that Edmund Burke could have some sympathy for the American
Revolution but none for the French.)

Both for Locke and for the Whig Party in his day it was
necessary to maintain the historicity of an original social contract.
Far from being a philosopher's fancy, despised by practical
politicians, this putative original contract between king and people
is mentioned crucially in the operative resolutions of the House of
Commons on 28 and 29 January 1689. It was because, 'by the
advice of Jesuits and other wicked persons', James II had allegedly
broken 'the original contract between King and Parliament', that
the House declared the throne now 'vacant'; proceeding to offer it
to Dutch William and his royal English wife Mary.

The 'original contract' to which appeal was thus made was
supposed to have imposed limitations upon the king's government,
and it was thus necessarily violated by the attempt of James II to
make himself a despot, his proper powers subject to no such
limitation. It is, of course, of the very nature of any contract to
impose limitations. For contracts essentially involve give and take:
each party giving, or at least promising to give, some restriction or
limitation upon their own conduct; in return for taking, or at any
rate becoming entitled to receive, some contractually corresponding
restriction or limitation upon the conduct of the other.

(ii) Second, *The Social Contract* is a quite extraordinarily
brilliant book, replete with epigram and paradox. Its opening
sentence is as typical as it has been unforgettable: 'Man is born
free, yet everywhere he is in chains' (Rousseau 1762, I(i)). Then,
on the following page, one once-respected establishment figure is
seen off in three short, decisive sentences: 'Grotius denies that all
human power is established for the benefit of the governed, citing
slavery as an example. His usual method of reasoning is always to

present fact as a proof of right. A more logical method could be used, but not one more favourable to tyrants' (ibid., I(ii)). So how can the reader – especially the reader knowing something of the author's vagrant, feckless, and dissident life-style – believe that he was anything but devoted to liberty, and a hater of despotism?

Perhaps indeed he was; but, like so many others later, he failed to grasp the concrete consequences of his own high abstractions and paradoxical sleights of mind. Certainly we have, in studying or discussing Rousseau, to be constantly on guard against the collapsing of the distinction between two categorically different kinds of questions: on the one hand, psychologico-historical questions about what someone's true intentions were; and, on the other hand, logico-semantic questions about the necessary implications, and hence the meaning, of what that someone said – of the meaning, that is, of the sentences actually uttered or written.

(iii) A third continuing source of error is the failure to read *The Social Contract* as what it was, the climactic expression of all Rousseau's political thinking. This failure has been encouraged by the common practice of printing it before whatever *Discourses* are included in the same volume. But all three of these were in fact both composed and first published before *The Social Contract*: the *Discourse on the Arts and Sciences* in 1750; the *Discourse on the Origin of Inequality* in 1754; and the *Discourse on Political Economy* (as an article in Volume V of the great *Encyclopedia*) in 1755. Certainly both the second and the third of these *Discourses* provide valuable clues to the interpretation of *The Social Contract*.

(a) For instance, what the *Discourse on the Origin of Inequality* has to say concerning the consequences of appropriation is, both in style and in substance, just about as remote as could be from Locke. This is relevant to us now inasmuch as all truly liberal thinkers have insisted on the impossibility of maintaining individual liberties without a wide distribution of holdings of private property. Rousseau's characteristically sparkling and characteristically hostile statement comes at the very beginning of Part II of that second *Discourse*:

The first person who, having enclosed a bit of land, took it into his head to say 'This is mine' and found people simple enough to believe him, was the true founder of civil society. What crimes, wars, murders, what miseries and horrors would the human race have been spared, had someone pulled up the stakes or filled in the ditch and cried out to his fellow men: 'Do not listen to this impostor. You are lost if you forget that the fruits of the earth belong to all and the earth to no one!'

It may perhaps prove salutary to contrast this squib with the soberly magisterial ruling of the *Summa Theologica* (II (ii) Q66A2). Willing as always to learn from and, if possible, to improve upon Aristotle, Aquinas asserts that private property is necessary, for three reasons:

First, because each person takes more trouble to care for something that is his sole responsibility than for what is held in common or by many – for in such a case each individual shirks the work and leaves the responsibility to somebody else, which is what happens when too many officials are involved. Second, because human affairs are more efficiently organized if each person has his own responsibility to discharge; there would be chaos if everybody cared for everything. Third, because men live together in greater peace where everyone is content with his own. We do, in fact, notice that quarrels often break out amongst men who hold things in common without distinction.

(b)   Earlier, in Part I of the same *Discourse*, Rousseau had uttered what has proved to be a seminal falsehood. In distinguishing 'natural or physical' from 'moral or physical inequality' he asserted that the latter 'consists in different privileges enjoyed by some at the expense of others, such as being richer, more honoured, more powerful than they, or even causing themselves to be obeyed by them'.

This contention that one person's riches must always and necessarily be possessed 'at the expense of others', and thus result from the exploitation of those others, has since become a socialist staple. Yet a moment's thought should be sufficient to show that being richer than, is not in this respect like having power over, someone else. This socialist staple can be justified only on the basis of the obviously false assumption that all wealth of every kind – not only material goods but also insubstantial services – is produced, and would continue to be produced, regardless of expectations about who is going to enjoy those goods and services. For it is upon this assumption, and upon it alone, that we should become entitled to conclude that everything which collective (re)distributors might allocate to any one individual would have been equally available for an alternative (re)allocation to one of several others.

At present the most popular and certainly the most damaging derivation from this *marxisant* misconception is Third World Dependency Theory (Cardoso and Faletto, 1979; and cf. Harrison 1985, *passim*, and Novak 1982, chs 17–18). Its core theoretical thesis is that countries are poor and 'underdeveloped' always and only because they have been made poor and are kept 'underdeveloped' by capitalist, imperialist, and colonialist exploitation.

The essential justifying assumption in the case of countries is even more grotesque than that required for the argument about individuals. For it must be that what political philosophers have called 'the state of nature' was, or is, a satisfactory and rising standard of living for all (cf. Bauer 1976 and Bauer 1981). What is so damaging about this fashionable intellectual rubbish, and so much to be deplored by everyone sincerely concerned '*pour le soulèvement de la condition humaine*', is that it obstructs application of the vastly productive insights of that first and greatest masterpiece of development economics, *An Inquiry into the Nature and Causes of the Wealth of Nations* (Smith 1776).

(c) The second *Discourse*, the *Discourse on the Origin of Inequality*, also warns us how Rousseau's later talk of social contracts is to be construed. It has to be as was intended by Hobbes rather than by Locke:

> Let us therefore begin by putting aside all the facts, for they
> have no bearing on the question. The investigations that may be
> undertaken concerning this subject should not be taken for
> historical truth, but only for hypothetical and conditional
> reasonings, better suited to shedding light on the nature of
> things than to pointing out their true origin.

It, would, therefore, be inept to fault Rousseau's account of the origin of private property by objecting that the words in which 'this impostor' made his claim could not have been understood unless his society already possessed both an institution of private property and the vocabulary necessary for its operation.

Later, in Part II, Rousseau appears to derive from his

conception of the social contract a deceptively Lockian conclusion: it is, he says, 'a fundamental maxim of all political right, that people have given themselves leaders in order to defend their liberty and not to enslave themselves'. But we have to notice that Rousseau goes on at once, in the following sentence, to write: '*If we have a prince*, Pliny said to Trajan, *it is so that he may preserve us from having a master.*' The difference, which for Roussau was crucial, is explained earlier in the same paragraph: 'in the relations between men, the worst that can happen to someone is for him to see himself at the discretion of someone else'.

It was, presumably, the peculiarities and the limitations of his own vagabond experience which led Rousseau thus to rate as crucial the difference between, on the one hand, being compelled by a private person, and, on the other hand, being compelled by agents of the state. His enormously strong personal preference for the latter may be made to seem less eccentric and less exaggerated, even if no more sympathetic, if we compare it with the preferences of the people – and their name is, it appears, Legion – to whom the disciplines of production subject to the demands of the market appear intolerable, yet to whom the alternative of obedience to the collective authority controlling a command economy constitutes the supremely seductive ideal.

Certainly it was Rousseau's obsessional revulsion against private dependency, and his refusal to recognize subordination to state officials as another form of dependency, which misled him to introduce his perverse redefinition of the word 'liberty'. In the 'Letter to the Republic of Geneva', prefacing the *Discourse on the Origin of Inequality*, Rousseau considers where he would have chosen to be born, had he been offered such a choice. In answering this question he says: 'I would have wanted to live and die free, *that is to say*, subject to the laws in such wise that neither I nor anyone else could shake off their honourable yoke' (emphasis added).

This redefinitional manœuvre is in large part to be explained, although certainly not by the same token to be excused, by the fact that these particular laws are supposed to be both in the best interests of, and somehow self-imposed by, every individual subject to them. That Rousseau is indeed appealing to these two claims is made clear by the previous paragraph. His ideal birthplace would be a country where the sovereign and the people could have but one and the same interest, so that all the movements of the machine always tended to the common happiness. Since this could not have come about unless the people and the sovereign were one and the same person, it follows that I would have wished to be born under a democratic government, wisely tempered.

Even where both these two claims were correct it ought to be obvious that those subject to the resulting laws, regulations, and administrative orders would not, in respect of whatever was thereby mandated or forbidden, be free. If there is a law against it, with a penalty attached for disobedience, then I am precisely not free to disobey. It is, therefore, entirely correct to condemn Rousseau's 'misuse of the word "freedom"' (Russell 1945, p. 697). For by thus redefining it to mean something very like, or at least necessarily including, its opposite, constraint, Rousseau was precisely not offering anything which may properly be called an alternative conception of freedom – *positive* freedom, perhaps, as opposed to merely negative. So Russell's condemnation of Rousseau must, however regretfully, be extended to embrace Sir Isaiah Berlin. For, with a characteristic excess of liberal generosity to the enemies of liberalism, he entitled his Inaugural Lecture not 'Liberty and pseudo-liberty' but 'Two concepts of liberty' (Berlin 1969; and cf. ch. four, below).

In order to make out that in this ideal state the laws would be both in the interests of or for the good of, and somehow self-imposed by, all those subject to them Rousseau employed a further definitional manœuvre. The immediately more relevant element in this exercise is to be seen most clearly in the third *Discourse*: 'The first and most important maxim of legitimate or popular government, *that is to say, of a government that has the good of the populace for its object*, is therefore, as I have said, to follow the general will in all things' (emphasis added; and cf. pp. 32–4, above). It is no wonder that in March 1756, in a letter to Madame d'Epinay, Rousseau wrote: 'Learn my dictionary, my good friend, if you want to have us understand one another. Believe me, my terms rarely have the ordinary sense.'

2 Popular absolutism

There are in both the two later *Discourses* signs that some notion of a general will is moving to the centre of the intellectual stage. Thus, in the last sentence previously quoted, Rousseau reiterates that 'The first and most important maxim of legitimate or popular government . . . is . . . to follow the general will in all things.' In the *Discourse on the Origin of Inequality* he speaks both of 'the establishment of the body politic as a true contract between the populace and the leaders it chooses for itself', and of how, 'with respect to social relations, the populace has united all its wills into a single one'. But then, in the *Discourse on Political Economy*, he speaks of a general will as attached to a kind of organism – something which must grow up naturally rather than be produced by contractual artifice: 'The body politic . . . can be considered to be like a body that is organized, living and similar to that of a man.' It is, therefore, 'also a moral being which possesses a will'.

Before coming to grips with that notion as fully and finally deployed in *The Social Contract* we need to press two sharp points about these anticipations. First, that the organic analogy is downright incompatible with any idea of a contract. That idea, as was said before, is what must appeal to those who want only limited and responsible government, with heavy emphasis upon the rights of the individual against all comers – whether individual or collective. But in any organism organs are necessarily subordinate. They are not – unlike us humans – autonomous agents able to decide whether or not to serve and obey. It is a truth which – not very consistently – Rousseau himself stresses in the *Discourse on the Origin of Inequality*. Nor, as Leninists so love to say, is it an accident that this organic analogy has become the traditional favourite of authoritarians advocating total and unconditional obedience. Consider, for instance, how in Shakespeare's *Coriolanus* Menenius Agrippa labours to subdue the 'mutinous citizens' (I.i).

Second, notice that in the *Discourse on Political Economy* Rousseau explains that all societies and corporations develop general wills, which are distinct from, and sometimes contrary to, the private wills of their individual members: 'Every political society is composed of other smaller and different societies, each of which has its interests and maxims. . . . The will of these particular societies always has two relations: for the members of the association it is the general will; for the large society it is a particular will'. This, as has often been remarked, is a sound sociological observation, notwithstanding that to make it here scarcely consists with the earlier undertaking to put 'aside all the facts, for they have no bearing on the question'. Certainly too all organization persons have abundant occasion to contrast corporate interests and policies with the private interests and policies of officers and members.

But Rousseau takes a further, more precarious, step. Presumably because general wills are wills to promote the interests – and in that understanding – the good of the collectivities of which they are the general wills, he maintains that, at least in respect of those collectivities, they must be *morally* good:

> The body politic . . . is also a moral being which possesses a will; and this general will, which always tends towards the conservation and well-being of the whole and of each part . . . is for all the members of the state, in their relations both to one another and to the state, the rule of what is just and what is unjust.

Suppose that we waive possible objections about the meaning of that prematurely relativistic phrase 'morally good, at least in respect of these collectivities'. Still we have to protest that here Rousseau seems himself to be arguing in the fashion so fiercely faulted in Grotius: 'His . . . method of reasoning is . . . to present fact as a proof of right. A more logical method could be used, but not one more favourable to tyrants.'

(i) The first sentence of *The Social Contract*, in a sort of preface to Book I, announces the object of the whole exercise: 'I want to inquire whether there can be some legitimate and sure rule of administration in the civil order, taking men as they are and laws as they might be' (I, 17). Fair enough; note it well. We shall need to recall this splendidly forthright statement when it begins to emerge that the rule proposed – Submit always to the most general will – achieves inexpugnable sureness and legitimacy only at the cost of raising apparently insuperable difficulties for the deter- mination, in particular cases, of what its concrete content is.

Given the project propounded in that first sentence, the problem, as Rousseau sees it, is to 'find a form of association which defends and protects with all common forces the person and goods of each associate, and by means of which each one, while uniting with all, nevertheless obeys himself alone and remains as free as before'. This, he continues, 'is the fundamental problem for which the social contract provides the solution' (I(vi)).

So to specify the problem, in a manner making it necessarily insoluble, is to guarantee that nothing offered as a solution can truly be such. We should, therefore, expect to find that any attempt at what is bound to be a pseudo-solution generates preposterous paradox. And so we do! For Rousseau goes on immediately to promise an account of a 'social contract' which is, allegedly, for all of us, all get and no real give.

(ii) 'The clauses of this contract', Rousseau assures us, 'though perhaps they have never been formally promulgated . . . are everywhere the same, everywhere tacitly accepted and acknowledged.' Properly understood, they 'are all reducible to a single one, namely the total alienation of each associate, together with all his rights, to the entire community'. Every individual is supposed willingly to make, or to have made, this total and unconditional surrender to the totalitarian collective:

> For . . . since each person gives himself whole and entire, the situation is equal for everyone; and, since the situation is equal for everyone, no one has an interest in making it burdensome for the others . . . . Finally, in giving himself to all, each person gives himself to no one. And since there is no associate over whom he does not acquire the same right that he would grant others over himself, he gains the equivalent of everything he loses, along with a greater amount of force to preserve what he has. (I(vi))

The social compact is supposed in consequence to be 'reducible to the following terms. *Each of us places his person and all his power in common under the supreme direction of the general will; and as one we receive each member as an indivisible part of the whole*' (I(iv)).

It is very easy to see that we are here being deceived by pieces of ultra-swift sleight of mind. But it is not nearly so easy to spot how these quick tricks are taken. So soon, however, as we reread the key paragraphs slowly, carefully, and calmly, objections do begin to make themselves felt. For a start, this whole superlatively fast-moving virtuoso performance of intellectual prestidigitation proceeds at an excruciating ethereal level of abstraction. The moment we push down towards the everyday, pedestrian plane, populated by flesh-and-blood human beings, we have to notice that real people, though necessarily equal in their common humanity and consequent universal rights, are by nature rather rarely equal in anything else. We are also born into, or else in some other way acquire, all manner of different social relations, any of which may give rise to what we are so often expected to assume is the most infamous thing, social inequality (Flew 1976, ch. 4).

In this somewhat more this-worldly perspective what becomes of the contention that 'since each person gives himself whole and entire, the situation is equal for everyone; and, since the situation is equal for everyone, no one has an interest in making it burdensome for the others'? For all persons having holdings which are below the local average – to say nothing of often rather conspicuously underdeprived members of the New Class, with a class interest in procrustean policies (Flew 1981) – have an obvious interest in state-enforced redistribution. There are also, as all students of US budgets will know, possibilities of what in that country is called 'porkbarrelling'; possibilities which are realized whenever any 'special interest group' – a group usually consisting of above average well-off citizens – contrives to secure particular favours at the expense of general taxation. (This is the sort of thing to which the authors of *The Federalist Papers* were referring when they wrote about 'faction', and which they hoped that the proposed Constitution would at least discourage.)

So, if we remember that commitments made to other and more particular associations are almost always partial, why should our commitment to the most fundamental and comprehensive association have to be thus total and unconditional? Why should we give ourselves 'whole and entire' to an all-embracing and all-demanding collective rather than – more prudently and more modestly – agree to join with others in defending our and their rights by force of law?

The most central and the most fundamental objection, however, appeals to that frivolously formulated yet solidly sound principle of practical wisdom, TANSTAFL – There Are No Such Things As Free Lunches! Allow that, formally and superficially at any rate, Rousseau satisfies the requirement that any contract, to be a contract at all, must involve both parties in both giving and taking. For, 'since there is no associate over whom he does acquire the same right that he would grant others over himself, he gains the equivalent of everything he loses'. Nevertheless there is no doubt but that the TANSTAFL principle is violated by the final clause in that sentence: 'along with a greater amount of force to preserve what he has'. The support of that 'greater amount of force' neither is nor can be costless. Someone has to be compensated for the time and effort devoted to judicial and police work.

(iii) *'Each of us'*, it is alleged, *'places his person and all his power in common under the supreme direction of the general will; and as one we receive each member as an indivisible part of the whole.'* This hypothetical, not to say fictitious, theoretical transaction is supposed then to generate a sort of instant Superman – remotely reminiscent of the more solid and visible figure constituting the original frontispiece of *Leviathan*: 'At once, in place of the individual person of each contracting party, this act of association produces a moral and collective body composed of as many members as there are voices in the assembly, which receives from this same act its unity, its common *self*, its life and its will' (I(vi)).

(a) So now, what is the content of this general will and how is it to be identified? For, as we have seen, unless that content can be reliably determined the general will cannot serve as the promised 'legitimate and sure rule of administration in the civil order'. But, as is recognized rather rarely, Rousseau's claim to be operating with a genuinely applicable notion and not some kind of pseudo-concept is bound to be – to put it no stronger – seriously prejudiced, unless this putative reality can be, at least in principle, confidently and positively identified. (Cf. Flew 1987b on the putative concept of a substantial soul.) Rousseau himself, before attempting to offer directions on where some tolerably specific answer to these questions might be found, makes a stipulation which, though indispensable if he is to fulfil this project, is bound to make the problems of specification and identification even more intractable.

'This public person', Rousseau continues, 'takes the name . . . *sovereign* when it is active' (I(vi)). This 'sovereign, by the mere fact that it exists, is always what it should be' (I(vii)). Its will, therefore, being 'the general will, is always right and always tends towards the public utility' (II(iii)). The original of which 'always right' in the usual translation is 'toujours droit'. A better, yet still far from perfect, translation would be 'always upright'. For Rousseau's point is that, although it may be mistaken on some point of fact, the general will is always directed 'towards the public utility'.

Perhaps at this point we ought to notice, if only parenthetically, that Diderot had introduced his own conception of a general will into the treatment of individual morality in his *Encylopédie* articles. His contention there was that people as we actually are cannot be the final judges of what is just or unjust, right or wrong. The particular will of any individual must always be suspect. We have forever to be addressing ourselves for judgement to the general good and to the somehow correlative general will. Anyone who rejects it thereby renounces humanity and becomes 'denaturé'; or, as we might now wish to add, 'denaturée'. Such persons disqualify themselves from membership of the species.

The 'sovereign, by the mere fact that it exists, is always what it should be'. Its will, therefore, being 'the general will, is always right and always tends towards the public utility'. Rousseau's supporting argument runs:

> since the sovereign is formed entirely from the private individuals who make it up, it neither has nor could have any interest contrary to theirs. Hence, the sovereign power has no need to offer a guarantee to its subjects, since it is impossible for a body to want to harm all its members, and, as we will see later, it cannot harm any one of them in particular. (I(vii))

Of course we do not see anything of the kind, either later or at any other time. Maybe 'it is impossible for a body to want to harm *all* its members'. But every surgeon can tell of cases where to save a life it is necessary to amputate. Maybe, again, it makes no sense to suggest that the public interest of any association can be flatly contrary to the private interests of *all* its members. Yet everyone who has ever been actively involved in the affairs of any association must be able to cite plenty of instances in which the good of the organization called for heavy sacrifices of the private interests of *some* members. To deny, and to try to disprove, so manifest a truth is, and ought to be recognized as, the trademark of an utterly infatuated theoretician.

Furthermore, even if the sense of the general will necessarily 'tends towards the public utility' – towards, that is to say, the public interest, and hence, in that understanding, the public good – still it will not be always and by the same token moral. For the public interest, and in this understanding the public good, may not only demand overridings of particular private interests and private goods within the collective in question. It may also urge both overridings of interest, and even violations of rights, which are external to that collective.

This in his own way Rousseau concedes by arguing that 'when . . . partial associations come into being . . . the will of each of these associations becomes general in relation to the state' (II(iii)). Nor is it only the public, collective interest of partial associations which may conflict with the public, collective interest of the state. The public, collective interest, the 'national interest' of one state may conflict with both the national interests of other states and with the private interests of the citizens of those other states. Nor can we concede the logical legitimacy of the slide from interest first to good, and then from good to moral. It is a point elegantly enforceable by reiterating Rousseau's objection to Grotius: 'A more logical method could be used, but not one more favourable to tyrants.'

(b) Obnoxious though it is to contend that 'the sovereign power has no need to offer a guarantee to its subjects', this initial outrage is almost innocuous by comparison with the same chapter's concluding claim: 'Thus, in order for the social compact to avoid being an empty formula, it tacitly entails the commitment . . . that whoever refuses to obey the general will will be forced to do so by the entire body. *This means that he will be forced to be free*' (I(vii)): emphasis added).

That most notorious contention is sometimes glossed by reference to a later footnote: 'In Genoa, the word *libertas* can be read on the front of prisons and on the chains of galley-slaves . . . In a country where all such people were in the galleys, the most perfect liberty would be enjoyed' (IV(ii)). Certainly Rousseau did have one fair and true point there, albeit a point obscured and distorted by his provocative and sensationalized form of expression. For the rights and liberties of citizens can be effectively guaranteed by law only when would-be violators are deterred by the threat of punishment, and where actual violations are regularly punished.

Perhaps too it is just worth remarking that by forcing a child to study subjects which are initially uncongenial you may be ensuring that, in the future, the child will have a wider range of career possibilities from which to choose. But the persistent defender does justice neither to Rousseau's honesty, nor to his competence as a writer, by suggesting that he really meant something equally harmless and equally true when he said that the dissident 'will be forced to be free'.

3 Vanguards and voluntarism

There are two main sources for the appeal, to those seeing themselves as members of a vanguard party, of ideas of a general will; of a will, which is, it is claimed, both real and properly overriding because it is of its very nature in the interest of, and therefore for the good of, the collective whose general will it is supposed to be. It appeals, first, precisely because it is a will, and will is an activist and dynamic notion. The appeal in this particular case is especially strong, since the general will is in effect defined as legitimately all-overriding: 'the sovereign, by the mere fact that it exists, is always what it should be'; and its will, being 'the general will, is always right and always tends toward the public utility'.

Against the determinations of such a general will neither the ties of tradition nor the clauses of some alleged ancient or even perhaps purely notional contract can count for anything. Those who would preserve and who dare to defend such antique relics, and thus obstruct the path of popular progress, are thereby revealed as backward-lookers, reactionaries, enemies of the people.

(i) The second source for the appeal of Rousseau's idea to a certain sort of very practical political activists is one which was at the same time an embarrassment to Rousseau himself as a theoretician. For the stated object of the whole exercise was, it will be remembered, to discover 'some legitimate and sure rule of administration in the civil order, taking men as they are and laws as they might be'. But Rousseau, having satisfied himself that whatever accords with the general will must indeed be 'legitimate and sure', now finds himself unable to specify any discovery procedure which can be guaranteed to reveal, on any particular occasion, the actual sense of that general will. This very elusiveness is of course attractive to some, inasmuch as it means that there can be no decisive demonstration of the falsity of confident claims to be acting in accordance with this general will.

(a) At first it might seem as if the general will in Rousseau was going to turn out to be, or to be congruent with, the unanimous will of an assembly of all citizens. If so, then – as often – Rousseau would be harking back to an idealized picture of some Classical city-state: 'For either the will is general, or it is not. It is the will of either the people as a whole, or of only a part . . . . In the second case, it is merely a private will' (II(ii)).

This clear conclusion, however, is forthwith contradicted in a footnote: 'For a will to be general, it need not always be unanimous: however, it is necessary for all the votes to be counted. Any formal exclusion is a breach of generality.' Not one whit discomfited, it seems, Rousseau proceeds in the next chapter to insist that even unanimity would not be a sufficient criterion: 'There is often a great deal of difference between the will of all and the general will' (II(iii)).

Hegel, in Section 163 of his *Logic*, is keen to commend Rousseau's insistence: for he 'would have made a sounder contribution towards a theory of the State, if he had always kept this distinction in sight'. Although there is a conflict of opinion about the value of such success it would, surely, be unfair to suggest that Rousseau regularly failed to maintain the distinction? Certainly Hegel himself – with a contemporary's knowledge of the development of the great French Revolution through the Jacobin Terror to the establishment of Napoleon's Empire – was well aware of the way in which both rank-and-file members of vanguard parties and 'world-historical individuals' can conveniently become persuaded that they have been privileged to learn the authentic sense of the general will; and that these revelations may be vouchsafed to them not only without benefit of, but even contrary to, the verdicts of actual votings.

(b) It is, however, curious that, even though unanimity would not for Rousseau be sufficient, he does nevertheless allow some magic in a mere majority: 'There is often a great deal of difference between the will of all and the general will. The latter considers private interest and is merely the sum of private wills. But remove from these same wills the pluses and minuses that cancel each other out, and what remains as the sum of the differences is the general will' (II(iii)). What magic there seems to be is the mystery of mathematics. As so often in our age of computers, the only defence against deception is an acronymic principle – GIGO; which, being interpreted, is 'Garbage In, Garbage Out'. For, absent any miracles or magic, how do we become entitled to assume that the pluses and minuses will so providentially cancel out?

Rousseau also thinks to improve any electoral process which is admitted with various devices, none of which he even pretends to believe could be completely relied upon to yield the results desired, and most of which presuppose assumptions inconsistent with something previously asserted. It is when Rousseau suggests the questions – questions, as the Latin grammarians used to say, expecting the answer, 'Yes' – that those who were able to visit National Socialist Germany in the 1930s will be reminded of Hitler. For he made a practice of holding plebiscites, during which every hoarding demanded that everyone, '*Stimmt Ja!*'. Rousseau says (III(xviii)):

> The periodic assemblies I have spoken of earlier . . . which have as their sole object the preservation of the social treaty should always take place through two propositions . . . which are voted on separately:
>
> The first: *Does it please the sovereign to preserve the present form of government?*
>
> The second: *Does it please the people to leave its administration to those who are now in charge of it?*

Once corruption has set in 'the general will is no longer the will of all'. Yet even the venal citizen 'in selling his vote for money . . . does not extinguish the general will in himself; he evades it. The error he commits is that of . . . answering a different question from the one he was asked. Thus, instead of saying through his vote *it is advantageous to the state*, he says *it is advantageous to this man or that party*' (IV(i)).

But this is to assume, what before was sensibly denied, that, if only the responses are responses to the appropriate question, then they are bound to be correct. This same assumption is again, and rightly, rejected when, in the chapter immediately subsequent, Rousseau writes:

When a law is proposed . . . what is asked . . . is . . . whether or
not it conforms to the general will . . . Each man, in giving his
vote, states his opinion on this matter, and the declaration of the
general will is drawn from the counting of votes. *When,
therefore, the opinion contrary to mine prevails, this proves
merely that I was in error, and that what I took to be the general
will was not so.*

(IV(ii): emphasis added)

(c) Rousseau's last resort was to introduce the Legislator,
summoned to fulfil in the supposedly ideal state of *The Social
Contract* a function somewhat similar to that which, in the politics
of France during the first two or three decades after the Second
World War, General de Gaulle found for himself. Those whose
personal political memories do not extend so far may be helped
towards a sympathetic understanding by the telling of a mischievous
tale: perhaps not strictly true, but certainly *ben trovato*. A
psychologist studying the frequency of the occurrence of the first
person singular in the speeches of political leaders was puzzled by
the low score achieved by the General. This perplexity was only
resolved when the student noticed the extremely numerous
employments of the expression 'La France', and realized that this
subject identified himself absolutely with his country. 'The
Legislator', Rousseau tells us, 'is in every respect an extraordinary
man in the state. If he ought to be so by his genius, he is no less so
by his office, which is neither magistracy nor sovereignty. This
office, *which constitutes the republic*, does not enter into its
constitution' (II(vii): emphasis added).

Earlier we saw how Rousseau attempted to induce us to accept –
relying upon the putative magic of mathematics – that somehow
'the pluses and minuses' will 'cancel each other out, and what
remains as the sum of the differences' will be, or perhaps only may
be, 'the general will'. Now, finally, we have a *deus ex machina*
wheeled out onto the stage in order there to work the unfortunately
essential miracle. Like 'the fathers of nations' Rousseau, as the
dramatist of political theory, is forced 'to have recourse to the
intervention of heaven' in order to provide the criterial wisdom
which he cannot himself supply:

It is this sublime reason, transcending the plain man's
understanding, whose decisions the Legislator puts into the

mouth of the immortals in order by divine authority to compel those whom human prudence could not move. But not everybody is capable of making the gods speak or of being believed when he proclaims himself their interpreter. The great soul of the Legislator is the miracle which alone can prove his mission.

(II(vii))

What Rousseau's sometime benefactor and almost exact contemporary, in the final paragraph of Section X of the first *Enquiry*, said of the Christian religion may relevantly be repeated here as a suitably swinging, stinging comment upon Rousseau's political revelation: namely, that it 'not only was at first attended with miracles, but even at this day cannot be believed by any reasonable person without one'.

(ii) To illustrate the attraction which ideas of the real or general will of some collective have for voluntarists and for vanguards we cannot do better than look to Lenin and the Bolsheviks. For their October Revolution, rather than the National Socialist successor lauded by Leni Riefenstahl, truly was 'The Triumph of the Will'. Made in the name of, and supposedly in the interests of, the Russian proletariat, it was in fact led and dominated by an elite including almost no one with any real claim to be or even to have been a proletarian.

The voluntarism becomes most vivid when we recall that this revolution was made by professing Marxists, but at a time when and in a country where what had until April 1917 been agreed by all Marxists to be the conditions necessary for success were not satisfied. The gap between the actual will of the flesh-and-blood proletariat – to say nothing of that of the enormous non-proletarian majority – and the supposed real will of that proletariat as revealed to its self-appointed vanguard, yawned wide whenever any such actual wills were, however briefly, permitted to appear. This was most notoriously the case: both when the fairest and most comprehensive elections ever held resulted in a Constituent Assembly which the Bolsheviks forthwith dissolved by force; and, after the Civil War, in the savagely suppressed Kronstadt Revolt.

In *Our Revolution* (1922, p. 705) Lenin repeats his familiar defence of the Bolshevik coup and jeeringly recalls the objection: 'Russia has not attained the level of development of productive forces that makes socialism possible . . . . They keep repeating this incontrovertible proposition over the over again.' He makes no attempt to deny either the truth or the Marxist credentials of 'this incontrovertible proposition'. Instead he denies the political corollaries Marx drew from it: 'If a definite level of culture is required for the building of socialism, why cannot we begin by first achieving the prerequisites for that definite level of culture in a revolutionary way, and then, with the aid of the workers' and peasants' government and the Soviet system, proceed to overtake the other nations?'

There can, it seems, be no adequate answer to this challenge: if, that is, we are, with Lenin, but frankly, delighted to discount every objection deriving from the historical materialism of Marx; if, unlike Marx and unlike Lenin, we are ready to recognize that 'actually existing socialism' is a high-tech revival of oriental despotism (Shafarevitch 1980 and Wittfogel 1981); and if, with Lenin again, we construe his 'we' as referring to an elite endowed with, and eager to employ, unlimited and total dictatorial powers. This ruling elite, where what is curiously called a 'dictatorship of the proletariat' is in place, may sometimes consist, in effect, of a single person: 'The will of a class', in Lenin's own words, 'may sometimes be carried out by a dictator' (quoted Heller and Nekrich 1986, p.59). And the 'scientific definition' of the meaning of the word 'dictatorship' is, once again in Lenin's own words, 'power which is not limited by any laws, not bound by any rules, and based directly on force' (ibid., p. 62).

Chapter four

'Freedom is slavery!':
slogan for philosopher kings

'But if you want to be free, you've got to be a prisoner. It's the conditon of freedom – true freedom.'

'True freedom!' Anthony repeated in the parody of a clerical voice. 'I always love that kind of argument. The contrary of a thing isn't the contrary; oh, dear me, no! It's the thing itself, but as it *truly* is. Ask any die-hard what conservatism is; he'll tell you it's *true* socialism. And the brewer's trade papers; they're full of articles about the beauty of true temperance. Ordinary temperance is just gross refusal to drink; but true temperance, *true* temperance is something much more refined. True temperance is a bottle of claret with each meal and three double whiskies after dinner . . .'

'What's in a name?' Anthony went on. 'The answer is, practically everything, if the name's a good one. Freedom's a marvellous name. That's why you're so anxious to make use of it. You think that, if you call imprisonment true freedom, people will be attracted to the prison. And the worst of it is you're quite right.'

Aldous Huxley,
Eyeless in Gaza (p. 91)

The passage adopted as the epigraph for this chapter was first drawn to the attention of philosophers for providing an ideal illustration of persuasive definition (Stevenson 1938). This phenomenon consists in more or less surreptitiously so redefining some word or expression carrying strongly favourable or strongly unfavourable overtones that it now becomes correct to apply that word or that expression to a set of objects substantially different from that to which it was in its previous meaning correctly applicable. The object of the exercise is, of course, to persuade users of the words and the expressions so redefined to look upon the sets of objects to which these words or expressions have now become applicable with the same attitudes, favourable or unfavourable, as those which those users previously harboured towards members of those sets to which the same words and expressions had been correctly applicable in their previous understandings.

The expression 'persuasive definition' was originally employed as the title of an article; an article which later became a chapter in his book *Ethics and Language*. But the species flourishes best in political discourse. And such terms as 'liberty' and 'democracy' – terms with which we are at present most concerned – have been and are, for obvious reasons, especially exposed to persuasive redefinition: to liberate, an exultant Marcuse used to tell student mobs in the late 1960s, is to emancipate from 'repressive tolerance'; in Orwell's *1984* under Ingsoc (English Socialism) the telescreens are programmed to blare out the slogan, 'Freedom is Slavery!'; while Lenin, having himself originally insisted that undemocratic principles of party organization were required by the conditions of conflict with the tsarist autocracy, was later to recommend those same now to be permanent principles as those of 'democratic centralism' (Lenin 1902; and compare Flew 1979).

1 What is to be examined

Chapter four is in form an elaborate examination of *Freedom and Liberation* (Gibbs 1976). This examination is on two counts a worthwhile task. First because Gibbs' book is a sustained attempt by a professional philosopher to persuade us so to redefine the two key words that he becomes able to justify the forcible imposition of his own supposedly enlightened and more than purely personal ideals as constituting the true liberation of those to be thus compelled to conform. The fact that the book is a full-length development by a professional philosopher assures us that, in examining his case, we shall be confronting the argument for such 'positive freedom' at its strongest.

The second reason is that, although Gibbs genuflects towards the Marxist–Leninist *magisterium* sufficiently often to avoid excommunication from the Radical Philosophy Group, his main inspiration is in fact more Plato than any modern. It was, of course, the Plato of *The Republic* who first presented a vision of what was for him the ideal city state, ruled absolutely by an ideological oligarchy. It is always salutary to go back to the classics, and to labour to learn from them. It is even more salutary when these are the (capital C, Graeco-Roman) Classics.

(i) Plato's Guardians, also called by him Philosopher Kings, were to be, in a peculiarly strong sense, an ideological elite. For their rule was to be legitimated by their exclusive knowledge of the Platonic Ideas, supposedly constituting the true standards for values of every kind. (The word 'idea' is itself etymologically Greek.) These Philosopher Kings were thus to be both entitled and required to impose their own values upon the subordinate populace, by education, by propaganda (including the notorious 'Noble Lie'), and, if necessary, by force.

Certainly this ancient vision was in many ways very different both from that which inspired National Socialists and from that which still inspires Marxist–Leninists. Nevertheless there are also, in both cases, some fundamental and some superficial similarities. For instance: Plato and the National Socialists shared a constant concern with breeding. The master race elite destined to dominate Hitler's hoped-for Thousand Year Reich would have to be racially pure, while citizens of Plato's City Beautiful were to be allocated to the appropriate class or caste in accordance with their several genetically determined talents. (The 'Noble Lie' was a factitious aetiological myth, telling how members of Plato's three different classes or castes had come to have in their natures admixtures of, respectively, gold, copper, and iron: hence a contemporary critic's description of top-class Plato as 'The Golden Man'.)

Again, we might mention the too rarely noticed spiritual kinship between Plato's Guardians and Pol Pot's Khmer Rouge:

'All the people in the city who are more than ten years old,'
Socrates said, 'they will send out into the fields; and, taking hold
of the children away from the practices followed by their
parents, they will bring them up in their own customs and laws –
which will be as we have already described.'

(540E–541A)

(ii)   In his Preface, Gibbs asserts that 'The theory of freedom expounded in this book might be described not entirely ineptly as a form of liberalism' (1976, p. 8). We should perhaps be reminded of Schumpeter's remark about the socialists who, 'as a supreme but unintended compliment . . . have thought it wise to appropriate this label' (quoted Hayek 1978, p. 132). After explaining that he is himself, 'since the term has been preempted by defenders of a shallow and inadequate doctrine', willing to relinquish it, Gibbs concludes his preliminaries: 'it will be sufficiently obvious that this is not a tract *against* freedom' (Gibbs 1976, p. 8).

Yet, just as soon as we get into the main text, it begins to become clear to the alert that – apart from two or three pages of inconsistent backsliding (ibid., pp. 112 and 132 ff), occasioned by recalling belated insights in Plato's last, most disillusioned work, *The Laws* – 'a tract *against* freedom' is exactly what *Freedom and Liberation* is.

Such a reader will have formed strong suspicions by, at the latest, the time when Gibbs quotes, and – with a characteristic explosion against 'heartless *laissez-faire* policies' – dismisses, Berlin's definition: 'Political liberty . . . is simply the area within which a man can act unobstructed by others' (ibid., p. 24: quoted from Berlin 1969, p. 122). By the bottom of this page Gibbs has already begun to assure us that 'complete freedom is *more than* merely being *made* to do what is good; it consists in recognizing the good and doing it willingly' (emphasis added).

So it should come as no surprise to find J. S. Mill later hauled over the coals for, it is alleged, not owning up to having realized that 'freedom in the sense of personal autonomy is a very different thing from being allowed to do what one desires' (Gibbs 1976, p. 93). It is similarly unsurprising to learn that 'Moral freedom involves conformance [*sic*], not so much between what one is and what one wants to be, as between what one is and what one *ought* to be' (ibid., pp. 105–6).

Finally Gibbs gives an account of a free society which should, surely, win some sort of award for working three uses of the word 'make' – presumably to be understood here as a surreptitious synonym for 'compel' – into two short sentences: 'A free society is not simply one that *makes* its people do what is right and good. It is a society that . . . *makes* them do what is right and good by *making* them desire to do it understanding that it is right and good' (ibid., p. 109: some emphasis added, and some removed).

(iii)   Throughout *Freedom and Liberation* much is also disclosed, both directly and indirectly, about the Guardian elite which is to do all this making – the new Philosopher Kings who will, if all goes well, create, and impose their own values upon, what Gibbs still, despite all this authoritarian elitism, wants to credit as 'A free society'. Although he never actually employs these particular Platonic technicalities, both past and future quotations make it clear that to introduce them here is entirely fair and appropriate. But his lesser debts, to Marx and Lenin, begin to reveal themselves when Gibbs explains that, in order to get themselves upon their thrones, his Guardian elite will have to effect a revolution. For somewhat incongruously, and certainly without more than a few snide asides by way of explanation, this is to be revolution specifically against capitalism; a revolution involving 'fundamental changes in the economic framework'. Gibbs does no more than hint at what he would offer as his reasons for wanting to launch a revolution against what he takes to be the existing economic arrangements: 'The institutions of capitalism do not compose a stable system . . . . Calliclean libertinism is adopted as a principle of conduct' (ibid., p. 139): Callicles is represented in Plato's *Gorgias*). So what is to be done?:

> Without doubt, this charmless decaying polity needs some kind of revolution to restore its equilibrium and vigour . . . . But where are the engineers of revolution? Every great melioration that takes place in human affairs is initiated by some resolute organization, endowed with political wisdom. A revolutionary movement, if it is to succeed, must be in possession of a clear design for the social order it wishes to establish, and must be able to gain command of the means (including sufficient military power) to enforce execution of that design.
>
> (ibid., pp. 139–40)

As the red dawn draws near, Plato, it appears, is yielding place to Lenin, the Golden Man to the iron Bolshevik. But then, through another strange turn, it emerges that the true revolutionary party has yet to be constituted:

> There are few enlightened groups and persons of influence, who understand what is involved in a truly liberating reformation of society, and who are endeavouring to bring it about. We can

only hope that their numbers increase and that they find ways of uniting. With luck, they might still win the day.

(ibid., p. 141)

2 Misunderstanding the meaning of 'liberty'

Having grasped what Gibbs wants to do, we are now ready to discover how he sets about it. *Freedom and Liberation* was the second volume to appear in a series presenting 'Philosophy Now'. Our first clue lies in the repudiation of minute philosophy in the opening manifesto from the General Editor of the whole series. 'The books in this series', he says, 'are united by nothing except discontent with' an activity 'submissively dwindled into a humble academic specialism, on its own understanding isolated from substantive issues in other disciplines, from the practical problems facing society, and from contemporary Continental thought' (ibid., p. 6).

The author himself has a little more patience with logical analysis. Perhaps he at least half remembers that Plato wrote not only *The Republic* and *The Laws* but also *Theaetetus*. Nevertheless Gibbs still wants to mix up and confuse questions about meaning with questions of other, quite different kinds. He allows that 'Part of the enterprise must consist in reflecting on what may seem rather dull facts about the meaning of words', and that 'An adequate theory of freedom must have some congruity with [*sic*] ordinary linguistic usage'. But he completes the sentence of which the last quotation is the beginning by insisting that 'the problems are to a large extent psychological, moral and political problems' (ibid., p. 10).

(i) It is this insistence which leads him to reject Berlin's definition of 'political liberty', offering as his reason what is, among its other faults, and in an understanding which is not cant at all, simply irrelevant. 'Berlin's idea of freedom', Gibbs wails, 'could be invoked *as it stands*, without being misrepresented in any way, to justify heartless *laissez-faire* policies' (ibid., p. 23).

Let us, at least for the moment, put aside the questions whether to leave alone can never be to leave well alone, and whether '*laissez-faire* policies' must always and necessarily be heartless. For what is important here is to bring out that the Gibbs objection is both entirely beside the point and based on pervasive false assumptions. Whether or not 'Berlin's idea' could be so invoked is neither here nor there. Probably, given a little lawyerly ingenuity, almost any term could be put to some work in the development of a justification for almost anything. But about the correctness of any proposed descriptive definition the only question relevant is that of its 'congruity with ordinary linguistic usage'.

The reason why Gibbs thinks that his outraged cries are relevant lies in his forever hankering after a peculiar conception of what he proposes to go on calling freedom or liberty; a peculiar conception which will enable him to welcome this as always and everywhere, in all circumstances and without qualification, good. Indeed at times he appears to want to go even further, to maintain that it must itself embrace all goods of every kind. For his final chapter, 'Liberation and politics', begins: 'If perfect freedom encompasses the whole spectrum of human goods' – which I take him to be suggesting that it does – then 'a fully fledged political philosophy is needed to give an account of it' (ibid., p. 129). It is the more worthwhile to point out these misleading false assumptions in the case of liberty since, as we shall be seeing in Part II, both are paralleled in the development of what are offered as conceptions of justice.

This same ruinous insistence that nothing can truly be liberty, or true liberty, or perfect freedom, unless it is something which Gibbs could hail, if not as the sum of all goods, then at least as a good always and without qualification, occurs in *Freedom and Liberation* not once only, nor yet only once and again, but again and again and again. A page or so earlier, for instance, Gibbs writes:

> When a person can select any of several apparently flawless apples he *thinks* he has a free choice, but he will not think so if some of the apples are discovered to be rotten. . . . Being free to choose between likeable things is no advantage if, through ignorance or misjudgement, one is led to desire and choose things which are harmful. We want, surely, to be free to choose things that not only seem good but which really are good.
>
> (ibid., pp. 21–2)

(ii) No doubt this is what, on a great many occasions, we do want to be free to choose. Before proceeding with the argument, however, I have by the way to record that I am construing this 'we' as this time including the vulgar. That would certainly not be correct in some other cases. For example: at the end of a chapter on 'The direction of desire' Gibbs speaks with reproachful tolerance of 'depravity among adults whose desires have been irretrievably corrupted, and who would suffer great misery if they were forced to alter their ways . . . . Let us follow Mill's principle, permitting them to do as they like so long as they do it in private, and no one else is harmed' (ibid., p. 112). There the 'we' presumably has a more exclusive reference to the Guardian elect, who share with Gibbs all the right and good preferences.

It may be interesting further to interject that these, it seems, are: in opera, for *The Marriage of Figaro* over *Madam Butterfly* (ibid., pp. 19–20); in pubs, for real ale rather than the 'standardized pressurized, sweet indigestible muck that the big national breweries, with an eye to their profit, have conditioned the public to prefer' (ibid., p. 89); and, after 'one has been philosophizing all day', for 'taking a cross-country run' (ibid., p. 130). I am strongly tempted both to sound off about the unhappy experience of would-be consumers under 'actually existing socialism', and to point out that it is precisely 'with an eye to their profit' that several 'big national breweries', having identified an emerging demand, are now supplying real Guardian ales. Instead I will say only, and more generously, as a fellow alumnus of a British boarding school, how delightful it is, and how much in the spirit of *The Republic*, that Gibbs should be thus devoted to preserving a philosopher's mind in a healthy body.

No doubt – to return to the choosing of apples – we all do, on many occasions, want to choose between alternatives which do not merely seem to be but really are good. Yet this is no reason at all for saying that persons so unfortunate as to have chosen rotten apples, under the mistaken impression that these were all in splendid condition, have not freely and without coercion chosen whatever apples they have in fact chosen. If they think they have not so chosen, then they are in error. We might add too that – in their whingeing and whining refusal to accept responsibility for doing what, however excusably, they most manifestly have done – they display in this relatively trifling matter a mean-souled lack of moral fibre.

(iii)   Nor is it anywhere to the point to protest: 'Being free to choose between likeable things is no advantage if, through ignorance or misjudgment, one is led to desire and choose things which are harmful.' Whether or not it is an advantage is once again neither here nor there. The question is not whether it is in such circumstances an advantage to be free to choose, but whether people in those same circumstances have a free choice. And, of course, they do.

This is something of which on other occasions, Gibbs himself is well aware; as indeed, he could scarcely fail to be. At the very beginning of this chapter, and notwithstanding that he is going to put down, a mere dozen pages later, Berlin's negative definition of 'political liberty' as describing a 'merely nominal liberty' (ibid., p. 24), Gibbs recognizes what he christens 'prescriptive freedom' as something which is presumably not merely nominal: 'the idea of exemption from servitude and being allowed to do as one pleases . . . Prescriptive freedom is freedom from rules and rulers' (ibid., pp. 12–13). It is this same old original freedom – and again with no suggestion now that it is to be sneered at as negative, unreal, or merely nominal – of which Gibbs is speaking when he refers to Luther 'denouncing the German peasants, when they revolted against their princes and sought liberty for themselves' (ibid., p. 82). Most remarkably, it is still the same old original, genuine freedom which is under discussion in those curious backslidings in his final chapter.

There – sandwiched between the previously quoted proclamation that 'perfect freedom encompasses the whole spectrum of human goods' (p. 129) and the concluding call for the Guardian elite to gather its forces '(including sufficient military power)' in order to overthrow by revolutionary violence 'senescent capitalism, putrid with greed, luxury and lawlessness' (ibid., p. 140) – we can find an incongruous admission: 'The liberal political tradition is right to insist that human welfare requires a fair degree of liberty, understood simply as being allowed to do as one pleases, for good or ill' (ibid., p. 134). Earlier Gibbs made an even more remarkable admission: 'There may never have existed a society which granted its members more liberty than we citizens of England enjoy' (ibid., pp. 109–10).

3 Suggesting senses of 'freedom'

None of this liberal backsliding is permitted to detract from the bold convictions that a *truly* free society is 'one that makes its people do what is right and good', while also 'making them *desire* to do it *understanding* that it is right and good' (ibid., p. 109). Nor does it insinuate into his mind the slightest anxiety as to whether his own revolutionary elite would, if it were ever permitted to seize the desired dictatorial power, allow it to be, as of course we are agreed that it is, 'patent sophistry to argue that, in a juster, freer society than the one we know, the traditional liberties might be abolished completely' (ibid., p. 136). This patent sophism, after all, has been and is both presented and accepted by every Jacobin from Robespierre and Saint-Just, through Lenin and Trotsky, right up to Castro and Ho Chi Minh.

His brief encounter with 'insubstantial and sterile . . . liberal ideology' (ibid., p. 128) thus fails to produce any salutary effects upon Gibbs. The main reason for this failure lies in that prime, besetting confusion between, on the one hand, questions of what liberty and freedom are, and, on the other hand, questions whether some particular exercise or kind of exercise of either is or was or will be – in the phrase made famous by *1066 and All That* – 'a good thing'. About this, Bentham said what should but obviously will not be 'the last word: "Is not liberty to do evil, liberty? If not, what is it? Do we not say that it is necessary to take liberty from idiots and bad men because they abuse it?"' (quoted Berlin 1969, p.46).

(i) Another source of trouble, though different from, is nevertheless related to that examined in the preceding section 2. Gibbs, though not so impatient of philosophical underlabouring as his General Editor, is still in much too much of a hurry to get on to what the latter has proudly proclaimed to be 'the theory of freedom expounded in this book' (1976, p. 6).

In that, though not in its comparatively modest bulk, *Freedom and Liberation* is reminiscent of *A Theory of Justice*; a work about which much more will be said in Part II, below. For the author of that monster volume expresses his happiness 'to leave questions of meaning and definition aside and to get on with the task of developing a substantive theory of justice' (Rawls 1971, p. 579). In both cases this impatience makes it easier to present what is at least in part an essay in persuasive redefinition as something more and other than it is.

(a) In chapter 1, 'Freedom: a conceptual labyrinth', Gibbs begins: 'All men yearn to be free . . .' After giving several examples of expressions of this yearning, he concludes, sadly: 'Yet there is no general agreement about what, in its essence, freedom is' (1976, p. 9). The titles of the following four chapters all suggest that Gibbs is going to be dealing with what was, in chapter one, above, distinguished as the more fundamental of 'two quite different yet not unrelated understandings of the words "liberty" and "freedom"'. These titles are: 'Metaphysical determinism'; 'Metaphysical indeterminism'; 'Naturalistic determinism'; and 'The elements of freedom'. Yet all the examples to illustrate the universal yearning given by Gibbs here are examples of liberty and freedom in the less fundamental of those 'two quite different yet not unrelated understandings'. Nor, it seems, does he ever come to appreciate how important this distinction is.

Without attempting, however cursorily, to sort out what was actually being said in the various confusing particular cases which he had himself instanced, Gibbs went on at once to outline, in very general terms, his own first answer to the general question: 'Certainly it is possible to be confused or mistaken, and to deceive people, about what being free or being set free consists in.' Nevertheless, Gibbs suggests, the truth is that the word ' "freedom" means different things in different contexts . . . it has a number of meanings which, though distinct, are . . . related to each other in specifiable ways'. He therefore concludes 'that there is no single correct concept of freedom' (ibid., p. 9).

If only Gibbs had had the patience to consider his own initial illustrations carefully, he could scarcely have failed to realize that they were in fact all cases not of differences in meaning but of differences in reference. But that there are different constraints from which different sets of people yearn to be free has no tendency to show that the word 'freedom' has, in their several mouths, different meanings.

Still more unfortunate is the fact that, in the very same paragraph in which we were just now told that 'there is no single correct concept of freedom' – that very same paragraph in which we are also about to be warned that 'We are prone to misconceive and misrepresent this perplexingly polymorphous notion, to abstract from it something . . . which we take to be the real essence of freedom' – we are then told that, in the event, 'What is brought into being may be a negation of true freedom' (ibid., p. 10). Whatever can this 'negation of true freedom' be if it is not the negation of that allegedly nonsubsistent single correct concept of freedom?

(b)   First, to maintain that 'there is no single correct concept of freedom' and then to speak of something as a possible 'negation of true freedom' is, manifestly, to contradict yourself. Yet the fault here may perhaps be put down as venial if it is to be interpreted as an anticipatory, pre-emptive self-reproach. Could it be that Gibbs then was, at least for a moment, and if only semi-consciously, ashamed of his forthcoming performance – an exercise in persuasive redefinition which is supposed to justify in the name of liberty the revolutionary destruction of a social system which, on his own admission, guarantees liberties possibly more numerous than any other people have ever enjoyed? Certainly we ought to endorse the statement which Gibbs made immediately before the last sentence quoted: 'If such abstractions are employed as principles of social policy, there may be a high price to pay in human suffering' (ibid., p. 10).

Nor shall I refrain from adding – as a more private and personal manifesto – that, if there is such a high price to be paid in the present particular case, then it is my own most fervent, albeit hopeless, hope that it may be paid by the self-recruiting elite making such frivolous and wanton calls for revolution; rather than by the vulgar. We have deplorable tastes which give offence to our yet-to-be-anointed Philosopher Kings: – 'predilections squalid and degraded'; and 'desires . . . for expensive material goods and pleasures' (ibid., p. 110).

(ii)   One possible cause of a false appearance of ambiguity in uses of the words 'liberty' and 'freedom' was noticed in the previous subsection. Another is the fact that any liberties legally secured to one set of people are bound to be so secured at the price of possible liberties which might have been secured for others. It was again Bentham who most doggedly insisted upon the truth of this truism: 'Every law is an infraction of liberty.' For even when a law does secure some liberty for all of us, still it must at the same time prevent everyone from violating that liberty; the very laws which guarantee our liberties to cultivate our own gardens must do so by restricting everyone's liberty to vandalize the gardens of others.

This is a very simple principle. Yet it is one which you are sure to find very difficult to grasp if, with Gibbs and with so many others, you want to insist that any freedom – or any true or real or perfect freedom – is always and in all circumstances and without qualification good. Once that self-imposed handicap is abandoned, there is no difficulty in resolving the paradoxes with which Gibbs begins his whole discussion. For there is then no call to be surprised that two human sets should be in conflict, while members of both sincerely profess to be fighting for liberty. The questions to ask are: 'Liberty in what direction?; and 'Liberty for whom?'. It will be time to think of multiplying senses, or to speak of intractable antinomies, when we find conflicts between groups demanding either the same liberties for the same people or equal liberties for all.

(iii)   We have seen that Gibbs, in the second paragraph of his first chapter, both maintains that '"freedom" has a number of meanings which, though distinct are . . . related to each other in specifiable ways'; and insists 'that there is no single correct concept of freedom' (ibid., p. 9). Nevertheless, before that paragraph was out, he started to talk of 'a negation of true freedom' (ibid., p. 10). Later in the same chapter he lists supposed or proposed meanings, specifying ways in which they are related. It may be salutary to review what is in itself a somewhat unsatisfactory exercise.

(a)   The first supposed sense of 'freedom', which Gibbs labels 'prescriptive', and explains in a curiously constipated way, refers to what we have been calling legally guaranteed liberties: 'Prescriptive freedom is freedom from rules and rulers; still, where there is no authority and no law, there is no prescriptive freedom or bondage' (ibid., p. 13).

He proceeds next to 'distinguish and give appropriate designations to four kinds of non-prescriptive freedom attributable to persons' (ibid., p. 17). This is where he deploys most of his argument for the conclusion that 'A free society' is one in which people are *made* to do what is right and good, and *made* to like it, agreeing that it is right and good. The case thus developed is, surely, neither? Furthermore, and although nothing of importance depends on this, it would seem that for only one of what Gibbs wants to distinguish as these different senses is there an established usage, whether non-technical or even technical.

(b)   The scope of what Gibbs christens 'optative freedom' just is the scope of human action as such: 'Indeed', he says himself, 'any act is free to that extent; there is no *acting* without the possibility of abstaining from acting. If a person has absolutely no choice about what he does – if he unavoidably breaks a window, for example, having been thrown against it by a gust of wind – then what takes place is just a happening, not strictly speaking a human act' (ibid., p. 18).

So far so good: this most crucial point could scarcely have been better put. But then whatever warrant can there be for hypothesizing and labelling a fresh sense of 'free' appropriate always and only to action, and such that all and only action can and must be free? What is wrong with saying, more simply and tersely, that this or that person was in this or that dimension an agent; without droning on about their being, therefore, necessarily and tautologically endowed with optative freedom? And, furthermore, once you have grasped the essential nature of human agency, you should, surely, go on to bring out that and how this fundamental fact of our nature is presupposed by every question about both freedom and constraint?

(c)   The next fresh coinage is conative freedom. This time the description which Gibbs provides is not so satisfactory. But when we take this with his illustrations it becomes obvious both that he has in mind the altogether familiar distinction between acting under compulsion and acting freely – acting, that is, of one's own freewill; and that conative freedom is what one has in this second case. His own account runs: 'If someone does something out of fear, unwillingly, reluctantly, under duress, or *faute de mieux*, he does not do it of his own free will. Yet the act is voluntary; it does not take place without reference to the agent's will; he is not moved willy-nilly. As I said earlier, "free will" is a synonym for "optative freedom"' (ibid., p. 20: Gibbs omits the quotation marks which should surround the expression 'optative freedom').

This account is on two counts unsatisfactory. First, it is unsatisfactory in applying the word 'voluntary' to what is presented as, though not in so many words said to be, not done under compulsion. But did not Austin teach us that in ordinary, untechnical usage the voluntary is opposed neither to the non-voluntary nor to the involuntary but to the compulsory? Second, and more serious, after a correctly colloquial employment of the expression 'of his own free will' in the exploration of the nature of conative freedom, Gibbs proceeds to allow that 'free will' is a synonym for 'optative freedom'. Certainly, as he noticed two pages earlier, this claim does accord with the usage of many philosophers; a usage usually not recognized as being technical. But – as was argued in section 1 of chapter one, above – it is here, as so often, better to follow Berkeley by speaking with the vulgar while thinking with the learned.

(d) We have already approached the third Gibbs coinage in connection with the choice of apples. Here the free agent is taken to be free in precisely the same sense as before: he is not, that is to say, acting under compulsion. But, whereas in a case of the previous kind that agent may be confronted with only one single positively attractive option, in this kind there have to be at least two. The rationale runs: 'To have a choice, in the full sense, is to be able to choose between agreeable alternatives. I shall refer to this henceforward as *elective freedom*' (ibid., p. 21).

Certainly it is true that we do often say in cases of the second sort that the compelled (but not the free) agent had no choice, and could not have done otherwise. It is also very important to notice, as Gibbs does, that even in those compulsion cases, it is true to say that in other and more fundamental senses, there was a choice, and that something else could have been done. Yet none of this constitutes a reason for saying that in cases of the third kind the agent is free, in another sense of 'freedom'; much less for saying – as we saw earlier that Gibbs does also go on to say – that he only has a real choice, being truly free in yet another sense, when the options available, and in particular the option actually chosen, not merely seem to be but are good.

Thus Gibbs is already beginning to confound freedom to choose between alternatives with the actual achievement of approved ends. It is a kind of confusion lamentably common in our time. Another variety of this same kind of confusion is that of those sociologists and educationalists who systematically collapse the distinction between opportunity and outcome. Because some particular racial or social set is not represented in some particular occupational set in the same proportion as in the general population, it is immediately inferred that members of that particular racial or social set must have been 'denied access' by being subjected to some sort of hostile discrimination (Flew 1981, ch. 2, sections 4–5). It seems never to occur either to such professing social scientists, or to the laypersons whom they manage to misinform, that there may have been relevant differences not only in the natural talents and temperaments of, but also in the senses of the individual choices made by, members of whatever particular racial or social sets are from time to time in question.

(e)   It is, however, with his fourth and final supposed sort of freedom that Gibbs really goes to town. This discussion is also the prime manifestation of the author's resolve to mix up questions of meaning with questions of value. Thus he begins: 'The value of freedom depends on that of the goods which it is the power of achieving' (1976, p. 22). Maybe it does. But this is no way to start detecting a further sense of the word 'free'.

Gibbs continues: 'The most precious freedom of all is the power of avoiding the greatest evils and achieving the greatest goods . . . . The most appropriate epithet for this sovereign freedom would be "eudaimonic" . . . . I shall use the term *natural freedom*, since this is the power of attaining and enjoying the cardinal goods appropriate to our nature' (ibid., p. 22).

This may – or may not – be all very well. But the relevant question here is why it is represented as a kind of freedom. 'To furnish a person with natural freedom', Gibbs continues, 'would be to liberate him not just in this or that respect but completely . . . . Thus, whereas every other kind of freedom consists in *being able* to avoid evil and to do good, natural freedom consists primarily in *actually* being immune from the worst evils and *actually* achieving the supreme goods' (ibid., p. 22). The emphases, which are of course all his, make it more rather than less difficult to discover why Gibbs wants us to accept this unsolicited gift as that of a kind of freedom.

For his only answer he resorts to his own version of that most notorious conversation-stopper of decadent Scholasticism: 'Aristotle hath said it.' His answer reads: 'Aristotle defines *eudaimonia* as "activity of soul in accordance with perfect virtue" (*Nicomachean Ethics* 1102a 5): activity, not mere potentiality; practice of the good life, not simply possession of the capacity to live well. It involves *willingness* to use and extend one's human talents and powers' (1976, p. 22). But what is needed here Aristotle hath not even said. For this was his definition of nothing else but 'eudaimonia'. Allow that Gibbs would do a trifle better by calling his 'natural freedom' eudaimonic freedom. But the real scandal is not adjectival but substantive. It is to commend what is not freedom at all as not merely one kind but actually the highest kind.

4 Miscellaneous anti-liberal misconceptions

There would seem to be no grounds for believing that *Freedom and Liberation* has been especially influential. The reason for making so extensive an examination of its treatment of the title topics is that the book constitutes a compendium of all the commonest misunderstandings and misrepresentations. That examination can now conveniently be supplemented by a consideration of two or three further misunderstandings and misrepresentations widely prevalent among those disposed – with Gibbs – to dismiss classical liberalism as 'a shallow and inadequate doctrine' (ibid., p. 8).

(i)   Gibbs has a lot to say about 'The romantic libertarianism of John Stuart Mill' (ch. 6). Contributors to this Sussex series, 'Philosophers Now', are licensed to treat Mill with some respect because – unlike crude fellows who rail at all his works as 'nothing more than an exposition of the individualistic ideology of *laissez-faire* economics' – they have been made aware that:

> Marx himself said, 'It would be very wrong to class (Mill) with the herd of vulgar economic apologists' (*Capital* I, VI, xxiv, 5). Like most bourgeois intellectuals (including Marx) Mill detested the avaricious society that had made him. Mill was not a conscious or unconscious spokesman for capitalism.
>
> (ibid., p. 85)

Nevertheless there are some things which 'Indeed Mill says (showing his bourgeois streak?)', or which at any rate Gibbs says that Mill says, that come under the lash (ibid., p. 92). For instance: poor, capitalist-corrupted Mill is at one point denounced because 'He makes no attempt to give this fatuous and fantastic claim the support it calls for' (ibid., p. 90). What, then, was the object of such contempt? What Gibbs says is that 'He says, apparently with conviction, that grown persons are always the best judges of what is in their own interest.' But what, immediately after this, Mill is actually quoted as saying is something else altogether: 'With respect to his own feelings and circumstances, the most ordinary man and woman has means of knowledge immeasurably surpassing those that can possessed by anyone else.'

Now that, as a moment's thought should be sufficient to reveal, is by no means so silly as what Gibbs is condemning Mill for having said. The point is that, whereas there may be room for Guardians better able than we to determine our true needs and true interests, we are all our own best experts on what we like and dislike, what we want, and how we feel. This is why the National Union of Teachers, when it argues against giving parents the education vouchers which would enable them to take their children to whatever school is providing the kind of quality of teaching service which those parents *want*, boasts that its members are alone qualified to determine and to cater for the educational *needs* of all children (Flew 1987a).

That is also the reason why the likes of Abdul Kharume and Janos Kadar prefer a definition of the hooray-word 'democracy' which refers not to what, for better or for worse, uncoerced electors do actually choose, but instead to whatever the ruling elite determines to be the *real* interests of whatever it itself identifies as the *true* people. That too, allied with the fact that needs are customarily contrasted with luxuries, are good reasons why, in listening to the familiar, seductive slogan of the *Critique of the Gotha Programme*, we should hear not so much a promise of freedom and abundance as a threat of austerity and authoritarianism: 'From each according to their abilities, to each according to their needs' (Marx 1891, p. 23).

(ii)   Gibbs, as befits a would-be Philosopher King, longs to delegitimize Hume's Law and to 'transcend' the categorical distinction between fact and value. For, as he puts it, 'Liberal ideologists frequently invoke the positivist doctrine of a fact–value dichotomy, in support of libertarian social policies' (1976, p. 115). So Hume has to be seen off:

> Hume claims that morality cannot be derived from matters of fact, because it is impossible to move validly from 'is' to 'ought'. The argument is misconceived. If the difference between 'is' and 'ought' were to lend support for the theory of a dichotomy between facts and values, it would have to be the case that all factual statements were 'is'-statements and all value statements 'ought'-statements. But some 'is'-statements – for example, 'Fornication is disgraceful' – are value statements.
>
> (ibid., p. 116)

Gibbs here is referring to what has perhaps become the most often-quoted passage from all Hume's writings (Hume 1739–40,

III (i) 1, p. 469). Certainly Gibbs is not the first nor even by now the latest critic to be tripped up by Hume's irony, and to be found in consequence sprawling flat on his face. So, embarrassing though it is to repeat such a hackneyed and to him humiliating hermeneutic truth to a professional colleague, there is no alternative but to insist once again that Hume's contention concerned a distinction which too frequently is not made; yet which, he thought, always could be and should be. He was not maintaining that, notwithstanding that this distinction regularly and most fastidiously is made, it was left to a Scottish 'lad of pairts' to recognize, for the first time, that it always is made, and is 'of the last importance'. Had Hume in truth maintained the position so confidently and so contemptuously overwhelmed by Gibbs, then Hume's contention might well have been described as – to put a borrowed phrase to more appropriate use – 'fatuous and fantastic'.

(iii)   Gibbs is very free with his condemnations of 'heartless *laissez-faire* policies' (1976, p. 26) and of 'senescent capitalism, putrid with greed, luxury and lawlessness' (ibid., p. 160); as well as of 'your typical smug pillar of commercial society' (ibid., p. 105), and of any one else who can be put down as 'a conscious or unconscious spokesman for capitalism' (ibid., p. 85). But there is in *Freedom and Liberation* precious little indication of any serious study, either of the sort of social arrangements to be condemned so unreservedly, or of the alternatives now offered by 'actually existing socialism'. Gibbs is no more 'in possession of a clear design for the social order' which he 'wishes to establish' than was Marx in the nineteenth century or Lenin in October 1917. All this, when the stakes are so inordinately high, should be seen as scandalous frivolity.

(a)   Earlier we quoted the sentence: 'Berlin's idea of freedom, however, could be invoked as it stands, without being misrepresented in any way, to justify heartless *laissez-faire* policies' (ibid., p. 24). The two sentences immediately following, which presumably express the author's perverse misunderstanding of what it would be to implement such policies, read:

> If a ruler owns all the land and means of production, he need not burden his people with a multitude of laws and taxes. He need not make explicit demands, because his subjects have no choice but to sell him their labour, in order to survive.
>
> (ibid., p. 24)

But this is scarcely a description, even a very angrily distorted description, of a free, competitive, and pluralist economy – what the first and greatest of those 'vulgar economic apologists' called not capitalism but 'the natural system of perfect liberty and justice', or 'the obvious and simple system of natural liberty' (Smith 1776, IV (vii) 3 and IV (ix)). This Gibbs' description of 'heartless *laissez-faire*', like the reality of 'actually existing socialism', corresponds in this world most closely with what Marx knew as 'the Asiatic mode of production' and others have called 'oriental despotism' (Wittfogel 1981).

Since Gibbs and his associates in the Radical Philosophy Group will clearly be deaf to anything said by anyone who can be put down as 'a conscious or unconscious spokesman for capitalism', we can do no better here than quote the author of *The Revolution Betrayed*, describing what to the end of his days he always insisted on defending, with incorrigible stubbornness, as a Workers' State. Of course, after nearly three-quarters of a century of contemporary experience, we also have to recognize that, for those who are or hope to be among the commanding elite, the attraction of full socialism precisely is this promise of total power:

In a country where the sole employer is the State, opposition means death by slow starvation. The old principle, who does not work shall not eat, has been replaced by a new one: who does not obey shall not eat.

(Trotsky 1937, p. 76)

(b) Gibbs shows the same frivolity in his sole, qualified commendation of the putative track record of what he recognizes as 'actually existing socialism':

The Russians produce novels, symphonies and rockets at least as good as ours. The leaders of modern China have controlled the lives and thoughts of their people more than Mill would have conceived possible; yet the social and technological achievements of that same people during that same period have astonished the world.

(1976, p. 95)

Responsible, and sincerely benevolent enquirers, before deciding to recommend any similarly revolutionary road, would insist on making some comparisons of before and after; and on giving some consideration to relative costs. How, they would ask, do Soviet achievements since 1917 compare with those under the pre-revolutionary regime? (See, for instance, Heller and Nekrich 1986.) Or they might compare Soviet performance in any period with that of Japan since 1965 – the latter bought at no human costs remotely comparable with those incurred in the Civil War and the consequent famine (ibid.); in 'the liquidation of the kulaks as a class' (Conquest 1986); and in *The Great Terror* (Conquest 1968). As for the Communist record in China, the Small Helmsman and his associates might be themselves even more astonished than displeased were they to be presented with any claims about spectacular social and technological advances during the successive traumata of the Great Leap Forward, the Great Proletarian Cultural Revolution, and the dictatorship of the Gang of Four.

What is most shocking about the Gibbs proposals to establish a new order of Philosopher Kings is indeed the frivolous, unenquiring irresponsibility with which they are advanced, and the lack of any visible concern for the possible victims of his projected total transformation. In *The Law of Love and the Law of Violence* there is a passage, released only in 1917, which, though exceedingly harsh and even perhaps mistaken in its diagnosis of motivation, should be taken to heart by anyone contemplating any kind of violent political revolution. Tolstoy was writing of 'a regime which exists only in imagination'. His warning words carry far greater force now that regimes of the Soviet sort rule in reality more than a third of the peoples of the world:

> Understand then all of you, especially the young, that to want to impose on others by violent means a regime that you can only imagine is not only grossly ignorant but even criminal.
> Understand that such work, far from assuring the well-being of humanity is only a lie, a more or less unconscious hypocrisy, camouflaging the lowest passions we possess.
>
> (Tolstoy 1909, pp. 95–6)

Chapter five

Choices and wants: discrediting the actual

'Now, if to be filled with what nature demands is pleasant, that which is more really filled with real things will make a man rejoice more really and truly with true pleasure; while that which receives what is less real will be filled less really and certainly, and will receive more untrustworthy, and less true pleasure.'
'That is quite inevitable', he said.
'Then they who have no experience of insight and virtue, but spend their whole time in revelling and suchlike . . . cannot be satisfied inasmuch as what they are trying to fill is not the real and continent part of themselves, nor is what they are putting into it real.'
'Truly perfect, Socrates,' said Glaucon, 'is your utterance regarding the life of the vulgar.'

Plato, *The Republic* (585E–586B)

Chapter one began by 'distinguishing two quite different yet not unrelated understandings of the words "liberty" and "freedom".' It went on to notice how, in the name of science, B. F. Skinner and others have tried to make out that, in the more fundamental of these two understandings, there exists nothing to which these words can correctly be applied. But on the contrary, it was then argued, we could not, as we do, even understand that negative claim were we not all of us, as we are, in a position to know its falsity. It is, furthermore, an essential and distinguishing characteristic of human beings that we are agents: agents who, as such and necessarily, always could do other than we do do; and agents who, again as such and equally necessarily, are never absolutely necessitated to act as we do act. It is just this essential and distinguishing fact about our human nature which gives importance to questions about liberty and freedom in the other and less fundamental of the two understandings distinguished in that first chapter.

Chapter two argued both that, if any claim to universal natural rights is to be vindicated, then it can only be a claim to option as opposed to welfare rights, and that such a claim will certainly have to be somehow grounded upon the fact that, as agents, we are creatures who can, and cannot but, make choices. We are also creatures who, as rational beings, can both have and give reasons for pursuing ends for ourselves. It is as members of this very special species that we may – and, I would say, should – demand the right to be left to our own devices; provided only that, and only in so far as, the devices chosen do not violate the equal rights of any others.

Chapter three began by examining the teachings of *The Social Contract*, bringing out the incompatibility of justification by reference to a social contract with justification by reference to some purported General Will. It then went on to show the appeal possessed by notions of that second sort for all those who exercise or hope to exercise total power. Chapter four considered the most popular misconceptions about liberty, incidentally illuminating some of the ways in which its opponents would have us see them as in truth supporters; albeit, of course, as supporters primarily if not exclusively of supposed liberty of some higher sort – of 'positive liberty', of 'natural liberty', perhaps even of 'eudaimonistic liberty'.

Chapter five is going to draw these themes together. First, it will consider a common kind of systematic misrepresentation, under which what in reality constitute, for better or for worse, the actions of an agent – performances for which that agent may therefore in some way be held accountable – are instead put down as the behaviours of a patient – presumably, therefore, performances outwith that patient's control. Second, it will survey the main manœuvres by which reference to the actual and categorical wishes of individuals may be set aside in favour of pretended concern for their alleged needs, their putative interests, or their hypothetical real wills.

These misrepresentations and these manœuvres both result in a de-emphasizing or even denial of differences between individuals, and thus tend to subvert claims to the importance and value of individual liberty. The most extreme form of this de-emphasis or denial will be examined in chapter seven, below. For sponsors of procrustean programmes for compulsory equalization have argued – in the name of (social) justice – that all the differentiating chararcteristics of the intended subjects of these programmes (of us, that is, the unanointed vulgar) must be regarded as not truly and individually theirs (not, that is, as truly and individually ours). Instead all these differentiating characteristics are to be treated as properly a collective asset, or, presumably, as the case must often be, as a collective liability.

The common kind of systematic misrepresentation to be considered here consists in the overextension of the application of the concept of mental disease. The consideration of this connects closely with chapter four. For Plato seems to have been the first both to introduce this concept and to overextend its application (Flew 1973a, pp. 12–19; also n.22). This exercise played an important part in legitimizing the rule of his Philosopher Kings. It was too a sign of the shape of sinister things to come that, having introduced the concept precisely and only in order to further these legitimating political purposes, Plato immediately insisted upon its embracing all perceived delinquency. Those duly qualified as Guardians became by this diagnosis political doctors licensed to practise against such delinquents an incongruously penal form of what has since been christened 'orthopsychiatry'. (Readers of Samuel Butler's 1901 novel *Erewhon*, remembering his perhaps Platonically inspired Straighteners, may like to notice, as a memorable example of life imitating art, that in 1924 the American Orthopsychiatric Association was founded with the stated object of bringing together 'representatives of the neuro-psychiatric or medical view of crime'.) 'Orthos' is the Greek for 'straight' or 'correct'.

The promised discussion of those 'main manœuvres' in the present chapter connects equally closely with the business of both chapter four and chapter three. For the 'eudaimonistic' freedom which Gibbs wished to promote is not straightforwardly and unequivocally our freedom – our freedom to do what we ourselves do actually want to do. Instead it is doing (and wanting to do) whatever Gibbs and his fellow Guardians judge to be in our (best) interests and for our (true) good. Rousseau's General Will also was, notoriously, very far removed from the actual present will of some or even all: '*When, therefore, the opinion contrary to mine prevails, this proves merely that I was in error, and that what I took to be the general will was not so.*'

They are words which Trotsky might have pondered, after his decisive defeat, and while subjecting himself to the victors:

> None of us can be right against the Party. In the last instance the Party is always right, because it is the only historical instrument which the working class possesses for the solution of its fundamental tasks. I know that one cannot be right against the Party. One can be right only with the Party and through the Party, because History has not created any other way for the realization of one's rightness.
>
> (quoted Deutscher 1965, p. 139)

1 Plato, delinquency, and disease

The contention from which Plato derives his conclusion that all delinquency is the outcome of some psychological disorder or disease is a thesis which he represents as distinctively Socratic: 'No one willingly does wrong.' This traditional translation is, however, misleading: it suppresses the fact that the Greek verb rendered as 'does wrong' also means 'fails' or 'misses the mark'; and it puts the emphasis on the will, whereas Plato himself stressed the intellect. His general line was, since all men always and necessarily do whatever seems good to them, if they do what is in truth bad, then it can only be because they have mistaken appearance for reality. Since it was also assumed that whatever is good is also good for you, your characteristic and habitual evil-doing must manifest gross failure on your part to appreciate your own best interests; and this cannot but be diagnosed as a mental, indeed an intellectual, disorder.

According to Plato, delinquency consists in the failure of the elements of the soul to perform their functions harmoniously. This strictly parallels that failure of bodily organs to perform their functions harmoniously which, Plato takes it, is physical disease. Perhaps one reason why these Platonic anticipations of doctrines quite popular in some circles in our time have only rather recently been recognized as such is that the Classical Greek word, which in our language provides the etymological root for 'psychiatry' and kindred terms, is usually rendered as 'soul' rather than 'mind'; and souls, if such entities are allowed to exist at all, are nowadays thought to be the business of priests rather than of any kind of doctors.

When Philippe Pinel opened an emancipatory epoch by ordering that the chains be struck from the prisoners of La Salpêtrière, he insisted upon the crucial distinction between delinquent actions and the non-voluntary behaviour of victim patients – a distinction which, at least in the present context, Plato ignored: 'The mentally ill, far from being guilty persons who merit punishment, are sick people whose miserable state deserves all the consideration due to suffering humanity.'

Members of the British Royal Commission on the Law Relating to Mental Illness and Mental Deficiency were in the same tradition when they asserted, with satisfaction: 'The general public now know more about mental illness and are more sympathetic to people suffering from it than ever before' (*Report*, 1957, p. 2). Both passages emphasize two fundamental resemblances between disease, in the primary physical sense, and what is to be called mental disease: that in both cases something is wrong with the patient which is bad for that patient, and not necessarily for anyone else or for society as a whole; and that the patient, as is appropriately suggested by that choice of word, is with respect to this something victim rather than agent.

It is this and this alone which makes it possible for affliction with first a physical and then later by analogy a mental disease to be sometimes reasonably accounted an excuse. Thus, in what later turned out to have become a leading decision, Judge Somerville declared that 'there must be two constituent elements of legal responsibility in the commission of every crime, and no rule can be just and reasonable which fails to recognize either of them: (1) capacity of intellectual discrimination; and (2) freedom of the will.' Having earlier, with a fine sense of occasion, insisted that the Common Law is not 'like the law of the Medes and Persians, which could not be changed', and that 'its power of adaptation to new scientific discoveries, and the requirements of an everadvancing civilization . . . must not be unduly obstructed by the doctrine of *stare decisis*', Judge Somerville proceeded to conclude that, if it is true as a matter of fact that mental disease can so affect the mind 'as to subvert the freedom of the will, and thereby destroy the power of the victim to choose between right and wrong, although he perceive it', then the patient of such a disease must surely be, no matter how clear that perception, innocent victim rather than criminal agent (*Parson v. State* (1886) 81 Alabama 5772 So 854).

Substantially the same conclusion was reached by Sir James Fitzjames Stephen. He proposed three rules to replace the McNaghten two, offering these confidently as an account of what the law ought to be, and only slightly less confidently as an analysis of what really it was already:

> No act is a crime if the person who does it is at the time when it is done prevented (either by defective mental power or) by any disease affecting his mind: (a) from knowing the nature and quality of his act; or, (b) from knowing that the act is wrong; or, (c) from controlling his own conduct, unless the absence of the power of control had been produced by his own default.
>
> (Stephen 1904, pp. 20–1)

More than a half a century later, in 1953, Stephen's third rule was endorsed as a proposal by the Royal Commission on Capital Punishment, but without the final exception clause. They recommended a change in the law to require that 'the jury must be satisfied that, at the time of committing the act, the accused, as a result of disease of the mind or mental defect, either: (a) did not know the nature and quality of the act; or (b) did not know it was wrong; or (c) was incapable of preventing himself from committing it' (p. 39; and compare section 317). This recommendation is in effect identical with that included in the Model Penal Code of the American Law Institute:

> A person is not responsible for criminal conduct if at the time of such conduct, as a result of mental disease or defect, he lacks substantial capacity either to appreciate the criminality of his conduct or to conform his conduct to the requirements of the law.
>
> (section 4.01)

The same understanding of disease, whether physical or mental, is again presupposed by two enormously influential American decisions. Mental, like physical, disease is simply taken to be in itself or in its effects incapacitating, and whether someone is or is not the victim of any sort of disease is construed as purely matter of fact. Thus in the case of *State v. Jones* the Supreme Judicial Court of New Hampshire maintained that 'Whether the defendant had a mental disease . . . seems as much a question of fact as whether he had a bodily disease; and whether the killing of his wife was the product of that disease was also as clearly a matter of fact as whether thirst and a quickened pulse are the product of a fever.' The legal implications are obvious: 'no argument is needed to show that to hold that a man may be punished for what is the offspring of disease would be to hold that a man may be punished for disease. Any rule which makes that possible cannot be law' (NH (1871) 369 and 394). When in 1956 Judge Bazelon formulated what has since been christened the Durham Rule, he gave the alternative: 'simply, that an accused is not criminally responsible if his unlawful act was the product of mental disease or mental defect' (*Durham v. United States* (DC Cir. 1954) VS 214 F 2d 862).

2 Agents' actions or symptomatic spasms?

Section 1 deployed what may to some have seemed an excessively massive array of legal authority. Surely it is obvious that the Common Law, like uncorrupted common sense, can admit mental disease as extenuating or fully excusing only in so far as it is in some way, as physical disease is always popularly taken to be, either incapacitating or at any rate handicapping? Indeed it should be. But in this case we do need to put heavy emphasis upon something which ought to be obvious. For psychiatrists appear to be professionally inhibited against admitting the reality of the difference between behaviour which is and behaviour which is not subject to the behaver's will; and still more reluctant to accept the crucial importance of this difference, not only for the courts but also for psychiatry.

Because the psychiatric laity have not harboured a sufficiently constant awareness of this inhibition and of the consequent reluctance, the courts, especially but not only the courts of the USA, have on many occasions been misled: not only into allowing that a *mens rea* was not present when in truth it was; but also into admitting as mitigation the presence of psychiatrically recognized syndromes which should have been seen as at best irrelevant if not actually aggravating (Flew 1973a). In Britain, too, statute law prescribes that, when the syndrome of psychopathy is diagnosed, the 'patient' may be compulsorily committed for treatment by psychiatrists in an institution for the criminally insane. Yet the legal definition of this syndrome satisfies none of the three conditions of non-responsibility listed by Sir James Fitzjames Stephen:

> the psychopath makes nonsense of every attempt to distinguish the sick from the healthy delinquent by the presence or absence of . . . symptoms of mental disorder which are independent of his objectionable behaviour. In his case no such symptoms can be diagnosed because it is just the absence of them which causes him to be classed as psychopathic. He is in fact, *par excellence*, and without shame or qualification, the model of the circular process by which mental abnormality is inferred from anti-social behaviour while anti-social behaviour is explained by mental abnormality.
>
> (Wootton 1967, p. 250)

(i) Many otherwise perplexing performances can, once we take this inhibition and this reluctance into account, easily be explained. The inhibition itself and the consequent reluctance are in turn explicable by reference to the very widespread assumption that a truly scientific psychology cannot admit the reality of choice. This widespread assumption was examined and, hopefully, rebutted in section 1 of chapter one, above. So we now have a ready response to the challenge of one who was in his day the Dean of American Orthopsychiatry:

> Free will – to a lawyer – is not a philosophical theory or a religious concept or a scientific hypothesis. It is a given, a basic assumption in legal theory and practice. To the psychiatrist, this position is preposterous; he seeks a clear operational definition of 'free' and of 'will'.
>
> (Menninger 1968, pp. 196–7)

(a) That challenge has already been met here: by first providing not so much operational as ostensive definitions of the key terms; and then going on to argue that we could not even understand sentences in which these terms occur had we not enjoyed experience of the various realities to which they refer.

The failure, indeed the refusal, to take theoretical cognizance of the difference between what is and is not directly subject to an agent's will has obstructed understanding of – among many other things – the Freudian Unconscious.

In a nutshell the neglected point is that all Freud's talk about unconscious minds involved not one but two sorts of extension of the range of employment of such notions as motive, intention, purpose, wish, and desire – the notions, that is, involved in the explanation of human behaviour as the conduct of agents. For in this talk Freud employed these notions: not only when the behavers were not themselves aware that these were their motives, intentions, or what have you; but also when the behaviour to be explained was not under the direct control of the behaver (Flew 1978, ch. 8).

Trained as he had been in a hard Vienna school of necessitarian determinism, Freud remained always reluctant to speak clearly and openly of true actions as opposed to compulsive or reflex 'actions'; of what is and is not under the subjects' direct control. One result was that the most famous statement of the aims of his therapy is obscure, enigmatic, and mysteriously picturesque:

> To strengthen the ego; to make it more independent of the superego, to widen its field of vision and so to extend its field of vision that it can take over new portions of the id. *Where id was, ego shall be.*
>
> (Freud 1933, p. 106: emphasis added)

(b)   More curiously, and more unfortunately, the same reluctance afflicts most of those most active in the fight against political and religious persecution practised in the name of psychiatry. They have refrained from engaging with the general questions of the nature and scope of mental health or mental sickness. This is true, for instance, of the authors both of *Russia's Political Hospitals* (Bloch and Reddaway 1978) and of *New Religions and Mental Health* (Richardson 1980; but contrast Flew 1988). These friends of freedom and dignity have been urgently and creditably concerned to insist both that those Soviet dissidents who have been and still are being, in effect, put to the torture by KGB psychiatrists are afflicted by a form not of mental illness but of totalitarian tyranny, and that supposedly 'brainwashed' converts to eccentric so-called 'cult religions' must not be compulsorily 'deprogrammed' back into the religious or secular mainstream. Regrettably, however, these true freedom-fighters have not taken time to spell out what should and should not make some syndrome a mental disease or mental illness, and hence a suitable condition for medical treatment.

In particular they have failed to spell out the relevance and irrelevance of normality, distinguishing prescriptive from descriptive understandings of the word. In the most obvious, non-normative, purely statistical sense normality is absolutely nothing to the point. Disease or sickness can be perfectly normal, in the sense that most or even all members of some population are similarly afflicted; this was, apparently, the case with malaria in some marshy Mediterranean areas during the nineteenth century. Dissidence too, when it involves standing up against the overwhelming power of the Soviet state, is, in the same sense, to the last degree abnormal.

Nor again is it much use to deny, as Bloch and Reddaway do, that the dissidents so outrageously maltreated in the Serbsky Institute of Forensic Psychiatry or the Leningrad Special Psychiatric Hospital are abnormal in what is presumably some legitimately prescriptive sense. Or, rather, it is not much use to deny this unless you go on at once, as Bloch and Reddaway do not, to specify what these norms are and why they ought to be accepted as valid for all psychiatrists. For what the dissidents are so persistently and so heroically dissenting from are the official norms, established and maintained by the Party and the government. Within the USSR, therefore, dissidents as such are, in both these two obvious understandings, paradigmatically abnormal.

(ii) What we need is at least a preliminary definition of 'disease' or 'illness'; with some account of what kind of abnormality, if any, is involved. The Compact Edition of the *Oxford English Dictionary* defines 'health' thus: 'Soundness of body; that condition in which its functions are duly and efficiently discharged.' 'Disease' becomes, correspondingly, 'A condition of the body, or of some part or organ of the body, in which its functions are disturbed or deranged.'

(a) This is a viable notion of disease, and one with which pure scientists can work without thereby and necessarily making any disputatious normative commitments. For certainly it is possible to achieve agreement of the function or functions of some organ; and to achieve this even when all available specimens are, through their inability to fulfil that function or those functions, to be accounted defective. During the Second World War German technical intelligence, working with nothing but mutilated specimens, succeeded in reconstructing both the blueprints and the operating manual for the US Norden bombsight. Yet all the conclusions of these German experts were correct conclusions about purely factual matters.

This can be a most instructive illustration. But it has to be used with care. Since bombsights are not organisms but artifacts the entire bombsight has a function or purpose; namely, that which it was originally designed to fulfil. Organisms, however, are not artifacts. They, and consequently we, were not made but – as Topsy so famously and so sensibly insisted – 'just growed'. Hence the argument that, because the organs all have their functions within and in the service of the organism, therefore the organism as a whole must have a function, does not go through. In the *Nicomachean Ethics* Aristotle asked:

> Must we not rather assume that, just as the eye, the hand, the foot and each of the various members of the body manifestly has a certain function of its own, so a human being also has a certain function over and above all the functions of his particular members?
>
> (I (vii) 11:1097B 31–3)

The answer is, emphatically: 'No!' But, to continue, the definitions given in the *Oxford English Dictionary* are completely general. They aim to epitomize health and disease not in man only but in the brutes and in plants also. The human organism, is, however, different. For to say of disease in a person that it is 'A condition of the body, or of some part or organ of the body, in which its functions are disturbed or deranged' should be to provoke the question whether these functions do or do not include the performance of any kinds of action.

The response to this gets us to the heart of the matter. For the concept of capability, of what we can or cannot do if we try, is central to the notion of (physical) health – at least in its primary application to human beings. For people to be fit is not for them to do, but only to be able to do, whatever it is which they are fit to do. Certainly, to be fit to do what a sick or otherwise unfit person cannot do, does in fact always require the actual or potential proper functioning of organs which never are subject to the will. Nevertheless the criterion of a fit person's fitness is, not the propriety of these actual or hypothetical ongoings, but rather that person's capacities for not necessarily proper activity.

If, therefore, a definition of 'disease' in terms of the disturbance or derangement of functions is to be retained, we shall have to take it that the function of whatever is normally subject to our wills precisely is to be in this normal way thus subject; while at least the prime function of those organs not subject to our wills must, correspondingly, be to ensure the continuing efficiency and due subordination of those organs which normally are so subordinate. (Death, as the end of all fitness for anything, is the ultimate limiting case of total malfunctioning.)

(b)   So far we have both been insisting that our idea of mental health must be modelled upon that of (physical) health, and construing and employing the expressions 'mental disease' and 'mental illness' as substantially synonymous. The case for continuing in the first contention has, if anything, grown even stronger since it was made in Flew 1973a. But on the second count the proposals put forward in an article 'On the distinction between disease and illness' must at least be mentioned.

> It is disease, the theoretical concept that applies indifferently to organisms of all species [which] is to be analyzed in biological rather than ethical terms. The point is that illnesses are merely a subclass of diseases, namely those diseases that have certain normative feature . . . . An illness must be, first, a reasonably *serious* disease with incapacitating effects that make it undesirable . . . . Secondly, to call a disease an illness is to view its owner as deserving special treatment and diminished moral accountability.
>
> (Boorse 1975, p. 56)

Boorse writes as if he were doing no more than explicate a distinction already embodied in established usage. His very title refers to the 'the distinction' rather than a distinction. Certainly it requires no preternaturally sensitive ear either to insist that the syndromes distinguished and labelled in the course of pure biological research should be rated diseases rather than illnesses, or to refuse to tolerate the describing of so very tolerable an affliction as athlete's foot as an illness. No doubt Boorse is right too in his claim that medical textbooks count every kind of physiological disorder as a disease; that they include among the diseased both the victims of gunshot wounds and persons born blind as well as the syphilitic. But that, as he appreciates, is not lay usage. More seriously, even the professionals appear inclined to construe the terms 'health', 'disease', and 'disorder' as all essentially prescriptive. Again, Boorse himself notes and protests this fact: 'With few exceptions, clinicians and philosophers are agreed that health is an essentially evaluative notion. According to this consensus view, a value-free science of health is impossible' (ibid., p. 50).

It therefore seems reasonable to suggest that Boorse is being too modest. What he is doing is, rather, recommending a measure of conceptual reform, but a measure possessing the great practical political merit of going with rather than against the grain of our linguistic habits. What still has to be shown, if it can be shown, is that the 'consensus view', expressed in the final sentence of the last quotation, is wrong.

3 Disease, disability, and dissidence

The Nature of Disease is a systematic yet still blessedly brief treatise by a practising psychiatrist, who has also enjoyed a thorough training in philosophy (Reznek 1987). Sometimes somewhat technical, the book contains chapters on such topics as 'Invention or discovery?', 'Taxonomic realism 1: natural kinds', 'Taxonomic realism 2: semantics', 'The normal and the pathological', 'The concept of function', and 'The concept of harm'. Committed as he is to 'this consensus view' the author concludes that he is 'not able to show that Russian psychiatrists have made a factual mistake in classifying political dissidence as a disease', notwithstanding that 'we can still defend our values' (ibid., pp. 221–3).

(i) Nevertheless it has to be said that Reznek is regrettably reluctant actually to do so, by repudiating those of his Soviet colleagues who have operated and still are operating as agents of the KGB rather than serving as doctors in the true traditions of Hippocratic medicine, serving their patients. He prefers to slip away to more comfortably academic, less urgently contemporary, consensus condemnation of Adolf Hitler: 'an evil man' (ibid., pp.

171 and 211). Immediately to the present point, Reznek appears never to entertain the eirenic thought that the concept of disease may contain both descriptive and prescriptive elements, and thus be both essentially evaluative-prescriptive and essentially descriptive-factual.

(a) By far the most serious fault of the book, and the most relevant to us, is the failure, or the refusal, to take account of the crucial difference between what is and is not subject to the will; between those movements in or of human bodies which are or are part of the actions of agents and those which are items of the uncontrollable behaviour of those same organisms. Let us – proceeding like Boorse with, rather than against, the grain of previously established usage – attach the label 'movings' to movements of the former (active) kind and 'motions' to those of the latter (passive) sort.

Sometimes it might seem that Reznek is simply unable to see such differences. Thus, after quoting Lady Wootton's definition of 'mental health' in terms of *abilities*, he uncomprehendingly objects: 'Any non-conformist could legitimately be labelled as mentally ill on such an account' (ibid., p. 120). But at other times it seems that we should be speaking not of a failure but of a refusal; a refusal perhaps inspired by a misguided ideal of psychological science, and hence of psychiatry, which cannot admit the reality of choice.

It is indeed both odd and suggestive that, when Reznek mentions an article arguing that mental disease must involve a measure of incapacitation, it is merely to fault it for maintaining something which he is himself going to maintain in a later chapter. Thus that article is quoted as, and forthwith dismissed for, contending that we can have a 'non-prescriptive ideal norm . . . defined in terms of the fulfilling of the functions which organs and organisms appear to have, yet have not, been designed to fulfill' (ibid., p. 95). Yet the following chapter concludes that 'There is an objective and value-free fact . . . whether a part has a function, and just what that function is' (ibid., p. 119).

Whether achieved by oversight or by self-denying ordinance, Reznek's exclusion of a crucial point from all consideration carries most unfortunate consequences. Some of these he recognizes. For he regrets his inability 'to show that Russian psychiatrists have made a factual mistake in classifying political dissidence as a disease'.

But now: if once incapacitation is accepted as a criterion of mental disease, then it becomes immediately obvious, first, that those put down by Dr Snezhnevsky and his associates as suffering from a peculiar form of schizophrenia – a very peculiar form manifesting itself in 'reformist delusions' – are not in fact afflicted with any relevant variety of incapacitation, whether intellectual or physical; and, hence, that to describe the condition of these KGB victims as diseased is factually false. (It would, however, be too kind to speak here solely of mistakes: unless, that is, the English word is employed mischievously to suggest its Russian equivalent – since Khruschev the established official euphemism for reluctantly and belatedly admitted Bolshevik wickednesses.)

(b)   This first chapter of *The Nature of Disease* is entitled 'Introduction: medicine and the need for philosophy'. In it Reznek reviews a series of conditions which some have wanted to characterize as disease syndromes, arguing that 'philosophical clarification' is needed in order to settle the question whether these characterizations are correct (ibid., p. 11). But in his final chapter, with the work of 'philosophical clarification' concluded, he reconsiders only three members of the original series, while for none of these is he prepared to provide a categorical and definitive answer.

If only Reznek had been willing to accept that the proper function of whatever is normally subject to the will just is to be subject to the will, and hence that incapacitation must in human beings be one criterion of disease – or, at any rate, of illness – then he would have become able to answer all or almost all of his original questions in very short order. As it was, his conclusions had to be tentative:

All this means that there is no easy solution to the classificatory problems with which I started. To judge that homosexuality is a disease, we have to first make a value-judgment. We have first to judge that we would be worse off if we were homosexual. If we have judged that we were worse off being homosexual, we have still to discover what process produces homosexuality before we can conclude that it is a disease. If homosexuality is the result of the normal process of learning, then it will not be a disease. On the other hand, if it is the product of some abnormal (hormonal) process, then it can qualify as a disease.

Similarly, to decide whether smoking is a disease, we have to first judge that smoking is harmful. Having judged this, we have to discover what sort of process leads to the acquisition of the destructive pattern of behaviour. If it is a matter of simple habit formation (that is, a normal process), then we cannot conclude that smoking is a disease.

(ibid., p. 212)

Part of the trouble is failure to specify exactly what it is which is alleged to be a disease. In the case of homosexuality, for instance, is it the orientation or the activities? Presumably it is, at least primarily, the latter. For why should anyone worry about the orientation, save in so far as it tends to consummate itself in disfavoured behaviour? But, if it is activities which we are talking about, then what reason is there for holding that homosexuals are any less self-controllable than heterosexuals?

A similar failure infects Reznek's treatment of masturbation, and of several other 'normal conditions', which 'have been classified as diseases and subjected to horrifying treatments' (ibid., p. 4). For, on the same page, he quotes a passage from 'The great English psychiatrist, Henry Maudsley', which shows that Maudsley's mistake was to believe masturbatory activities causative rather than symptomatic of mental disease: 'The habit of self-abuse notably *gives rise to* a particular and disagreeable form of insanity' (ibid., p. 4: emphasis added).

The habit of smoking comes into the picture because a 'Manchester general practitioner, Dr Chris Steele, prescribed Nicorcttc, a nicotine-containing chewing gum enabling heavy smokers to give up smoking, for some of his patients. He charged this to the National Health Service (NHS)' (ibid., p. 3). He was, apparently, supported by 'The local medical committees'. But the responsible Minister objected; realizing that, if this became standard practice, 'It would cost the British taxpayer £20 million a year' (ibid., p. 3).

Reznek's own comment is: 'here too a philosopher would have been invaluable' (ibid., p. 4). Perhaps; but, manifestly, that depends on which philosopher it is proposed to call in evidence. For it is neither necessary nor relevant 'to discover what sort of process leads to the acquisition of the destructive pattern of behaviour'. Instead it is sufficient to insist that this habit, like other human habits, can be broken by the habituated agent; albeit, no doubt, only by great efforts and with much difficulty. One comparatively easy way is that prescribed by Dr Steele; to substitute an alternative, less harmful addiction.

By picking on harm in general as the crux, rather than on incapacitation and perhaps suffering, Reznek makes not only diagnosis but also treatment more disputatious than they need be. For it is certainly a matter of fact, albeit one about which often the truth may be difficult to discover, whether some set of movements was, in our suggested terminology, agent movings or mere motions. Again, although other people may be in a better position than I to determine what is in general harmful to me, it is only very exceptionally that they can be better placed to judge what in particular is or is not subject to my will. And, as chapter four should have reminded us, even when I can be persuaded that something is indeed good for me, I shall not necessarily either want that good or be disposed to welcome the interferences of those eager to ensure that I have it.

(ii)   Questions about the nature of mental disease or mental illness have been treated at some length. For it is only in this deeper perspective that we become able to appreciate the ultimate significance of current misrepresentations. Immediately, defence lawyers, pleading that their clients were patients of some mental disease rather than agents properly held accountable for their deeds done, must appear to be acting in their interests. Certainly that is how the defendants themselves see it. For where are those who do not want to escape conviction for committing the crimes of which they are accused?

The further and perhaps less welcome implications of a psychiatric diagnosis begin to emerge when we ask why the insanity defence 'has been notably unattractive to defendants (except when capital punishment was in prospect) . . . . The reason, of course, is that the insanity defense usually brings not freedom but commitment for an entirely indeterminate period' (De Reuck and Porter 1968, pp. 188–9).

Thus Daniel McNaghten himself – unlike the fictional anti-hero of Robert Travers' filmed novel *Anatomy of a Murder* – did not walk (or drive) from the court a free man after his acquittal as 'not guilty on the grounds of insanity'. Instead he spent the remaining 22 years of his natural life in continuous confinement. The crucial

point was put very clearly, indeed with characteristic brutality, by
F. H. Bradley:

> There is a way of thinking and feeling about punishment, not
> uncommon in our days, which exhibits a high degree of
> inconsistency. It more or less explicitly accepts the doctrine that
> crime (all or some of it) is mere disease . . . . And, rightly from
> this ground, a protest is made against such unwilled defects
> being imputed and judged of morally . . . Justice is the
> assignment of benefit and injury according to desert; but this
> man is not a moral agent . . . surely what follows is that justice is
> indifferent to his case.
>
> (Bradley 1894, I, pp. 155–6)

To be punished, even to be punished with a severity of which
Bradley would have approved, is to be treated as a person with
still a dignity deriving from your very accountability as the
responsible agent. To be diagnosed as mentally diseased is to be
put down, at least in respect of the behaviour taken to be
symptomatic of the syndrome in question, as not an agent at all;
and hence, at least to that extent, as something less than a person.
Whenever such a diagnosis is correct, these consequences follow,
and must be accepted as, however unwelcome, fact. It becomes
then the business of the psychiatrists, as quickly and as best they
may, to restore their patients to their former full freedom and
dignity as persons.

Certainly it is in part because a day in the Serbsky Institute for
Forensic Psychiatry can be even more awful than 'A Day in the
Life of Ivan Denisovitch' that the KGB has developed the practice
of incarcerating intractable dissidents in such 'mental hospitals'.
But the main reason, surely, is the desire to delegitimate their
protests by pretending that these were not, and are not, the
deliberate actions of rational agents but rather the symptomatic
spasms of a sort of physical and intellectual defectives:

> To be 'cured' against one's will, and cured of states which we
> may not regard as disease, is to be put on a level with those who
> have not yet reached the age of reason, or those who never will,
> to be classed with infants, imbeciles, and domestic animals. But
> to be punished, however severely, because we have deserved it,

because we 'ought to have known better' is to be treated as a human person.

(Lewis 1972, pp. 242–3)

4 The logic of wants and needs

Chapter three examined the way in which a party of the vanguard can claim to be expert in determining the general or real will of some collective, and construe this pretended expertise as justification for overriding the actual wishes of any or even all members of that collective. The final section 4 of chapter four contrasted wants and wishes with interests and needs: whereas I remain the best expert on my own actual wishes and wants, others may claim special skills in identifying my true needs or my real interests.

(i) Since such pretended identifications can and often do provide the basis for in some way discounting or discrediting actual, present, wishes and wants, it becomes relevant to uncover the logical relations and the lacks of logical relations between these various ideas. Task number one is to spell out four conceptual truths about needs.

(a) The first is implicit in what has been said already, but has now to be made explicit. It is that we may want what we do not need, and need what we do not want.

(b) The second is that the satisfaction of people's needs must be in their interests, or in some other way good for them. If you need medical attention, for instance, then getting this must be in itself, and all other things being equal, good for you; even if your likely conduct on your return to health is such as to make the whole business anything but good for others. Again, if I prescribe something which you definitely do not want, as what is required to meet some need of yours, then I must in consistency at least pretend that my prescription is to your ultimate advantage: 'What you need is a thorough thrashing, which will do you a power of good'; or 'What you need is a few months in an infantry training depot, which will make a man out of you.'

(c) The third is that what is needed is supposed to be needed not for its own sake but as a means to the fulfilment of some further function, purpose, or end. If I want to climb this particular route, then there may be no further answer to the question 'Why?' Suggestions that I could get to the top more easily and more quickly by train or by helicopter may simply miss the point – that what I want is to climb, and to climb this particular routè. Yet if I say that I need something it is never inept to ask: 'What for?' I need food and drink in order to maintain life and health; I need a lift in order to get me to Manchester in the morning; and so on. But if I claim just to need something, but not for the sake of anything further, then what I really have is not a need at all, but only a wish or craving.

(d)   A fourth analytical point is suggested by the conclusion: 'A need, therefore, is a legitimate or morally sanctioned demand' (Minogue 1963, p. 46). The same writer later quotes Simone Weil: 'Where there is a need, there is also an obligation.' But then he makes in his own person the much more cautious assertion: 'Desire may be capricious; need always claims to be taken seriously' (ibid., p. 103).

The truth, surely, is significantly different. Certainly there is always about any need something hypothetically, if only hypothetically, imperative. For to say that this or that is needed is to say that it is a necessity for the fulfilment of some function, or purpose, or end. If I want any of those fulfilments then I must have those necessities. But this is by no means to say either that that function, purpose, or end is 'legitimate or morally sanctioned', or that this necessary means to it is also licit. Much less is it to say positively that 'there is an obligation' upon everyone to assist all others to secure their every genuine need. It is not incoherent to assert that people need to do things, which ought not to be done, if they are to achieve objectives, which in any case they ought not to be pursuing: 'They needed to employ every instrument of terror if they were to secure their firm control over the countries which their armies had conquered.' Nor is it improper to speak of needing to do or to have this or that in order successfully to pursue what is admittedly only a pastime: 'We shall need to do much better in the scrum if we are to have any chance of winning on Saturday week.'

On the other hand we do often contrast basic human need – what is needed simply to sustain life, or to maintain whatever is taken to be the minimum tolerable standard of living – with luxuries and frivolities. No doubt Simone Weil had this contrast in mind when she said what she said. But it is only some needs that are thus distinguished – those essential to certain minimum or otherwise approved ends. That fact is the decisive reason why all needs cannot as such and necessarily be, as both she and Minogue maintain, 'legitimate or morally sanctioned'.

(ii)   All this raises, as it was intended to raise, the question of the relations between professional or other people offering skilled services and the public who may from time to time wish to make use of these services. A consideration of these relations will bring out, first, that although our needs cannot be identified with our wants, it is nevertheless impossible completely to separate the two, and, second, that although some expert may be qualified to tell me what I need for this or that end, there is no room for an expertise referring not to means only but to ends.

Suppose that I visit, as I often do, my local DIY shop owner. I tell him about a job I want to do. He from his expert knowledge can, and does, help me. He explains what I need, and then sells me whatever it is which I need for the job but do not already have. But no expert knowledge would enable him to discern what I need if I did not tell him what I want. It is just the same with a visit to a solicitor, or a surveyor, or an architect. They have to discover what I want before they can begin to bring their expert knowledge to bear in order to advise me on my needs. The reason why a doctor is, generally, able to prescribe for the needs of his patients without first asking them what they want is that he can take it for granted that they want to be as fit and as free from pain as they can be.

These are all simple cases of employment of experts to determine needs, as means to the achievement of the actual and present ends of their employer. But there are, of course, also cases where the need or the supposed need relates to some want which cannot be expressed immediately, or which would or will be felt only on certain hypothetical conditions, or even one which it is thought ideally ought to be, rather than actually is or will be, felt by the person to whom that need is attributed. The first thing to stress about all such complicated and off-centre cases is that they do still manifest, in the various ways just indicated, the same logical link between a person's needs and that same person's wants.

A second point to be emphasized, most strongly, is that the further we get from actual and present desires, the more dubious becomes the status of the expert, and the more questionable his putative expertise. The first harmless step is when the need corresponds to a want which, although not in fact felt at the moment of prescription, will be felt as soon as the expert communicates some relevant item of his own knowledge: 'You need to have that treated at once; or the infection will spread, and you will lose the whole arm.' But at the end of the road there is the Guardian elite, whose absolute power is warranted by nothing else but a putative expertise consisting precisely and only in alleged privileged access to the objectives which it is contended that everyone ought to pursue. (See *The Republic* 484A–485C and 487C–489C; and compare Bambrough 1967.)

(iii)   It is today common to excoriate elitism, without making clear whether the objection extends to every form of selection for quality; and, if not, why not. If it really does then those who employ the word as a term of abuse – and, even in what Tom Lehrer would have us call Edbiz, they are all too numerous – betray thereby not only academic education but also every other form of striving after excellence. Suppose however that the epithet has to remain dyslogistic, demanding some suitably obnoxious reference. Then it would surely be much better to specify the obnoxiousness as being that of pretending to enjoy privileged Guardian access to ultimately authoritative values, and of claiming as a consequence to possess the right by all available means to impose what are alleged to be uniquely authentic ends.

(a)   There was a time when socialists, and especially Marxist socialists, used to promise that socialism would have done with the economics of scarcity. When once the productive possibilities of capitalism had been exhausted, then the revolutionary abolition of those capitalist relations of production which had now become fetters on the forces of production would unleash a new age of abundance. Now that experience of 'actually existing socialism' has exposed the falsity of that promise to all those willing to learn, the preferred alternative apologetic is an attempt to discredit all those wants which are in fact so much more richly and successfully satisfied through the instrumentality of persons hoping to profit from so doing. It is, of course, the so much condemned 'greed' of capitalist producers which constrains them to compete for the custom of consumers, by serving them to their satisfaction: private vices, perhaps; public benefits, undoubtedly (Mandeville 1725).

One prime source of material for such new apologetic

constructions is *The Affluent Society*, published shortly before its author announced his own conversion to socialism. He starts with a warning, immediately ignored: 'Nothing in economics so quickly marks an individual as incompletely trained as a disposition to remark on the legitimacy of the desire for more food and the frivolity of the desire for a more elaborate automobile' (Galbraith 1958, p. 147).

Certainly there are some important purposes for which such distinctions can and should be made. But the basis which Galbraith proposes will not do:

> If the individual's wants are to be urgent they must be original with himself. They cannot be urgent if they must be contrived for him. The fact that wants can be synthesized by advertising, catalyzed by salesmanship, and shaped by the discreet manipulations of the persuaders shows that they are not very urgent.
>
> (ibid., p. 158)

This purple passage takes no tricks here, for two reasons. First, commercial advertisers – those monster bogey-persons of the New Left – are not in fact secret and irresistible manipulators. They operate in the open, sometimes effectively and sometimes in-effectively, attempting to inform and to persuade. In this they are entirely at one with Galbraith who, as has often been remarked, would have been equally successful on Madison Avenue. We must not, and need not, allow ourselves to be misled by his hard-sell eloquence. Desires are not being implanted by compulsory brain surgery or surreptitiously conditioned by subliminal reinforcers. (In Britain the only case of such abuse so far exposed was a subliminal presentation of an offensive image of the chairman of the 'ultra right-wing' Freedom Association by the non-commercial BBC.) And, furthermore, by comparison with the amounts directed to establishing and maintaining brand loyalty or to telling possible buyers about what is available where and for how much, precious little advertising is designed to arouse desires for products which people have heard about but not previously wanted.

The second, more philosophical objection is that only a man's most elemental and least differentiated desires can be 'original with himself' if this means, as it must, altogether uninfluenced by the environment: 'The innate wants are probably confined to food, shelter and sex. All the rest we learn to desire because we see others enjoying various things. To say that a desire is not important because it is not innate is to say that the whole cultural achievement of man is not important' (Hayek 1967, p. 314). Indeed even this is still too weak. For the particular directions of our tastes in food, housing, and sex are not, surely, genetically determined.

Nor must we overlook that at the time of writing Galbraith, like the present writer, and like so many of the others inclined to despise and to discount the desires allegedly 'contrived for' the vulgar by commercial advertising, was a university teacher. I hope that we were both labouring then, and not without success, to arouse interest in our subjects, even enthusiasm, among students who most surely were not all born economists or born philosophers. So what price now Galbraith's final, supposedly damning reproach:

> If the individual's wants are to be urgent they must be original with himself. They cannot be urgent if they must be contrived for him. And above all they must not *be contrived by the process of production by which they are satisfied.*
>
> (Galbraith 1958, pp.152–3: emphasis added)

(b)   Galbraith is a mild and moderate man, but misguided. No one could describe the author of 'In defense of radicalism' as either mild or moderate (Nielsen 1974; and compare Flew 1974). Nielsen, who continues to be perhaps the most prolific philosopher within the Marxist–Leninist obedience, contends that he and his fellow revolutionaries must not allow the actual desires and values of any of those disposed to oppose the revolution to count for anything. It is hard to be sure. But it seems that it is precisely and only because these unfortunates are or eventually will be opponents of the revolution favoured by Nielsen that they are to be put down as inconsiderable 'manipulated men', living in a less than fully human because 'ideologically drugged state'. Certainly we are never told how Nielsen and his political associates have themselves contrived to escape that masterful ideological manipulation which supposedly holds all their opponents in thrall.

We are, however, assured that Nielsen is not 'suggesting that a small tightly-knit group of intelligentsia [and] class-conscious workers' should try 'to impose socialism all from above' (ibid., p. 65). He could have had us all fooled! For he had just said:

radical workers and intelligentsia should not be afraid to regard themselves as a vanguard, and should not lack the courage to insist on a vision of society – a positive conception of a truly human life – which does not correspond to the only one prevailing in our intellectually and emotionally drugged capitalist mass culture. And if the situation ever becomes ripe for this vanguard to translate such a vision of society into a social reality, they must not hold back from such a translation because they fear imparting or inculcating, through structural means, a set of values that some plain, but manipulated men, would not in their ideologically drugged state choose . . .

This may sound – brought up as we have been in a liberal ethos – like an invitation to tyranny, but if it is done with integrity and with a full commitment to socialist and indeed egalitarian values, this must not and indeed will not be so.

(ibid., pp. 62–3)

Yes, this does sound like an invitation to tyranny. But – to parody a later and funnier Marx – do not be misled. It is. When Plato in *The Republic* was dreaming dreams of his own ideal city, stately as a Dorian temple, he did for one uneasy moment wonder how his 'guard dogs' were to be inhibited from themselves preying upon 'the sheep'. Plato then saw 'the chief safeguard' in their 'being really well educated' (416A–B). He never got around to suggesting any other.

Nielsen, who claims to be no dreamer bringing news from nowhere but a 'scientifically oriented realist', a 'tough-minded man' possessing Marxist clues to history, can do no better than simply to assert that 'this must not and indeed will not' happen. For Nielsen the sole but supposedly sufficient guarantee is not strict Platonic education, but 'a full commitment to socialist and indeed egalitarian values'.

Yet this allegedly adequate guarantee surely has been and is, on his view, provided by all Marxist–Leninist parties, past, present, and to come? And Nielsen – who, unlike Gibbs, is certainly well read in the basic scriptures of Marxism–Leninism – must, in at least one corner of his mind, know perfectly well that extra-legal and unlimited power, totalitarian and hence all-controlling and all-intrusive power, dictatorial and therefore necessarily tyrannical power, absolute and total power for the individual or the collective manipulating the party machine; Nielsen must know that that, most emphatically, is the constantly and repeatedly stated essence of Leninism.

Section 4 of chapter four, above, accused Gibbs of both frivolity and inhumanity. For he put forward proposals for a Platonizing revolution: apparently without having given any serious study to the track records of any of those Marxist–Leninist parties, which have seized and maintained power, establishing 'actually existing socialism'; and certainly without showing any signs of concern for the innumerable victims of these revolutionary triumphs. The same charges must rest against Nielsen, but with far greater force. For his commitment is explicitly, exclusively, and categorically to Marxist–Leninist revolution. He aspires to become the iron Bolshevik; where Gibbs is, rather hesitantly, rather more the Golden Man.

In concluding that same chapter with a quotation from Tolstoy's jottings on *The Law of Love and the Law of Violence* there seemed to be some reason to suggest that that work was 'exceedingly harsh and perhaps mistaken in its diagnosis of motivation'. But how can we now refuse to concur in charges of hypocrisy against all these procrusteans who, while professing 'a full commitment to socialist and indeed egalitarian values', demand dramatically unequal power over the benighted vulgar? In the name of their own pretended moral and intellectual superiority, these people are demanding unequal power, and no doubt in practice equally unequal perquisites, for themselves and for other would-be members of an elite of professing egalitarians (Flew 1981). So, once again, we have to insist, with Lenin, '*Kto, kogo*?' [Who, whom?]: who will equalize these equalizers?

Part II

Chapter six

The geography of justice

'For if I do not know what justice is I am scarcely likely to find out whether it is an excellence, and whether its possessor is happy or not happy.'

Plato, *The Republic* (354C)

There is in fact a vast hole in his 600-page book which should be occupied by a thorough account of the meanings of these words, which is the only thing which can establish the logical rules which govern moral argument. If we do not have such an account, we shall never be able to distinguish between what we have to avoid saying if we are not to contradict ourselves or commit other logical errors, and what we have to avoid saying if we are to agree with Rawls and his coterie.

R. M. Hare, 'Critical notice of *A Theory of Justice'* (p. 147)

Part II like Part I is beginning with an extensive preliminary survey of the local logical geography: it was solely for alliteration that chapter one had the title 'The logic of liberty' whereas chapter six is 'The geography of justice'. Since John Rawls published *A Theory of Justice* all discussions of at any rate social or distributive justice have had to come to terms with this book. It begins by distinguishing conceptions of justice from the concept of justice (Rawls 1971, p. 5). But Rawls does not develop this distinction. Nor, it appears, does he perceive its real relevance to his own enterprise.

What needs to be spelt out is the distinction between, on the one hand, providing an explication of the concept of justice, perhaps by giving a formal and general definition of the word 'justice', and, on the other hand, developing a conception of what – substantively and particularly – justice actually requires. For it is entirely possible, and common, for people to disagree pretty profoundly in their conceptions of justice, or chastity, or whatever else, while nevertheless all employing the same concept, and hence the same definition of the word. Indeed, unless they are in this most fundamental though tenuous form of agreement, their different conceptions cannot be different conceptions of justice, or of chastity, or of whatever else is supposed to be under discussion.

This is the relevance which, apparently, Rawls never perceived. For – as was noted in passing in section 3 of chapter four, above – he wanted 'to leave questions of meaning and definition aside and to get on with the task of developing a substantive theory of justice' (ibid., p. 579). He must thus have become the first person ever to produce what purports to be a treatise on justice which can find no room even to quote, much less to discuss, any version of the traditional definition. By this misguided omission Rawls exposes himself to the objection that what he commends as a conception of justice just is not, whatever its other merits, a conception of justice at all (Matson 1978; and compare Flew 1981, ch. 3).

If we are ready to refer, as all previous treatise writers surely have been, to that most famous epitome, the *Institutes* of Justinian, we will find there that the mark of a just person is *Constans et perpetua voluntas jus suum cuique tribuere* [A constant and perpetual will to yield to each their own]. That last crucial phrase – *suum cuique tribuere* – can be traced back through such earlier Roman jurists as Ulpian until at last it is discovered first in the definition wrongly rejected by Plato's Socrates. Ulpian prefaced the same key phrase with two further clauses, making his own definition run: *Honeste vivere, neminem laedere, suum cuique tribuere* [To live honestly, to injure no one, and to yield to each their own]. In *The Republic*, after old Cephalus has been politely seen off, his son Polemarchus 'inherits the argument'. Following the poet Simonides, and improving on his father, Polemarchus suggests that justice is 'to render to each their due' (331E).

To become fully adequate any of these traditional formulations would no doubt need both polishing and supplementation. But at this stage it is sufficient to establish that the essential element is some variation on the theme of yielding, or allotting, or assigning, or resigning, to each their own, their due, their several and presumably often very different deserts and entitlements. For we have at once to indicate, what we shall be considering more fully in chapter seven, that Rawls dismisses any suggestion of individual deserts, refuses to admit individual entitlements, and never even notices that he is himself making a massive assumption of collective entitlement.

From this, as we noticed earlier, he proceeds to argue – it seems, as so often, altogether unaware of the devastating implications of what he is saying – that everyone's individual talents should all be considered a strictly collective asset. Rawls thus becomes committed to delegitimizing the differentiating characteristics of every individual member of his projected Great Society; making its citizens species beings in a sense surely stronger than anything urged even by the young Marx (Marx 1843 and 1844).

But now, if both ideas of desert and of possibly unmerited entitlement are indeed essential to the concept of justice, then it follows that a theory which finds room neither for deserts nor for possibly unmerited entitlements, however powerful its other claims to our acceptance, cannot be admitted as a theory of justice. Therefore, too, for Nozick to try to distinguish his own account as 'The Entitlement Theory', and for hostile critics to want to condemn it as such, was as if someone had laboured to pick out one particular conception of chastity as being peculiarly concerned with sexual restraint, while opponents had been proposing on the same account to dismiss it as an altogether unacceptable conception of *chastity* (Nozick 1975, p. 150).

1 Justice as a particular virtue

Sometimes, for a brief and hesitating moment, Rawls does seem to glimpse the possibility that such a charge might rest against his own project. For, in a revealingly confused way, his Preface offers the forthcoming attraction of 'justice as fairness' as an alternative to what has been, he maintains, the previous programme: 'During much of modern philosophy the predominant systematic theory has been some form of utilitarianism.' This has had well-girded opponents: 'But they failed, I believe, to construct a workable and systematic moral conception to oppose it . . . . What I have attempted to do is . . . to offer an alternative systematic account of justice that is superior, or so I argue, to the dominant utilitarianism of the tradition' (Rawls 1971, pp. vii–viii).

(i)   But a 'systematic theory' or a 'systematic moral conception' cannot at one and the same time also constitute an account, whether systematic or otherwise, of only one particular virtue, however important and perhaps transcendent. Rawls, despite having chosen *A Theory of Justice* for his title, never in this book recognizes any need to choose between, on the one hand, producing a rival to the whole of Mill 1861 – by developing an account of morality in general – and, on the other hand, by concentrating upon the particular virtue of justice, producing a rival only to chapter 5. (The apter comparison would perhaps have been with Sidgwick, *The Methods of Ethics*, if only because of the similarity in bulk. But let that pass.)

Yet in an earlier article, which has since come to be seen as a trailer for his book, Rawls began by explaining that he was going to discuss justice in the narrower sense in which it is 'but *one* of many virtues', and protested that he would certainly not be deploying 'an all-embracing vision of a good society' (Rawls 1958, p. 165).

What was, surely, the most percipient of all the critical notices hailed '*A Theory of Justice* . . . as the long awaited successor to Rousseau's *Social Contract* . . . the rock on which the Church of Equality can properly be founded in our time' (Nisbet 1974, p. 107). But the author – no devotee of either Rousseau or Rawls – refuses to refrain from remarking the enormous differences in respect of literary and intellectual style: 'I do not know when I have read a book so dense in its rhetoric, so thicketlike in the form of its argument. One has the feeling that the book was not so much written as accumulated over the years, like some of the mansions of the South' (ibid., p. 108).

Nevertheless there is one significant exception to the general rule of turgid dullness. For, after the briefest of prefatory programmatic paragraphs, the first sentence is electrifying: 'Justice is the first virtue of social institutions, as truth is of systems of thought' (Rawls 1971, p. 3). Just as Rousseau's exclamation about man being born free but being everywhere in chains is the axiom from which he derives an entire republic of virtue, total in its dedication to equality, so that formidable sentence may be seen as the rock on which Rawls proposes to build his own future community of virtue – of justice, he calls it, ultimately understood as prescribing a somewhat qualified equality of outcome. The entire, enormous Book of Rawls is a development of that opening theme:

> Each person possesses an inviolability founded on justice that even the welfare of society as a whole cannot override. For this reason justice denies that the loss of freedom for some is made right by a greater good shared by others. It does not allow that the sacrifices imposed on a few are outweighed by the larger sum of advantages enjoyed by the many. The only thing that permits us to acquiesce in an erroneous theory is the lack of a better one; analogously, an injustice is tolerable only when it is necessary to avoid an even greater injustice. Being first virtues of human activities, truth and justice are uncompromising.
>
> (ibid., pp. 3–4)

Overwhelmed by an eloquence which they will not meet again for many a long page, readers rarely ask whether justice is indeed in the first place a virtue of social institutions, or whether, even if it is, it is the first virtue of any institutions other than courts of justice. For even, or perhaps especially, in courts concerned with crimes there is usually provision for appeals to mercy; and, when these appeals are granted, justice has precisely not been uncompromising.

(ii) Another traditionally recognized virtue with which it was once customary to contrast justice is charity: both in the narrower, popular sense in which we might speak of 'charitable contributions' or of (in fact highly politicized) 'charities' such as War on Want or Christian Aid; and in the wider, more technical sense in which old-fashioned and still authentically Christian theologians employ both 'love' and 'charity' as equivalent to the Latin *caritas* and the Greek *agape*.

In the last fifty years distinctions between the claims of justice, on the one hand, and of charity on the second and broader understanding, on the other, seem to have dropped out of moral philosophy, or at least receded very much into the background – casualties no doubt of the concurrent, explosive, imperial expansion of the colonialist concept of (social) justice.

But it is relevant to notice that in the late 1930s a Master of Balliol preached in his college chapel a sermon on the Pauline text, that 'love is the fulfilling of the law'; the key word 'fulfilling' involving, of course, in this context supplementation rather than implementation (Lindsay 1940). Ten years earlier the leading Aristotelian scholar of his generation had published Gifford Lectures on *The Right and the Good* (W. D. Ross 1930). Among the classical philosophers we may think of Kant's characteristic contributions as referring to the particular sphere of justice and rights; while Humean sympathy belongs rather to that other morality of love.

Three decades later a political philosopher observed that 'the gradual extension of the scope of rights means that the concept of justice gradually takes over more of what formerly came under the concept of charity' (Raphael 1964, p. 101). Earlier he had asked: 'Would anyone say that the Welfare State is a charity organization, or deny that it is a more just . . . society than one in which the relief of basic needs is left to private generosity? Would anyone say that the provision of uneconomic transport services to remote, sparsely populated areas of Britain is charitable rather than fair?' (ibid., p. 149).

Clearly these were questions expecting the answer, 'No'. Yet, even if we allow that the alternatives of *charity* and *justice* are here exclusive, we cannot go on to assume that they must be exhaustive also. For in the modern period the first founder of what came to be called a Welfare State was Count Otto von Bismarck; and his reasons were, surely, purely power-political *raisons d'état*? He would never have conceded that tax-financed education or tax-supported pensions were owed to all as a matter of moral right and elementary justice. He never claimed, nor would anyone ever have believed him if he had, that, in his sponsoring of such measures, he was exercising charity in either the broader or the narrower understanding. (Had any opponent ever suggested to Bismarck that there has to be some limit to tax-financed expenditure on health, education, and welfare, the last thing of which he would ever have accused them was a heartless lack of compassion!)

There have always been, though their number is in progressive decline, proudly self-reliant persons reluctant to accept welfare hand-outs precisely because they do perceive these as 'charity'.

Their objection is not met by replying that there are now state-maintained entitlements and state-created rights to these benefits. For that objection refers to moral entitlements and moral rights.

Recently there has been an attempt to derive from the duty to charity, in the narrower sense, both a legitimation for the extraction of all the taxes required to pay for the Welfare State, and support for the conventional wisdom which holds that its benefits are all, at least to its more needy beneficiaries, due as a matter of (social) justice (P. Russell 1987). The legitimation suggested is at one and the same time both inadequate and superfluous. It is inadequate because only a comparatively small and declining proportion of state spending on the provision of health, education, and welfare services in fact goes to people who are unable to help themselves; and who would remain so even if taxation, presently taking between 40 and 50 per cent of GNP, were significantly reduced (Harris and Seldon 1987). It is superfluous because, as we shall be seeing in chapter nine, the principle of a state-maintained welfare floor is not now generally in dispute.

Nor can the conventional wisdom here derive any support from the duty to charity. For to provide such support the duty to give would have to be linked with a complementary right to receive. But the truth is that the situation of the recipient of charity is analogous to that of the third party beneficiary of a promise. As mentioned in chapter two, above, if Jack promises Jill that he will give some sum as a present to Tim, then Jack does thereby create a kind of right. But it is Jill's right to the fulfilment of Jack's promise, not Tim's right to receive that present.

(iii) What Nisbet percipiently if unenthusiastically hailed as 'the long-awaited successor to Rousseau's *Social Contract*' opens with a manifesto declaring the indefeasibility of the claims of justice. The two previous subsections of the present section 1 pointed out that, on the contrary, these claims sometimes may or even must be overridden by those of mercy, or transcended by those of charity. Yet there is a truth about justice which may have been what misled Rawls to maintain its absolute indefeasibility. This truth is that the claims of justice are minimal and basic, and of a kind which, by common consent, may properly be enforced by the public power.

A cynic has described 'social justice' as an euphemistic

expression for gift-wrapping programmes which their proposers intend to implement by flouting the principles of justice. Certainly, to describe any proposals as being mandated by justice is, just as long as that description is accepted as proper, to add to their appeal. The proposers are thus enabled to see themselves as playing the John Wayne role in a blessedly unregenerate Western movie: 'doing what a man has to do' in order to ensure that the good people win and that the baddies get their just deserts. (Who of us, after all, are so mean-spirited as never to have indulged in such fantasies?) The proposers are also by the same verbal manœuvre enabled to misrepresent their political opponents as systematic and dedicated enemies of justice: which, as we shall see in subsequent chapters, they indignantly do.

The main reason, however, for misappropriating the expression 'social justice' as a description of the objectives of programmes which have little or nothing to do with justice, in any traditional understanding of that term, is in order to meet a possible objection. 'By what right,' the objector might ask, 'are you planning to impose your individual and personal ideal of the good society upon everyone, by collective force?' But, if and in so far as it is a matter not of a purely individual and personal ideal but of fundamental justice, then there is an entirely decisive answer ready:

> Mere justice is, upon most occasions, but a negative virtue, and
> only hinders us from hurting our neighbour. The man who
> barely abstains from violating either the person, or the estate, or
> the reputation of his neighbours, has, surely, little positive merit.
> *He fulfils, however, all the rules of what is peculiarly called*
> *justice, and does everything which his equals can with propriety*
> *force him to do, or which they can punish him for not doing.*
> (Smith 1759, II (ii) I: emphasis added)

2 Plato and (social) justice

Although his book is called *A Theory of Justice*, without prefix or suffix, Rawls from the very beginning indicates that this is too broad a description of its actual scope: 'Our topic is that of social justice. For us the primary subject of justice is the basic structure of society, or more exactly, the way in which the major social institutions distribute fundamental rights and duties and determine the division of advantages from social cooperation' (Rawls 1971, p. 7).

This explanation of how he intends to construe the expression 'social justice' fails to make explicit what it is which, by the insertion of the adjective 'social', is here being excluded from consideration. It is said that, for an examination paper in Political Philosophy, Austin once set the question: 'Power politics: what other sorts are there?' Since Hume was by no means either the first nor the only philosopher to make some distinction between social and non-social virtues (by him distinguished awkwardly as artificial and natural), and since everyone recognizing such a distinction is bound to want to put justice in the former class, anyone owes their public an explanation if they choose to use what, since its first employment in Mill 1861, has become a cant expression.

It is a pity that Rawls was not more willing to learn from his Classical predecessors, and especially from *The Republic*. There are only two footnote mentions: one a repudiation of anything like the Noble Lie; and the other a reference to Plato's employment of a notion of a social contract. Rawls might with profit have noticed a seminal remark in *The Open Society*: Plato's persuasive redefinition does 'not . . . touch the essence of what men generally mean by justice', but instead sums up a conception of 'social justice' (Popper 1966, I, p. 247).

In insisting that an examination of justice 'writ large' in the polis must be the prudent preliminary to detecting it 'writ small' in the individual (368C–369A), Plato's procedure was in the beginning the same as that of Rawls; although their purposes, and still more their ultimate destinations, were very different. The substantive 'principles of social justice' favoured by Plato could scarcely have been less egalitarian. For he was committed to what he intended to be a sharply class-divided society, but one in which the almost entirely hereditary classes would have been bound to become in practice castes. More to the present point, he did, however unsuccessfully, try to ensure that it really was justice he was talking about.

Rawls, by contrast, so far from proposing even eventually to check his own findings about justice 'writ large' in society against tutored or untutored beliefs about what is assumed to be the same virtue 'writ small' in individuals, seems instead to want actually to disqualify such scrutiny as irrelevant. No wonder that one of his Harvard colleagues in despair asked how, if 'no micro counter-example' is admissible against a principle 'to be applied only to the fundamental macrostructure of the whole society', these findings are to be assessed (Nozick 1975, p. 204).

(i)   In complete contrast with Rawls, Plato begins *The Republic* – traditionally subtitled 'Concerning Justice' – by seeking a definition. Nor does Plato anticipate Rawls in mistaking 'the primary subject of justice' to be 'the basic structure of society'. (Since he was himself, so far as we know, the first to engage in this kind of radically reconstructive social criticism, it would scarcely have been possible for him to make this mistake!) Instead in Book I, which may well have been written separately and only later redeployed as the prelude to Books II–X, Socrates is made to address the problem in a way perfectly parallel to that previously followed in dialogues concerned with virtues such as courage, piety, or temperance; virtues which no one, surely, has ever believed to be characteristic primarily of social institutions? It is at the very end of this book that Socrates is scripted to give the warning which serves as the first epigraph for the present chapter.

It was there, following Simonides and improving on his own father, that Polemarchus suggested that justice is 'to render to each their due' (331E). Since we have already urged that Polemarchus has grasped the heart of the matter, it will be as well to dispose now of the objections offered by Plato's Socrates. Since Plato is writing (or rewriting) the script, and since he (now) wants to promote both his own persuasive redefinition and the new social order from which that redefinition is to be abstracted as an epitome, these objections are in the dialogue allowed by one and all to be decisive. Disposals are worthwhile, because similar objections are still offered to definitions of other terms, and similarly mistaken to be decisive.

(a)   Even before the intervention of Polemarchus, Socrates offers a marginal or puzzle case as an allegedly knock-down refutation of an earlier suggestion. Suppose we had borrowed weapons from someone who then went mad, then surely it would not be right or just to return these; or even, while the frenzy lasted, to speak the truth, the whole truth, and nothing but the truth? Socrates concludes: 'Then this is not the definition of "justice", to speak the truth and give back what one has received?' (331D).

Certainly that earlier suggestion was unsatisfactory. Yet this is not the way to refute it. It is easy enough to think up possible situations in which it would be wrong to follow the ordinary moral rules. But this does not show that these ordinary rules already make adequate internal provision for such exceptional cases: quite the reverse. Both correct formulations of such rules, and faithfully descriptive definitions of their key terms, must embrace rather than rectify all the shortcomings of the established conceptual order. (When, but only when, we have achieved a thorough understanding of that order do we become ready to propose reforms both practical and promising of actual improvement.)

(b)   When he comes to the Polemarchan definition, 'to render to each their due', Socrates goes on to develop a more radically misguided critique. He begins by seducing Polemarchus into two fundamental errors. Then he persuades him to accept that what are in truth the unacceptably paradoxical consequences of these two errors, are instead the unavoidable implications of the definition which is under examination.

The first of the two seductions is into the scandalously corrupt notion that the distributions of justice may properly be determined by the likes and dislikes of the distributors. The second is into the no less wrongheaded yet still characteristically Socratic nostrum that the virtues are skills, rather than dispositions. Bringing both together Socrates asks: 'Then what does the skill we call justice supply, and to whom?' Polemarchus is duly scripted to reply: 'If we are to be consistent, Socrates, it must be the skill to provide benefits to friends and to do harm to enemies' (332D).

The second misconception, already noticed in chapter four, above, is not relevant now. To dispose of the first we have to remind ourselves why the figure of Justice is represented as wearing a blindfold. It is because those who are to do justice are by their cloth commanded to operate 'without fear or favour'. Here favour simply is advantaging your friends and disadvantaging your enemies, rather than rendering to each and all whatever is – altogether independent of any likes or dislikes or yours, or theirs, or mine – their due.

(ii)   The fear of which the same fine old phrase speaks is, presumably, a fear of overweening powers and distorting interests.

This other exclusion, therefore, is more relevant to the suggestion made by Thrasymachus. When Socrates and Polemarchus have at last and not very elegantly set aside the irrelevancy of reference to either friends or enemies, and while they are engaged in an improving conversation about the wrongfulness of ever harming anyone at all, Thrasymachus makes his notorious interruption: 'Listen then. For I say that justice is nothing else but the advantage of the stronger' (338C).

The response from Socrates was labouring. He never seized hold of the crux (Flew 1973b). It is worthwhile to develop a more compelling critique both because, until what by the near glacial standards of philosophy counts as very recently, the same applied to what was usually offered to students as an up-to-date alternative; and because every period, and ours perhaps more than most, has its Thrasymacheans. For instance, on 4 February 1931 *Pravda* reported that the supreme Thrasymachean of the twentieth century, J. V. Stalin, had ruled: 'If you are backward, if you are weak, that means that you are wrong and can be beaten and enslaved. If you are mighty, that means that you are right, and people have to beware of you.'

(a)   The crux for us is that the whole point and purpose of appealing to justice is as to a tribunal necessarily impartial between, and altogether independent of, all manner of conflicting wishes and incompatible interests. It is one thing to maintain that there are not, and could not be, objective standards of the sort thus presupposed. It is quite another to propose to build a denial of that presupposition into your definition of the word 'justice'. For to define that word in terms of any such particular wishes or particular interests cannot but be utterly wrong, and wholly destructive of the concept which it purports to explicate.

What Thrasymachus himself urges in support of this pretended definition is an orgy of perversely irrelevant, proto-Marxist cynicism. Bad, powerful ruling classes and bad, powerful ruling men are all the time making out that what the likes of the hardbitten Thrasymachus without difficulty recognize to be nothing but matters of the selfish individual or group interests of those men or classes constitute in truth the binding imperatives of justice. Had he been scripted to speak not Attic Greek but modern English his protest would surely have taken the form of what is today the favourite idiom of angry debunkers: 'When those hypocrites say – splendidly – this or that, then what they really mean is – sordidly – the other.'

But, of course, 'the other' is precisely not what the words actually uttered by 'those hypocrites' really mean. If it were, then there would have been no hypocrisy to denounce; only a perhaps commendable candour. The debunker's occupation would be gone. The other relevantly misleading modern idiom is that in which an epigram about something is misrepresented as a definition of the word 'something'. People preening themselves on account of their new 'definitions' of the Roman genius as 'an infinite capacity for making drains', or of tanks as 'armoured and mechanized firepower', are not claiming credit for contributions to a future dictionary. Thrasymachus too, although his notorious intervention was both made and examined as if it provided a possible alternative to the Polemarchan proposal, should surely be seen as indulging in an angry aphorism rather than making a constructive philosophical contribution.

(b) It is often and with reason asserted that Thrasymachus and Cleitophon in *The Republic*, as well as such similar characters as Callicles in *Gorgias*, are spokesmen for ideas which were very much part of the contemporary intellectual scene. It is also sometimes said that these ideas find expression in the Melian Dialogue. This comes in the *History* of Thucydides (V 89), and is a dramatic reconstruction of exchanges between the representatives of a great power – Athens – and those of a tiny island state – Melos. The Athenians wish with as little fuss as possible to subjugate this would-be neutralist island, which falls unambiguously within their traditional sphere of influence. In fact they do, when the dialogue is over, 'normalize' the situation by an exercise of overwhelming naval force.

The introduction of the word 'normalize' is intended to suggest a contemporary comparison. For, after the Prague Spring of 1968, in which a new leadership of the Czechoslovak Communist Party announced a policy for 'socialism with a human face', they were later summoned to a dialogue with Soviet representatives at Cierna nad Tisou. Although no official transcript has ever been published, it is clear from the private reports of Czech and Slovak participants that the Cierna and the Melian Dialogues were extraordinarily similar in substance. The ends of the affairs were also similar. For finally, in accordance with what was belatedly to be formulated and labelled as the Brezhnev Doctrine, the Soviets ordered in the tanks of normalization.

The discussion of the present subsection can therefore be memorably rounded off, and its conclusions elegantly enforced, by considering how the first of these two dialogues proceeds. The Athenians begin by indicating the framework which they think appropriate to discussion between insiders:

> We on our side will not offer a lengthy speech which no one would believe, with a lot of fine talk about how it is our right to have an empire because we defeated the Persians, or that we are coming against you now because we have been wronged; and we do not expect you to think to persuade us that the reason why you did not join our camp was that you are kith and kin of the Spartans who originally settled Melos, or that you have done us no injury.

After these fifth-century BC equivalents of dismissing appeals to services rendered in the Great Anti-Fascist War, or of eschewing calls for the promotion of 'socialism with a human face', the Athenians continue:

> Rather we expect you to try to do what is possible on the basis of the true thoughts of both parties, since you know and we know that it is part of the human condition to choose justice only when the balance of power is even, and those who have the advantage do what they have the power to do while the weak acquiesce.

The Melians have to accept that they cannot here appeal to justice. So they try an appeal to expediency, the accepted antithesis. This has, of course, to be at least primarily a matter of what is alleged to be expedient (not for them but) *for the Athenians*:

> Well, we consider that it is expedient that you should not destroy something which is for the general good. (The word has to be 'expedient' since you have in this way laid down that we must speak of advantage rather than justice.)

(iii) It is only in Book II – when the purist might say that Plato's philosophical examination of justice has been, however unsatisfactorily, completed – that he starts to lay down what Rawls and those who work in his tradition would call 'principles of social justice'. These are the principles of Plato's utopia, of Kallipolis, the City Beautiful. The dramatic reason for introducing this account is that it will be easier to read the physiognomy of justice writ large in a (city) state rather than writ small in the individual: 'Justice can be a characteristic of a single individual or of a whole city, can it not? . . . We may therefore find justice on a grander scale in the larger thing, and easier to get hold of' (368E).

In contrast to Rawls, Plato, while painting the picture of his utopia, is abstemious in his employment of either the Greek word translated 'justice' or its derivatives. He is well into Book IV before he launches his notably artificial programme for picking out where in his supposedly ideal city justice would reside. It is supposed to be thanks to the wisdom and the courage of, respectively, the ruling Guardians and their soldier Auxiliaries that the city can be described as possessing these first two of Plato's four cardinal virtues. Temperance or self-discipline allegedly characterizes the whole society in respect of its consensus concerning who should rule and who be ruled.

Justice, Plato concludes, is a matter of all doing their own things; provided always that this is interpreted as meaning that everyone is fulfilling their several proper functions in the hierarchy. Writ large in the city justice is to do your assigned job as a member of that class to which it has pleased your genes to call you; and not aspiring to a status for which neither by your genes nor by your education are you fitted. Writ small in the individual justice becomes, correspondingly, a matter of the three so curiously congruent elements in the soul fulfilling their different functions, and maintaining their several own proper places in the hierarchy of human nature.

Suppose that we waive any Aristotelian questions about possible systematic ambiguity as between city and citizen applications for the term translated 'justice'. Still it should immediately be obvious that no account on these lines could yield a correct, purely descriptive definition. For the distinctions between the three classes in Plato's ideal state, and between the corresponding three elements in actual human nature, did not in fact result, nor could they have resulted, from any logical analysis of the everyday Greek concept the word for which we translate as justice. Nevertheless Plato, unlike Rawls, does recognize some obligations to relate his definition to ordinary usage.

It is altogether irrelevant to argue for a supposedly descriptive definition of 'justice' by maintaining that anyone whose psychology is in sound shape can in fact be confidently expected to act in every way as they should; and, in particular, to act justly. On the other hand, the notions of our all doing our several and often different own things, or of our all fulfilling our several and often different functions, are by no means impossibly far removed from those of the Simonidean definition.

Certainly there is in *The Republic* no such enormous gulf as we find with Rawls: the gulf, that is, between the common concept of justice as allowing to each their own – a concept which Rawls lacks the patience to explore; and his own (social) 'justice as fairness' – presenting the friends of (social) justice as those striving to establish or maintain arrangements under which no one (or, rather, no set) becomes or remains better off than any other – except, that is, in so far as this offensive superiority tends somehow to improve the position of the least advantaged (not individuals but) set. What a distinguished economic journalist said of Rawls is not so true of Plato – his 'theory contains very little "justice" in the sense in which the word is normally used' (Brittan 1975, p. 24).

3 Aristotle and (distributive) justice

It is notorious that the egalitarian principles recommended by *A Theory of Justice* are somehow derived from an hypothetical social contract made behind 'a veil of ignorance' (Rawls 1971, p. 12). In our time, and after what some may find the endearing frankness of the author's confession – 'We want to define the original position so that we get the desired solution' (ibid., p. 161) – it should come as no surprise that the curiously deprived creatures set up in that 'original position' cannot but 'acknowledge the first principle of justice as one requiring an equal distribution. Indeed, this principle is so obvious that we would expect it to occur to anyone immediately' (ibid., pp. 150–1).

What is less easy to follow is the route which Rawls takes in order to reach his own final, more qualified, verdict: 'Inequalities are permissible when they maximize, or at least all contribute to, the long-term expectations of the least fortunate group in society' (ibid., p. 151). Limitations upon that allegedly obvious 'first principle' are easy enough to justify but, once given that it is supposed to be a first principle of *justice*, far from easy to justicize; that is, show to be *just* (Frankena 1965).

For consider: if justice mandates 'an equal distribution', and if too – as that initial trumpet-blast proclaimed – the claims of justice are altogether indefeasible, then these two premises together must yield the conclusion that everyone has an absolute right not to be excelled; as well, presumably, as a peremptory duty not to excel. So it will not be members of the least advantaged set alone, but absolutely everyone falling below the going average, who will have somehow to be induced to waive their basic Rawlsian right not to be excelled.

Rawls recognizes that his principles justicize dog-in-the-manger demands from all the members of any less advantaged set, although – very understandably – he chooses not to stress this unlovely implication: 'Those who have been favoured by nature, whoever they are, may gain from their good fortune *only* in terms that improve the situation of those who have lost out' (1971, p. 101: emphasis added).

Again, and presumably , because we are supposed to be discussing justice rather than charity, Rawls refuses so much as even to hint at the possibility that it might sometimes be proper to take account of the absolute rather than the relative situation of whoever happen to constitute the least advantaged set. Yet he somehow fails to see that his 'first principle of justice' must endow not only the least advantaged, but also all the merely less advantaged, with similarly indefeasible albeit substantially lesser claims.

Rawls makes many more references to Aristotle than to Plato. But these are not those which might have been expected. Thus, remarkably, Rawls does not compare and then inevitably contrast the assumptions and the extension of the comparative critiques of different kinds of constitution which Aristotle provides in the *Politics* with those of his own investigations into 'the basic structure of society, or more exactly, the way in which the major social institutions distribute fundamental rights and duties and determine the division of advantages from social cooperation' (ibid., p. 7). Even more remarkable, like so many others nowadays eager to propound conceptions of distributive justice, Rawls appears never to have attended to those sections of the *Nicomachean Ethics* in which Aristotle originally introduced the very concept of distributive justice.

(i)   When we do attend to Aristotle's treatment the first thing which should strike us is that, unlike Rawls and so many of our other contemporaries, Aristotle does not assume either that everything is up for grabs, subject to no prior claims, or that all goods which any individual is entitled to have ought to be, or to have been, assigned to that individual by some sovereign collective.

The first of these assumptions is made by Rawls, quite unequivocally, when he takes it for granted that all the wealth already produced, plus all the wealth which may in the future be produced within the temporarily unknown territories inhabited by his contracting parties, is available, freely and subject to no prior claims, for distribution or redistribution at the absolute discretion of those contracting parties. With regard to the second assumption the situation is less clear-cut, since Rawls fails even to make, much less to insist upon, the crucial distinction between actively intended and purely passive distributions or assignings. (Objects or characteristics may be found to be normally or abnormally distributed without this having resulted from the activities of any intending distributor.)

There is, however, no question but that there are many passages which may fairly be construed as carrying an implication of intentional action; and, by all those who welcome that implication, they certainly have been. Rawls lays it down, for instance, that 'The justice of a social scheme depends upon how fundamental rights and duties are *assigned*' (ibid., p. 7: emphasis added). Both assumptions may be seen together in the injunction to 'assume that the chief primary goods *at the disposition of society* are rights and liberties, powers and opportunities, income and wealth . . . . All social values – liberty and opportunity, income and wealth, and the bases of self-respect – *are to be distributed equally* unless an unequal distribution . . . is to everyone's advantage' (ibid., p. 62: emphasis added).

It remains an unsolved mystery why the expression 'to everyone's advantage' is by Rawls first characterized as ambiguous (ibid., p. 61), and then eventually read as equivalent to 'to the advantage of the least advantaged group'. It is a confusion not found in Rawls 1958. But that is by the way. The next directly relevant task before we come to Aristotle's own words is to introduce some related distinctions.

First, there is a world of difference between, on the one hand, providing an environment in which certain human performances become possible, or even likely, and, on the other hand, compelling, or otherwise necessitating, the occurrence of those performances. Had Gibbs begun his investigations of *Freedom and Liberation* by distinguishing two fundamentally different understandings of 'free' and of 'liberty', and had he then gone on to notice that both persons acting under compulsion and persons acting freely are agents, he might eventually have come to realize that people may be induced to act in two radically different ways: by persuasion; or by compulsion. Given all this Gibbs might then have diverted much of the force of the objection to his definition of a free society as one which *makes* people do this that, and the other. But this diversion could have been achieved only at the possibly unacceptable price of disowning all ambitions to become a member of an elite imposing his ideals by force.

The second preliminary, and obviously related distinction, is between the state, an essentially coercive institution, and the society or the community. In the *Politics* Aristotle employs the word 'polis' in both these senses, but unfortunately without either making the distinction explicit or holding to it firmly and consistently. It is, however, clear that at the beginning of Book III he is talking about the state, whereas in Book I his concern is with the community (F. D. Miller 1974).

Finally we need to notice that it may be misleading, as it certainly is unsociological, to speak – as many, including Rawls and perhaps most professing sociologists, so often do speak – as if everything which results or is done within any society is, or at any rate ought to be, intentionally brought about by such hypostatized Super-Agents as Society and/or its Major Institutions. It sometimes seems as if the Scottish Founding Fathers of that most undisciplined of disciplines laboured in vain. For those great men were above all concerned to show how much even of what looks like the product of intention and design either happens in fact to have been, or sometimes must have been, an unintended by-product of intended action (Flew 1985, ch. 3).

Once we have become fully seized of these various essentials we can scarcely fail to appreciate that, since the centralized collective assignment of all goods to individuals as the mere creatures of society is not the inescapable and universal norm, as these lamentable ways of talking falsely suggest that it must be, then, for anyone wanting to ensure that in the future it will be, it is necessary to excogitate a compelling case. Simply to assert that it is all manifestly mandated by the indefeasible imperatives of social justice is not sufficient.

(ii) What is indeed obvious from even the most cursory reading of Book V of the *Nicomachean Ethics* is that Aristotle was not a client of either of the two huge assumptions into which Rawls and so many of our own contemporaries fall so easily, and with so little awareness of possible alternatives. Justice, Aristotle holds, is of two kinds: distributive; and corrective. The former 'is exercised in distributions of honour or of wealth or of anything else which is to be divided among those who have a share in the constitution; since in these it is possible for one to have an allocation either equal or unequal to that of another' (1130B 30–4).

(a) A generation dazed and deafened by the drum-beat rhetoric of 'equality and social justice' will no doubt at first be inclined to construe these words as making the very modern assumption that there either is or ought to be an active redistribution of all goods. Yet so anachronistic a reading is ruled out as Aristotle proceeds, first, to entertain the oligarchic suggestion that the relevant criterion of entitlement might be the possession of wealth, and then to conclude that this 'Justice in distributing common property . . . when a distribution is made from the common stock . . . will follow the same ratio as that between the amounts which the several persons have contributed to the common stock' (1131B 28–33). The common stocks from which these distributions are to be made clearly cannot be the only stocks there are. Throughout, therefore, Aristotle is presupposing the subsistence of private holdings justly or at least not unjustly acquired, holdings which presumably did not all result from previous public distributions.

It is unfortunate that in his discussion Aristotle ventures no illustrations. One which he might have used is provided by the famous occasion when the citizens of Athens wondered whether to share out unexpectedly large profits from the state silver mines at Laureion as a poll dividend, but were instead persuaded by Themistocles to put defence first. They in fact used the money to build ships in which they shortly afterwards won the Battle of Salamis.

Suppose that we here follow the Athenians in refusing to entertain any claims on behalf of the slave miners. Then this truly was Manna-from-Heaven, a windfall gain to the achievement of which no citizen had contributed anything. So the choice between an equal distribution among all the citizens or a use for a public purpose might well appear appropriate.

I do not know whether the Athenian navy had an institution of prize money, such as is familiar to all readers of the Hornblower stories of C. S. Forester. But if it did, this would have provided Aristotle with an illustration of the application of the different principle of allocation according to contribution. The reason why the Captain's share was in those days so spectacularly unequal was that it was thought, whether rightly or wrongly, that his contribution to the taking of the prize would normally amount to roughly that of the whole of the rest of the crew put together.

(b)   There are two reasons why Rawls is able to be so sure that his hypothetical contractors would 'acknowledge as the first principle of justice one requiring an equal distribution', and why this principle seems so obvious both to him and to so many others. These reasons arise from the ways in which 'the original position' is so set up as to ensure this antecedently desired outcome. Since, as has been stressed already, everything is assumed to be freely available for collective (re) distribution, no one can end up with a larger holding than anyone else unless that larger share is assigned collectively. But then, as we shall be seeing in chapter seven, there is a further assumption to guarantee that no one can have a larger legitimate claim on this common kitty than anyone else.

Similar assumptions, similarly unwarranted, have been made, both previously and subsequently, by others arguing for similarly egalitarian conclusions. Many before the appearance of the Book of Rawls were misguided by the statement: 'If I have a cake, and there are ten persons among whom I wish to divide it, then if I give exactly one tenth to each, this will not . . . call for justification; whereas if I depart from this principle of equal division I am expected to produce a special reason' (Berlin 1956, p. 305; and cf. Flew 1981, pp. 87 ff).

If the cake can be assumed to be of the distributor's own baking, made from her own materials, and if it is allowed that none of the distrubutees have any special claim upon her generosity, then this is no doubt all very well. But to think in this way of the entire social product of any but the most totally socialist society is preposterous. That is to collapse the crucial distinctions made in the previous subsection: it confuses society with the state; and it mistakes the social product to be the product of some hypostatized single being, Society. But the total product is entirely composed of myriad elements each of which was actually produced by particular individuals or particular firms; while what and all – windfalls excepted – that is available to (non-socialist) states for (re) distribution must previously have been taken from the citizen producers, hopefully not without their consent.

Given that there are several other cases in which Rawls fails to appreciate what might be thought obvious implications of important assumptions and assertions, it is perhaps not so very surprising that he is unable to discern this categorically socialist commitment in 'the original position'. Certainly he believes that he is neutral: in the eventual position 'the means of production may or may not be privately owned' (Rawls 1971, p. 66).

What is more surprising is that a self-conscious socialist should have described Rawls as presenting 'A Liberal Theory of Justice' (Barry 1973), and that a highly sophisticated and equally self-conscious liberal also accepts him as one of us (Gray 1986). It may be that they, like the Marxists so heavily overrepresented in Daniels 1975, were swept away by the manifestly sincere insistence upon the priority of liberty. As a true liberal attracted by this insistence, or as Marxists repelled, they all joined with Rawls in failing to recognize that, as is argued so forcefully in Nozick 1974, patterned distributions of wealth and income, whether egalitarian or any other, can be established and maintained only by an ever-intrusive and coercive central authority.

What is not merely surprising but scandalous is that some political and social philosophers have persisted with the Rawlsian assumption that all wealth and income can properly be treated as a collective windfall gain, and this without making any attempt to overcome the radical objections brought by Nozick and others.

Ackerman, for instance, in order to justify 'an egalitarian decision rule' (1980, p. 66) sets up what, with a nod towards Putney and the New Model Army, we might call the Spaceship Debates. In this swinging, hi-tech updating of Rawls the hypothetical debates of the hypothetical contracting parties take place in a spaceship approaching a planet endowed with a unique economic resource. In direct and deliberate defiance of Nozick's objections Ackerman labels this wonder substance 'manna, which can be transformed into any of the familiar objects of our own world' (p. 24; and compare Flew 1983b).

It is, you might say, not Manna-from-Heaven but Manna-in-the-Heavens. 'Finally', we should not be utterly flabbergasted to learn, 'the Commander . . . takes the floor to announce that every adult citizen will, on landing, be awarded an equal share of manna' (ibid., p. 168). It is equally unsurprising to find Ackerman arranging for that Commander to be of what those fashionably ignorant of traditional grammar characterize as the feminine gender. (Although *mädchen* is neuter its referents, most happily, are not.)

(iii)   Aristotle did not himself refer either to bumper profits in the state silver mines or to the institution of naval prize money. Yet the quotations given in the previous subsection were surely enough to establish that, unlike the parties contracting behind 'The Veil of Ignorance', he was not inclined to 'acknowledge as the first principle of justice one requiring an equal distribution' (Rawls 1971, pp. 150–1).

Certainly this was not the principle which he described as 'commending itself to all without proof'. The passage so concluding begins: 'Now, given that unjust conduct and the unjust man are equal, it is clear that there is a mean or average between inequalities; and that this is equality, since whatever action admits of more or less admits of equality too. If, therefore, injustice is inequality, justice is equality – a view which commends itself to all without proof' (1131A 10–4).

So there, someone might interject, Aristotle hath said it: 'injustice is inequality, justice is equality'. Everyone knows, and always has known, that the enforcement of equality is the mandate of justice: 'it will make the community more equal, and therefore' – we are assured, as if this is an obvious, logically compulsive, immediate inference – 'and therefore more just' (Dworkin 1977, p. 252).

No, not so. Certainly Aristotle wrote the words quoted as his in the previous paragraph. But that was not what he meant by them. For he continued immediately:

So it follows necessarily that justice involves at least four terms: both two persons for whom it is just and two shares which are just. And there will be the same equality between the shares as between the persons, since the ratio between the shares will be equal to the ratio between the persons. *For if the persons are not equal they will not have equal shares.*

(1131A 19–26: emphasis added)

That last sentence puts an altogether fresh complexion upon the whole affair. It now emerges that everyone accepts without proof: not the substantial practical prescription that distributive justice requires that every person, or every citizen, enjoys an equal share of every kind of good; but instead some more formal principle to the effect that it is a universal and necessary feature of any system of justice that it treats all (relevantly) like cases alike. Such a principle is indeed essential. It is, therefore, important to appreciate that and how it differs from any substantive egalitarian norm. The crux, as put in a famous essay, is simple: 'All rules by definition, entail a measure of equality' (Berlin 1956, p. 305).

Similarly James Fitzjames Stephen was able to conclude 'that the only shape in which equality is really connected with justice is this – justice presupposes general rules . . . . If these general rules are to be maintained at all, it is obvious that they must be applied equally to every case which satisfies their terms' (Stephen 1873, p. 199; and compare Sidgwick 1901, p. 293 and A. Ross 1959, pp. 268 and 273).

Where rules are not being followed, rules as such necessarily applying to all who satisfy their terms, there can be no rule of law; and hence no question of any established laws being either just or unjust. But although any rules of justice, simply as rules, must apply equally to all those who satisfy their terms, this conceptual truth carries no further implication that everyone subject to any set of such rules has to be treated alike. On the contrary: it is, for instance, beyond dispute that every system of criminal justice must require that offenders be treated differently from people who have not offended.

4 Procrusteanism, or justice?

So the great principle of equality before the law cannot and does not mean that a just system of laws will treat everyone exactly alike; much less that it will strive to equalize the conditions of all its subjects. What it does in fact mean is that the law ought to take account only of whatever differences are properly relevant.

Certainly, there may in many cases be reasonable disagreement as to what differences are and are not relevant. But it is quite another matter, and pretty heroic, not to say reckless, to maintain that no differences at all are relevant, that nothing can give rise to any – or at any rate to any substantial – inequality of desert or entitlement.

That that reckless ruling should today appear so obvious not only to Rawls but also to many others constitutes a remarkable index both of oversophistication and of parochialism. For, once the basic Manna-from-Heaven assumption is seen for what it is, it really does become obvious that, wherever it may end, the always defeasible presumption from which the inquiry should start is, not that everyone's holdings should be (made) equal, unless sufficient reason is found why someone should have more or less than the average; but that everyone should continue to hold what they have, and to get what they can – save in so far as it can be shown that such possession, or such getting, is morally illicit. Possession thus becomes nine points even of the moral law; although to say this is still precisely not to dismiss unheard possible challenges to any and every actual holding or getting.

After this it ought perhaps to be unnecessary to emphasize again that references in the present chapter to the Classical contributions of Plato and Aristotle have not been made in hopes of establishing by appealing to their authority any substantive conclusions. There has not been here and there will not be, any attempt to refute Rawls or anyone else by revealing that and where their teachings contradict those of The Philosopher. The primary purpose was, rather, to bring out how necessary it is for anyone putting forward a programme for compulsory state-enforced redistribution to present sufficient justifying reasons, not only for maintaining that certain persons or certain sets of persons ideally ought to have more, but also – much less easily done – for urging that this provision should, as a matter of simple justice, be effected by forcible seizures and transfers from the holdings of those who otherwise would be better off. The main object was to show where the burden of proof lies, and what most needs to be proved; as well as to suggest, rather than definitively to show, that that burden not merely has not been but in fact cannot be sustained.

Chapter seven

Annihilating the individual

> As always, the big Musical Tower was playing the March of the United State with all its pipes. The Numbers, hundreds, thousands of Numbers in light blue unifs (probably a derivative of the ancient uniform) with golden badges on the chest – the State number of each one, male or female – the Numbers were walking slowly, four abreast, exaltedly keeping step. I, we four, were but one of the innumerable waves of a powerful torrent: to my left, 0–90 . . . to my right two unknown Numbers, a she-Number and a he-Number.
>
> Eugeny Zamiatin, *We* (pp. 6–7)

> Most educators and laymen evidently feel that an individual's genes are his, and that they entitle him to whatever advantages he can get from them . . . . For a thoroughgoing egalitarian, however, inequality that derives from biology ought to be as *repulsive* as inequality that derives from early socialisation.
>
> Christopher Jencks *et al., Inequality*
> (p. 73: emphasis added)

Suppose we allow, as everyone ought, that the claims of justice, although not absolutely indefeasible, must nevertheless be always both considerable and compelling. And suppose, forthwith and very fashionably, we proceed to mistake it that to 'make a community more equal' is thereby and necessarily to make it 'more just'. Then we become committed either, on the one hand, to denying that there are or could be any such things either as deserts or as entitlements which are not deserved, or, on the other hand, to continuing still, while admitting that there are, to insist that in fact no differences obtain, and hence no inequalities, as between at least the sum totals of all the actual deserts and not-deserved entitlements of different individuals.

Furthermore, and whether or not the equalities desired are believed to be mandated by justice, all those who are in the present understanding egalitarians acquire by that commitment a strong incentive to try to make out that whatever observed differences between individuals are considered sufficiently important to be condemned as inequalities must have resulted from some sort of environmental determination.

To the extent that such egalitarians recognize that some of the widest of the actual differences just cannot be explained in exclusively environmental terms, they have to reconcile themselves to the deferment of the full realization of their ideals. Complete satisfaction now has to wait until such time as it may become possible to produce future generations consisting, in effect, of substantially identical twins.

There is in our time a widespread reluctance to recognize the genetic component in any adequate explanation of actual differences, and a zeal to prevent research on those differences which most manifestly cannot be explained without reference to genetics. Or, if the research can no longer be prevented, there are strenuous efforts to suppress the findings. (See, for instance, Jensen 1972, Davis 1986, and Halstead 1987.)

Certainly it is, as Leninists so love to say, no accident that all the most famous of twentieth-century utopias – Zamiatin's *We*, Huxley's *Brave New World*, and Orwell's *1984* – as well as such lesser works as Jerome's *New Utopia* and Hartley's *Facial Justice*, have not merely been, but have by their authors been intended as, nightmare visions of ultimates in deindividualizing equalization. Equally certainly, whatever Bob Dylan's intentions in 'I shall be free No 10', he too presented a repellent vision of such an ultimate; but this time, for once, without any exceptional ruling class of exceptionally unequal equalizers:

> I'm just average, common too
> I'm just like him, the same as you,
> I'm everybody's brother and son,
> I ain't no different from anyone.
> Ain't no use to talk to me,
> It's just the same as talking to you.

1 Individual differences and (social) justice

A Theory of Justice proceeds, as has here been more than once reproachfully noted, without preliminary conceptual underlabouring, 'to get on with the task of developing a substantive theory of justice' (Rawls 1971, p. 579). Behind 'The Veil of Ignorance', theoretical fictions, stripped of all knowledge of every differentiating characteristic making them individual human beings, consider the terms of their timeless and hypothetical future social contract. In this situation, as has been noted before, 'the sensible thing . . . is to acknowledge as the first principle of justice one requiring an equal distribution'. To which Rawls then adds, brightly: 'Indeed, this principle is so obvious that we would expect it to occur to anyone immediately' (ibid., p. 150).

(i)   Certainly it is obvious that, given the creatures – we can scarcely dignify such epistemological zombies with the description 'persons' – and given the situation stipulated, a contract could be made, if at all, only on fundamentally egalitarian terms. (That qualification 'if at all' has to go in in order to allow for doubts whether any existing system of positive law would concede that creatures in 'the original postion' were competent to make a contract.)

Suppose, however, that everything so far is indeed obvious. It still remains neither obvious nor even true that this is either the same thing as, or a sufficient reason for saying, that all actual flesh-and-blood (adult) human beings are, as 'the first principle of justice', entitled to an equal share in all relevant goods; whenever and however these goods may arise or may have arisen; and by whomsoever they may be or may have been produced.

(a)   In order to bring out the crucial reason why for Rawls his commended conclusion became 'so obvious', we have to take account of both of his two stated purposes in hanging up 'The Veil of Ignorance'. It is usual to discuss this comprehensive blinkering as stipulated solely in order to secure impartiality. This makes the whole exercise a dramatization of the colourless Humean appeal to the ideally impartial spectator (Hare 1973). Certainly Rawls does mention this as one purpose: 'We should insure further that particular inclinations and aspirations, and person's conceptions of their good, do not affect the principles adopted' (Rawls 1971,

p. 18). But the stated primary aim is quite different, and altogether preposterous:

> Once we decide to look for a conception of justice that nullifies the accidents of natural endowment and the contingencies of social circumstance as counters in the quest for political and economic advantage, we are led to these principles. *They express the result of leaving aside those aspects of the social world that seem arbitrary from a moral point of view.*
>
> (ibid., p. 15: emphasis added)

What is primarily preposterous is to present this (if not exactly self-denying then at any rate) individuality-denying ordinance as a first and necessary step towards developing a conception of, in particular, *justice*. Certainly, if all possible grounds for any differences in deserts and entitlements are thus to be dismissed as morally irrelevant, then indeed – always allowing that anyone is still to be allowed to deserve or to be entitled to anything at all – it does become obvious that everyone's deserts and entitlements must be equal. Yet it is precisely and only upon what individuals severally and individually are, and have done or failed to do, that all their several and surely often very unequal particular deserts and entitlements cannot but be based. It is, therefore, bizarre so superciliously to dismiss it all as, 'from a moral point of view', irrelevant.

(b) Nevertheless, even if this is the heart of the matter, it is by no means the end of the affair. For here the failures of Rawls to discern what are damaging and should be obvious implications become truly heroic. They start in the manner of Rousseau, the style of a *philosophe*: by 'laying facts aside, as they do not affect the question'.

Having thus put down all circumstantial and integral differences between individual human beings as – 'from a moral point of view' – irrelevant, Rawls goes on almost immediately, and suffering no apparent philosophic qualms about consistency, to deploy the classical objection to any kind of utilitarianism: namely, that it 'does not take seriously the distinction between persons' (ibid., p. 27).

That indeed is an objection which to many of us might indeed appear decisive. So how can Rawls continue not to see that it applies with at least equal force to his own account of 'justice as fairness'? For this, we must never forget, was offered as a supposedly superior alternative to all the various forms of utilitarianism; which, according to Rawls, have: 'During much of modern moral philosophy', provided 'the predominant systematic theory' (ibid., p. vii).

Again, throughout the whole book there is emphasis upon the value of self-respect: 'On several occasions I have mentioned that perhaps the most important primary good is self-respect' (ibid., p. 40). Certainly no one devoted to human freedom and dignity will dissent. But how can this insistence consist with the summonses, first, to dismiss 'the accidents of natural endowment and the contingencies of social circumstance' as irrelevant and arbitrary, 'from a moral point of view', and then, as we shall soon see, 'to regard the distribution of natural abilities as a collective asset'?

These two summonses carry, surely, two implications? First, that we are indeed 'from a moral point of view', and in the present context, interchangeably equal. Second, and consequently, that nothing which could distinguish any one individual from any other – including even their own conduct – is truly and ultimately either part of them or something for which they are individually responsible. (Here for Rawls is where the buck never stops.)

So where is anyone now to find any legitimate basis for individual self-respect? In one vital way this last concept resembles those of deserts, rights, and entitlements: they all have to be grounded in facts, or alleged facts, about the persons who are characterized by them or who lay claim to them. But suppose that the indifferentiable atoms of a society of social justice, Rawlsian style, were each to seek grounds for their individual self-respect. Then they would presumably, be permitted to refer only to those characteristics which all persons – or, at most, all persons in their particular society – have in common. So, at least 'from a moral point of view', Rawls' people would become, as has been suggested before, and no doubt in a sense somewhat different from that of the young Marx of 1843 and 1844, species beings; and nothing else whatsoever but.

(ii) Although such blinkered and de-individualized zombies would find an ultra-egalitarianism 'obvious', Rawls himself contrives somehow to discover that, in the last analysis, what must emerge are two substantially different yet still enviously egalitarian 'principles of justice' (ibid., pp. 60–5).

The insertion of the adverb 'enviously' is fair, since the Rawls 'Difference Principle' – unlike a generously Italian insistence upon satisfying, simply and solely, the conditions of Pareto optimality – does not permit advances beyond 'the benchmark of equality' if these merely leave no one absolutely worse off, without positively benefiting the least advantaged. For Rawls rules: 'Inequalities are permissible [only] when they maximize, or at least all contribute to, the long-term expectations of the least fortunate group in society' (ibid., p. 151).

(a) Although it is of justice that these two principles are supposed to be principles, Rawls refuses to say outright that those to whom goods are thereunder to be assigned either deserve or are otherwise entitled to the goods. His reasons are, first, that all proposed grounds of either desert or entitlement strike him as 'arbitrary from a moral point of view' (ibid., p. 15); and, second, that he is unhappy about even the notions themselves and the possibility of their application anywhere.

That 'the accidents of natural endowment and the contingencies of social circumstance' are 'arbitrary from a moral point of view' Rawls argues on two counts: first, that these natural endowments are not themselves deserved; and, second, that, in consequence, what they make possible cannot be either itself deserved or a proper basis of desert. The more fundamental notion that anyone might be entitled, have a moral right, to anything which they had neither earned nor deserved is not entertained at all. As Rawls sees it, the crux is that 'the natural distribution of abilities and talents' is the (morally arbitrary) outcome of a 'natural lottery'. And, furthermore: 'Even the willingness to make an effort, to try, and so to be deserving in the ordinary sense is itself dependent upon happy family and social circumstances' (ibid., p. 74).

(b) It thus becomes clear that Rawls would be hard put to disagree with the Harvard colleague who, as we saw earlier, wrote: 'A scientific analysis shifts both the responsibility and the achievement to the environment' (Skinner 1971, p. 25). But that colleague is eager, as he himself would put it, to advance *Beyond Freedom and Dignity*. Rawls, on the contrary, insists both that, in order to realize his ideal of (social) justice there must be a priority for liberty, and 'that perhaps the most important primary good is self-respect'.

No doubt, for Humean reasons, there is no strict and formal inconsistency between the cherishing of a priority for liberty and an acceptance of Skinnerian assertions about total environmental determination and the unreality of choice. It may even be that the concepts of individual self-respect and of individual human dignity can theoretically consist with the collectivism of characteristics which Rawls proposes. But we certainly are in both cases dealing with uncomfortable bedfellows, having poor prospects for a lasting marriage:

> If individual diversity were not the universal rule, then the argument for liberty would be weak indeed. For if individuals were as interchangeable as ants, why should anyone worry about maximising the opportunity for every person to develop . . . to the fullest extent possible?
>
> (Rothbard 1976, pp. x–xi)

2 Individual deserts and 'genetic inheritances'

Notice that in arguing for his proposed collective confiscation of all individual genetic inheritances Rawls is not saying, what no one should dispute, that our 'inherited' natural endowments are neither deserved nor undeserved; that the notion of desert does not apply. His is a much stronger claim, carrying an important practical implication: it is a matter of 'principle that undeserved inequalities call for redress; and since inequalities of birth and natural endowment are undeserved, these inequalities are to be somehow compensated for' (Rawls 1971, p. 100).

(i) The reason why this argument appears to go through is that the word 'undeserved' does indeed usually carry overtones of outrage, calling for redress. What is needed now is to introduce a third category of the not-deserved to cover what is neither, meritoriously, deserved nor, scandalously, undeserved. Although the introduction of such categories is a characteristically Aristotelian move, Aristotle himself unfortunately saw no occasion to make it in the present case. The *Rhetoric* contrasts deserved with undeserved pain:

> Pain at unmerited good fortune is, in one sense, opposite to pain

at unmerited bad fortune . . . Both feelings are associated with
good moral character; it is our duty both to feel sympathy and
pity for unmerited distress, and to feel indignation at unmerited
prosperity; for whatever is undeserved is unjust.

(1386B 10–15)

Rawls too, recognizing likewise only the deserved and the
undeserved but never the not-deserved, continues:

We see then that the difference principle represents, in effect,
an agreement to regard the distribution of natural talents as a
common asset and to share in the benefits of this distribution
whatever it turns out to be. Those who have been favored by
nature, whoever they are, may gain from their good fortune
only on terms that improve the situation of those who have lost
out.

(Rawls 1971, p. 101: emphasis added)

Or later, in other words: 'The two principles are equivalent . . .
to an undertaking to regard the distribution of natural abilities as a
collective asset, so that the more fortunate are to benefit *only* in
ways that help those who have lost out' (ibid., p. 179: emphasis
added).

(a)   This is another place in the argument where the failure to
distinguish active distributions from those for which no agents were
responsible is crucial. It is also one of the few places where explicit
reference is made to a traditional requisite of justice, redress. Nor
is the contention that justice requires redress for the injustices
allegedly produced by this putative 'natural lottery' peculiar to
Rawls. So it becomes important to challenge the basic assumption:
that there has through 'genetic inheritance' been an active and
hence possibly just or unjust distribution, to antecedently existing
human individuals, of natural assets and natural liabilities. It is an
assumption which a moment's thought will show to be altogether
inept and unwarranted. We therefore have another ever-welcome
occasion to quote the most acerbic of Classical scholars: 'Three
minutes thought would suffice to find this out; but thought is
irksome, and three minutes is a long time' (Housman 1931, p. xi).

Although some may overlook, no one can deny, the fact that
our several and various 'genetic inheritances' were not actively
willed over to us as individual legatees. For to whom were those

various bodily parts, talents, and dispositions – all of which, uninstructedly, we should most of us have been inclined to describe as our own – originally allocated; or by whom were they originally inherited? And who were all the others among whom God or Nature might have made a different and fairer allocation of all such things? These, surely, are not contingent acquisitions but elements of what we severally and individually are? So now, given that there never has been and never could have been any active distribution of genetic 'legacies', and that in such contexts all talk of genetic inheritances becomes grossly misleading, it is to the point to quote a philosophical comment:

> A bare fact, or state of affairs, which nobody can change, may be a good or bad, but not just or unjust. To apply the term 'just' to circumstances other than human actions or rules governing them is a category mistake. Only if we mean to blame a personal creator does it make sense to describe it as unjust that someone has been born with a physical defect, or been stricken with a disease or has suffered the loss of a loved one.
>
> (Hayek 1976, pp. 31–2)

(b)   This philosophical comment Rawls and other proponents of a collectivization of characteristics can perhaps afford to concede. The more profound objection, which must be more difficult to meet, and with which they may find it harder to live, begins by repeating the question: 'Just who are these people who are supposed to have inherited their several "genetic inheritances"? Who are the equals?'

Certainly my particular double-helix is not something which I have earned or deserved. But then neither was it either inherited or acquired by Deed of Gift; nor yet is it a windfall which I was so fortunate or unfortunate as to happen to pick up. Instead it is something at any rate some large part of the consequences of which must be allowed to be essential to what I individually am. Admitted that I can significantly suppose that my genes had been in some comparatively modest way different; just as I can suppose that I had been born on a different date, or raised in a slightly different way. But any drastic supposition in either direction ceases by that token to be a supposition, about *me*. For I just am the person who was born to such and such parents, with such and such a constitution, and so on. Although I can know what it is like to be a very different person, very differently circumstanced, I cannot by that token understand a suggestion that I might either be or become a person born at a different time, in another country, and to different parents.

It is very easy here to collapse the crucial distinctions. It is one thing, and perfectly sensible, to ask what it would have been like to have been Napoleon. It is quite another, and strictly self-contradictory, to ask what it would have been like *for me* to have been Napoleon. The case runs parallel with that of witnessing my own funeral: I can imagine what it will be like (for someone else) to witness my funeral; but I cannot without self-contradiction speak of *my* witnessing *my own* funeral (Flew 1987b, ch. 7).

(c)   Recognition here of the truth that each of us essentially is a son or a daughter of our own particular parents provides occasion to remark that Rawls, like most contemporary egalitarians, refrains from spelling out or advertising the implications of his ideals for the future of the institution of the family. Perhaps out of prudence, the most which he is prepared to say is much too little:

> The consistent application of the principle of fair opportunity requires us to view persons independently from the influences of their social position. But how far should this tendency be carried? It seems that even when fair opportunity (as it has been defined) is satisfied, the family will lead to unequal chances between individuals . . . . Is the family to be abolished then? Taken by itself and given a certain primacy, the idea of equal opportunity inclines in this direction. But within the context of the theory of justice as a whole, there is much less urgency to take this course.
>
> (Rawls 1971, p.511; and cf. Nisbet 1974, *ad fin.* and Nisbet 1976, *passim*).

(ii)   A further and more widely comprehensive objection to the proposed collectivization of all individual human characteristics is that it will not do to argue, with Rawls and with so many others, from the premise that our natural characteristics are not themselves deserved, to the conclusion that what they make possible cannot be either itself deserved or a proper basis of desert. The desired conclusion simply does not follow. That Rawls is indeed resting his case upon this invalid argument becomes still clearer when we attend to another passage. It was one quoted – and, on behalf of

'R. H. Tawney and Richard Titmuss and . . . the Labour Party', enthusiastically endorsed – in what the trade must have relished as perhaps the most unqualified of all the 'rave reviews' (Hampshire 1972, p. 34).

(a)   Rawls is talking about the earnings and attainments of 'those who, with the prospect of improving their condition, have done what the system announces that it will reward' (Rawls 1971, p. 103). Maybe in some contexts we are allowed to allow that they are 'entitled to their advantages'; which here means the earnings which their various natural advantages alone made possible. But then, what about those natural advantages themselves? The answer to that question, Rawls believes, will show that in the last analysis no one truly deserves anything:

> Perhaps some will argue that the person with greater natural endowments deserves those assets and the superior character that made their development possible. Because he is more worthy in this sense, he deserves the greater advantages that he could achieve with them. This view, however, is surely incorrect. It seems to be one of the fixed points of our considered judgments that no one deserves his place in the distribution of native endowments, any more than one deserves one's initial starting place in society.
>
> (ibid., pp. 103–4)

Hampshire never protested that Rawls was here erecting, and then – to his and Hampshire's satisfaction – forthwith demolishing a straw man. Instead he seizes the opportunity to renew his own long-running war against desert. But those of us who do still wish to conserve this endangered concept refer, as bases of good or ill desert, not to anyone's native talents or temperament, but to what they have actually done or abstained from doing. Rawls himself appears to be at least half aware that that is the natural habitat of the concept. For, in the sentence immediately following the one with which Hampshire ended his quotation, Rawls concedes: 'The notion of desert seems not to apply to these cases' (ibid., p. 104). Yet he still continues to insist that, by showing that natural endowments cannot be said to have been deserved, he has shown that we cannot acquire deserts by employing those endowments.

Both Rawls and Hampshire thus assume both that no one can be entitled to anything which they have not deserved, and, hence, that nothing can be either earned or deserved unless everything which makes the earning or the desert possible was itself earned or deserved. Rawls makes the first when he takes it that he can dispose of any claim that someone might be entitled to 'the greater advantages' achieved by the employment of 'greater natural endowments' simply by showing that these latter were not themselves earned or deserved. The same first assumption is perhaps also, but less obviously, involved in the making of the second.

Both assumptions are ruinously wrong Since an examination of the second will yield conclusions needed in a critique of the first, let us begin with the second. The crux is that, whereas entitlement does not entail desert, desert itself does logically presuppose entitlement. So if it really were true that nothing could be either earned or deserved unless everything which made the earning or the desert possible was itself earned or deserved, then the moral would be, not that we are not, as it happens, 'deserving ultimate subjects', but that this complex notion is itself ultimately incoherent.

(b) It may be helpful here to remind ourselves of the parallel contention that I cannot properly be accountable for actions springing from desires which I never chose to have. For, certainly, I can choose to acquire or to lose some tastes; and, given time and persistence, succeed. I can decide to acquire a taste for beer, or to lose my craving for tobacco. It is nevertheless incoherent to suggest that I might have chosen all my desires, from the beginning. With no desires and no inclinations no one could ever act or choose at all (Flew 1978, pp. 77–8 and 193). So, if to be 'an ultimately responsible subject' it really was necessary to have chosen all one's original desires, then the correct conclusion would again be that this notion too is ultimately incoherent.

Similarly, to act in any of the various ways which can on occasion constitute earning or deserving, I have to have some talents, some temperament; as well indeed as some desires and some inclinations. I have, in a word, to be already a person. So, while some of my personal characteristics may be products of my own earlier endeavours, I cannot possibly have earned or deserved everything that I am and ever was, from the beginning. None of this, however, has any tendency to show that actual flesh-and-blood individual people, who cannot have earned or deserved everything they are, cannot be entitled to their own natural talents and other characteristics; and entitled also to what they may succeed in earning or deserving by their employment of these talents, and of all the rest of what they have, and are.

3 Actual entitlements, but not deserved

Since entitlements are normative rather than physical resources their subsistence can be demonstrated to an opponent only by showing that it follows from prescriptive premises which that opponent cannot but accept. In arguing with Rawls, or with anyone else sharing his socialist starting-place, the obvious prescriptive premise from which to work is their claim that all wealth, whether already produced or in the future to be produced, is or will be available for (re)distribution, free of any legitimate individual prior claims, at the absolute discretion of the collective.

Two things need to be noted more often than they are. First, that the extension of the expression 'all wealth' must embrace not only all material goods but also all tradable services. Second, that in the most advanced economies the latter constitute an ever-increasing proportion of the total. But such economically valued services either are or otherwise involve human actions. So to insist that these too should be regarded as collective property is to take a giant step towards an annihilation of the intractably individual, autonomous agent. In the future United State of *We* the sole relic of personal responsibility is for the capital offence of dissidence:

> Piously and gratefully I would kiss the punishing hand of the Well-Doer at the last moment. I have this right with regard to the United State: to receive my punishment. And I shall not give up this right. No Number ought, or dares, to refuse this one personal, and therefore most precious privilege.
>
> (Zamiatin 1924, pp. 108–9)

(i)   In chapter 11, 'Two principles of justice', Rawls maintains that these 'are a special case of a more general conception'; which is concerned with (the goods or, perhaps, it is only) 'the chief primary goods at the disposition of society'. As an expression of this 'more general conception' he offers the formula: 'All social values – liberty and opportunity, income and wealth, and the bases of self-respect – are to be distributed equally unless an unequal distribution of any, or all, of these values is to everyone's advantage' (Rawls 1971, p. 62). As has been noted before, 'everyone's' here must not be construed as meaning what everyone else would mean by that word. With Rawls, as with Rousseau, the reader is required to master an idiosyncratic vocabulary.

The previous quotation should make it clear beyond dispute that Rawls, from the beginning and throughout, indeed is making the same enormous socialist assumption as was made in the blurb of Michael Harrington's *The Twilight of American Capitalism*: 'A notable study which analyzes reasons why sharp inequalities in the sharing of *the nation's* wealth are inevitable outcomes of American capitalism' (Harrington 1977: emphasis added). So two questions arise at once: first, why should it be assumed that all this is freely available for (re)distribution; and, second, even if it is, why should it be assumed that this (re)distribution is properly to be continued within the (by them) temporarily unknown in-group of hypothetically contracting parties?

Rawls is quite explicit in limiting himself to (social) justice within a single society: 'I shall be satisfied if it is possible to formulate a reasonable conception of justice for the basic structure of society conceived for the time being as a closed system isolated from other societies' (Rawls 1971, p. 8). At first blush this restriction seems sensible. After all, if it is going to take 600 or more pages 'to formulate a reasonable conception of justice for the basic structure' of one isolated society, then what chance could there be of ever completing the corresponding job assignment for a whole United Nations? So why not at least for the moment confine ourselves, as J. V. Stalin might have said, to 'Social Justice in One Country'? (Actually he would not; preferring, as he did, to maintain that 'Not abstract justice but socially necessary labour time justifies socialism!')

The objection to the limitation thus announced is that, if and in so far as the two principles of Rawls, or indeed any others, are supposed to be principles of justice, then they have to be applicable universally. It therefore becomes permissible to limit the distribution to a particular set of privileged recipients only when members of that set are equipped with legitimate particular claims upon whatever is to be distributed. In the present case the obvious ground for such proper privilege claims is membership in what is assumed to be the owning collective.

But collective ownership, like individual ownership, has itself in turn to be somehow grounded in deserts and/or entitlements which were not themselves deserved. Nor can the admission of the legitimacy of the latter be comfortably avoided. It is, of course, easy and agreeable to denounce (other people's) investment income: 'The existence of unearned income is wrong in itself no matter how it is distributed' (Gaitskell 1956, p. 6). But, provided that the parties to the Rawls contract belong to some generation other than the first, a large proportion of what is assumed to be their collective national property is bound to be a collective inheritance passed on from previous generations. It will be this inherited capital – capital of every kind – which alone makes possible higher individual and social wages than could be paid were the present generation starting from scratch.

Unless they admit, indeed insist upon, the moral legitimacy of some such entitlements – entitlements neither earned nor deserved – our egalitarians will find themselves, by their own misconceptions of justice, morally required to hand over, to assorted foreigners, not merely the tithes of generous charity but instead the greater part of all their capitals and incomes. For it is notorious that average incomes in many populous nations fall far below the official poverty lines for the USA or for any other First World country; and so on. Had this been perceived to be its main moral, we may doubt whether *A Theory of Justice* would have received quite such an enthusiastic, tickertape reception.

(ii)   In the previous subsection of the present section 3 the prescriptive premise employed to force the admission of morally legitimate entitlements which are not themselves deserved was a fundamental socialist assumption. It is worth supplementing the argument of that subsection by drawing upon another kind of premise for enforcing the same conclusion. Many political philosophers – like Hampshire in his 'Critical notice of *A Theory of Justice*' – simply take it for granted that there can be no legitimate entitlements which are not deserved; and then, in order to dispose of entitlements which are in some way earned or deserved, deploy a necessitarian deterministic case for concluding that there are and can be no such things as deserts.

(a)   Here the conceptual truth is not, as seems so often to be assumed, that entitlement presupposes desert, but rather, as has been suggested above, that desert presupposes entitlement – entitlement, that is, to whatever parts or attributes people may exercise or fail to exercise in the acquisition of good or ill desert. Certainly it is awkward to speak of property rights where the putative owner cannot be substantially distinguished from what is said to be owned. Very few of us, however, could bring ourselves to accept all the implications of denying to individuals some sort of necessarily not-deserved right or entitlement, not only to their several bodily parts, but also to those very various native talents and dispositions which are both inherent in and consequent upon their several and equally various physiological constitutions.

The most explosive way of challenging any such denial demands to know whether, in a world in which half the children were born with two eyes and half with none, and in which eye transplants were both possible and not unduly painful, the two-eyed would have no right to their second eyes, but should – as a matter presumably of (social) justice – be forced to surrender these unequal and hence illicit holdings to the transplant surgeons (Nozick 1975, pp. 207–8).

It would seem that, in consistency, Rawls and all who follow him ought to accept this consequence. For them, in the circumstances hypothesized, that would indeed be the imperative of social justice. Being himself no crazed, ferocious, fanatic Rawls would, once he realized that consequences of this kind are carried by one of his fundamental principles, presumably wish to reconsider first the proposed collectivization of characteristics and then, perhaps, the entire structure erected upon such truly revolutionary, socialist foundations.

(b)   To anyone who is quite happy to accept the consequences there is, surely, nothing more to be said? So let us now consider the notions involved in honest trade, and in earning under a contract of employment. For it is these, and not those of merit and desert, which are fundamental in what the father of classical economics called 'the obvious and simple system of natural liberty' (Smith 1776, IV (ix)). Notwithstanding that such misrepresentations are nowadays commonplace even among persons paid to know better, it is muddled, misinformed, and misinforming to maintain the contrary: 'Under the market, let us recall, the principle of desert reigned supreme – a man's deserts being estimated by the quantity of goods and services he brought to the market' (D. Miller 1976, p. 308).

It would appear that the writer, who has since aligned with the

Socialist Philosophy Group, derives his misunderstanding of a market economy from polemics against the Thatcher administrations published in the *Guardian* newspaper rather than from any firsthand study of *An Inquiry into the Nature and Causes of the Wealth of Nations*. For the truth is that markets are for and about trade. And the one universal and essential presupposition of (honest) trade is, not that everyone has earned or *deserved* what they either surrender or acquire, but that the sellers are *somehow entitled to* the goods or services which they offer for sale, while the buyers by buying them with resources to which they too are *somehow entitled* become in turn entitled to whatever it is that they have bought.

Nor is the notion of reward in place here: typically people are rewarded for some service which they have not contracted to perform – returning valued lost property, supplying information leading to the conviction of terrorists, or what have you. Trade and contract, which are the key notions, ultimately presuppose rights or entitlements which could not have been themselves obtained in any market. For the parties to a contract, like the intending acquirers of desert, have, as we have just seen, to be already entitled to whatever they propose to trade, or to employ in this acquisition.

Most of us acquire most if not all of our capitals and our incomes by trade; in return, that is, for services rendered under explicit or implicit contracts of employment. Providing always that there is nothing either immoral or criminal about these employments, our earnings thereunder constitute, surely, paradigm cases of just acquisition? But, if that is so, then it simply will not do – notwithstanding that it is continually being done – to start from what has been picked out as the fundamental property assumption of *A Theory of Justice*. It simply will not do, that is to say, to collect up, in thought, all the wealth already produced and in the future to be produced by all the individuals and firms in some society; to describe this as the total social product, conceived as the product of an hypostatized super-person, Society; and then take it for granted that this total social product is in fact now available, free of all prior claims, for redistribution among the members of that same hypostatized entity, Society, at its absolute collective discretion.

In undertaking any such redistributive enterprise the first

essential is somehow to delegitimize all those previous paradigm cases of legitimate acquisition. In so far as, in order to achieve this, it is necessary to propose the collectivization of all the characteristics which differentiate one human being from another, with the consequent effective annihilation of the individual, it is an enterprise carrying enormous costs; costs which should, surely, be altogether unacceptable? And, furthermore, until and unless this systematic delegitimation can somehow be achieved, the proper response to anyone putting forward their ideal pattern for the distribution of wealth and income, and urging that the redistributions necessary to produce and to maintain that ideal pattern should be effected by state power, has to be, irrrespective of the attractions of the particular ideal propounded, the same as that angrily made by Freud to the news that not his political but his medical doctors had contemplated lying to him: '*Mit welchem Recht?*' [By what right?]

4 Everywhere different, yet born identical?

So far, in the previous three sections of the present chapter, the concern has been with attempts somehow to discredit rather than outright to deny differences which might otherwise have been found intractable. The only differences which Platonizing political doctors and other would-be social engineers perceive as remaining forever intractable are those recognized to be the outcomes of genetic as opposed to environmental determination.

(i) Since the eighteenth century there have been people prepared to maintain that, with possibly a few exceptions at the extremes, all babies are the same at birth. In our own century such claims would seem to have been made primarily in the name of the social sciences. To minimize the extent and importance of any differences at birth which it is not longer possible to deny outright is for the practitioners of these studies an obvious, trades union, job-reservation interest (Flew 1976, ch. 4). For differences manifest at birth must be conceded to some rival band of brothers; whereas social science claims for its province whatever can be attributed to actions and interactions within the social environment.

That was perhaps the predominant reason why, in the late twenties – at a time when you could have your Ford in any colour you liked, just so long as black was your beautiful – the

Encyclopedia of the Social Sciences laid it on the line: 'at birth human infants, regardless of heredity, are as equal as Fords' (quoted Hayek 1978, p. 290). But the US Department of Labour was surely moved by wider considerations when in 1965 it announced: 'Intelligence potential is distributed among Negro infants in the same proportion and pattern as among Icelanders or Chinese, or any other groups . . . . There is absolutely no question of any genetic differential.' So too, and even more manifestly, were the members of the American Anthropological Association who, at their New Orleans Conference in 1970, resolved to repudiate:

> statements now appearing in the United States that Negroes are biologically and in innate mental ability inferior to whites, and reaffirm the fact that there is no scientifically established evidence to justify the exclusion of any race from the rights guaranteed by the Constitution of the United States.
>
> (Jensen 1972, p. 38)

(ii)   The first and by far the boldest of the three claims cited in the previous paragraph will not long detain any unprejudiced enquirer. For it must, by all who have been privileged to compare the development in the first weeks after birth of two children who were not identical twins, be known to be false.

Since the statements to which the assembled anthropologists were referring were inconsistent with nothing so far mentioned save the announcement by the US Department of Labour, and since, as we saw in chapter two, the equality presupposed by the Declaration of Independence is in no more than our essential and hence essentially equal humanity, the New Orleans conference was, however benign the intentions of the sponsors of this resolution, completely confused. They would have done better service to the Civil Rights cause had they refrained from thus associating it with a much less well-founded, would-be factual contention.

(a)   Maybe the most which anyone here can with complete cognitive propriety confidently claim to know is that whatever differences there actually are between the gene pools of different racial sets are differences only on average; except, of course, for those determining the defining racial differences themselves. (It really is very remarkable how rarely this awkward exception gets mentioned!) Only an extremely rash person, presumably misled by some strong occupational or ideological motivation, would be prepared to assert, at this stage of the game, that there are absolutely no genes more heavily represented in the gene pools of some racial sets than in those of others.

Although that genetic question is not of any wider importance, it is important to appreciate that and why it is not. What has to be asserted with all possible emphasis is that nothing which either has already been or is ever likely to be discovered about differences between the distributions of genes in the gene pools of different racial sets can provide any warrant for racism. For racism, in the strict and proper sense of the word, is self evidently wrong only and precisely because self-evidently unjust. In that strict and proper sense 'racism' is defined to mean the advantaging or disadvantaging of individuals for no other or better reasons than that those individuals happen to be members of this racial set rather than that.

To escape all danger of mistaking any actual or possible discoveries in this area for justifications of racism it is both necessary and sufficient to learn to identify two familiar fallacies. First, we have to subject ourselves to Hume's Law, forbidding the invalid deduction of committed conclusions about what allegedly *ought* to be from totally detached premises stating only what supposedly in fact *is* or *was* or *will be* the case.

The second fallacious form relevant here has no accepted name. It consists in moving from the general average in some set to a conclusion about a particular member of that set. It should be obvious that such arguments do not go through. The average height, for instance, of some set of people may be – say – 5 feet 9 inches notwithstanding that the height of every individual member of that set is either significantly more or significantly less.

(b) Thus to labour points which should be obvious to all is tiresome. Yet the tiresome task is sometimes necessary. For the precedent set in the early seventies by the Penguin Education Special *Race, Culture and Intelligence* continues to be followed in much of the proliferating 'anti-racist' literature of the eighties. In that sometime best-seller the crucial distinctions were neglected. No attempt was ever made to define such key terms as 'race', 'culture', and 'racism'. And, worst of all, some contributors were clearly clients of the fallacies just now described (Richardson and

Spears 1972; and cf. Flew 1976, ch. 5, Flew 1987a, ch. 5, and Palmer 1987).

(c)   The assumption that genes are distributed in the gene pools of any racial subset in exactly the same way as in the whole population of which these are subsets is one of many similar assumptions about similar distributions as between subsets and sets; assumptions which are nowadays constantly and without warrant made by those who would deduce unequal opportunities from evidence which by itself can establish no more than inequalities of outcome.

By comparison with most of these, distributional congruence of set and subset gene pools is a quite tolerable working assumption. For whereas it can rarely if ever be known to be true, it is at least not in most cases known to be false. There is, on the other hand, an enormous amount of evidence showing – not only as between one racial or social subset and another but also as between the same subsets at different times – vast differences in the distributions of various acquired characteristics making for economic or political success. Sowell 1981 constitutes the richest treasury of such material, although almost all his other books are relevant.

(iii)   The first three sections of this chapter examined attempts to delegitimize admitted and admittedly important differences between individual human beings. This final section 4 has been noticing attempts to deny that there actually are any such differences which are genetically as opposed to environmentally determined. All this, as well as much which was discussed in earlier chapters, is reminiscent of Plato's demand to be allowed to start *The Republic* with a clean slate; a call curiously incongruous with the aspiration, expressed elsewhere in the same work, to become a kind of political doctor. At one point Plato's mouthpiece Socrates explains how, after long and rigorous training in the hard science of dialectics, the Guardian elite, endowed now with absolute power, are to make and to maintain a new order, forgetting and falsifying its past:

> They will take the city and characters of men, as they might a tablet, and first wipe it clean – no easy task – this would be their first point of difference from the others, that they would refuse to take in hand either individual or state, or to legislate before they either received a clean slate or themselves made it clean.
>
> (501A)

Chapter eight

Equal outcomes, or equal justice?

> What I hope to have made clear is that the phrase 'social justice' is not, as most people probably feel, an innocent expression of goodwill towards the less fortunate, but . . . a dishonest insinuation that one ought to agree to a demand of some special interest . . . I may, as a result of long endeavours to trace the destructive effect which the invocation of 'social justice' has had on our moral sensitivity, and of again and again finding even eminent thinkers thoughtlessly using the phrase, have become unduly allergic to it, but I have come to feel strongly that the greatest service I can still render to my fellow men would be that I could make . . . speakers and writers . . . thoroughly ashamed . . . to employ the term 'social justice'.
>
> F. A. Hayek,
> *The Mirage of Social Justice* (p. 97)

A craving for a clean canvas, though often sympathetically understandable, must be altogether incongruous with any kind of medical practice. For the business of doctors has to start with diagnoses of the present conditions of patients who would not have come for treatment in the first place had those conditions been by them perceived as being perfectly clean and without blemish. The same craving ill befits also those sincerely seeking to discover the mandates of justice. For what everyone severally deserves, or to what they are otherwise entitled, depends entirely upon who they are; on what they have done or failed to do; and on what they have already acquired, whether by unrequited gift, or by contractual exchange, or by that special and most important form of exchange constituted by earning under contract of employment.

Justice therefore becomes an essentially backward-looking notion. That, for instance, is why the 'Shane' figures in good, old-original American Western movies, or the 'Four Just Men' of England's Edgar Wallace, cannot begin to do the justice 'which a man has to do' without some preparatory research into the conduct and background of all the various persons concerned; and into their several and consequent, and consequently often very different, deserts and entitlements.

The newer ideal of equality of outcome, equality of welfare, is by contrast essentially forward-looking. It commits its proponents to disregarding the past as irrelevant: their ideal future is to be very different and much more, if never perhaps perfectly, equal. That is why anyone attempting systematically to justify the currently common identification of the imposition of this procrustean ideal with the enforcement of a kind of justice would be facing a formidable and perhaps impossible task. It would be so much easier, if only they could bring themselves to resign the enormous propaganda advantages of that identification, to present their own fresh and future-oriented ideal neither as, nor as a part of, but rather as a rival to justice – the pursuit of which they should therefore see and condemn as reactionary, backward-looking, irrelevant, unsociological, antique, and even gothic.

The phrase has to be not 'has faced' or 'faces' but 'would be facing'. For the most prominent protagonists of such procrustean ideals have preferred either simply to take it for granted that we may immediately infer 'more just' from 'more equal', or, if they attempted anything somewhat more elaborate, simply to assume that some sort of clean slate or clean canvas is the appropriate starting-place.

One rule-proving exception is a paper discussing what are perceived as 'Impediments to radical egalitarianism' (Nielsen 1981; and compare Flew 1983c, pp. 168 ff). This kind of egalitarianism is construed as involving 'a conception of social justice I call *justice as equality* . . . Justice in society as a whole ought to be understood as a complete equality of the overall level of benefits and burdens of each member of that society' (Nielsen 1981, p. 121). Nielsen is unusual in that he both recognizes the present objection and states it fairly and fully. He also, with truth, adds that it 'has been argued most intransigently by Antony Flew' (ibid., p. 122n).

What Nielsen significantly fails to do is to offer a relevant response. He seems to have been distracted from this subsidiary task by concern to show that his stated Radical egalitarian ideals could be realized; and that at no unacceptable cost. Thus distracted he does no more than attempt to make out that, in the future Cloud-cuckoo-land of his dreams, there would be and could be no significantly unequal entitlements. (It is perhaps also just worth saying that deserts are not mentioned. This contrasts with Rawls, who, as has been said before, while explicit in his discounting of deserts, appears never to recognize the possibility of entitlements which are not in any way deserved.)

The decisive objection, therefore, to Nielsen's attempted response is that, however true any of his supposed hypothetical truths may be about his Cloud-cuckoo-land, still they cannot be anything but totally irrelevant to the task of refuting the original objection which he undertook to refute. Maybe we can imagine a set-up in which everyone's deserts and entitlements would be as near as makes no matter equal. Yet this is not to begin to show that justice is not an essentially backward-looking notion, or that, always and everywhere, in the real world, justice demands the allocation to everybody of equal shares of everything.

So that original objection still stands. It has to be stated once again, no less intransigently than before. Since procrustean ideals are essentially forward-looking, clear-headed and honest procrusteans ought to abandon all pretences that, in promoting these, they are instead promoting some ideal of justice. For this is, equally essentially, backward-looking. Since the propaganda advantages of these pretences are so enormous, and since the attractions of self-images as disinterested crusaders after justice are so great, it would be unrealistic to expect much immediate response to such appeals for truth in advertising.

In this, if in nothing else, the scientifically minded and future–oriented reformers who want to replace criminal justice by orthopsychiatry set a most commendable example. Thus the man who was for years the recognized doyen of that discipline had no backward-looking scruples, and no inhibitions against projecting what to dissident diehards will appear an unlovely image. In a book aggressively entitled *The Crime of Punishment*, he wrote:

The very word 'justice' irritates scientists. No surgeon expects to be asked whether an operation for cancer is just or not. No doctor will be reproached on the grounds that the dose of penicillin he has prescribed is less or more than justice would stipulate. Behavioural scientists regard it as equally absurd to invoke the question of justice . . . . This (to the scientist) is a matter of public safety and amicable coexistence, not justice.

(Menninger 1968, p. 17)

1 Hayek's last mission

Certainly the expression 'social justice' is often employed in ways which would warrant all the cynical and despairing comments of its critics, and more: social justice is what my party proposes and my opponents oppose; social justice is what A and B agree that C should be made to do for D (Sumner 1883); 'social justice' is a euphemism employed to embrace any condition which the employer would like to see brought about, often in violation of the most ordinary principles of justice; and so on.

But what does require explanation is how Hayek contrived to conclude that always this was all that there was to it. For in his Preface to the book from which the epigrah of this chapter is taken he asserted 'that the people who habitually employ the phrase simply do not know themselves what they mean by it, and just use it as an assertion that a claim is justified without giving a reason for it' (Hayek 1976, p. xi).

His insufficient reason for reaching this conclusion was given there as part of an account of the circumstances which 'have contributed to delay the publication of the second volume of this work'. The chief such circumstance was 'dissatisfaction with the original version of the central chapter . . . in which I had tried to show for a large number of instances that what was claimed as demanded by "social justice" could not be justice because the underlying consideration (one could hardly call it a principle) was not capable of general application' (ibid., p. xi).

(i)   Hayek's final conclusion not merely does not follow from the premise from which it is here derived but is also in any case much too strong. It does not follow because the fact that social justice is not a kind of justice is no sufficient reason for saying that the expression 'social justice' is altogether meaningless. It is much too strong because nowadays politicians, both professional and amateur, especially those professing to be either democratic socialists or social democrats, are forever talking of equality and social justice; without seeing fit to indicate how, if at all, that word is supposed to differ from that expression in either meaning or reference. There is also an enormous and ever-growing literature of a more academic kind in which economic is either associated or even identified with social justice, while both are taken to mandate a (always to some extent qualified) universal equality of both income and wealth (and hence of economic outcome).

(a)   While, therefore, it is very much to the point to ask if social justice so conceived really is a kind of justice, or how it is proposed to limit or to qualify the supposedly ideal equality of outcome, or whether there is here any system of principles capable of consistent application, it is going too far to maintain that 'social justice' is an expression empty of all meaning.

To the first of these good questions the response, for reasons to be indicated later, should be that in the usage presently under discussion 'social' becomes an *alienans* adjective. Hence social justice is no more a sort of justice than positive freedom, Soviet democracy, or Bombay duck are – respectively – kinds of freedom, of democracy or of duck. But the inclusion of an *alienans* adjective does not make an expression wholly meaningless. If this were so such expressions could not be so effectively misleading as they often are.

It is perhaps in part by reference to the previous felt lack of any even halfway satisfactory answers to the second two good questions that we may begin to explain the extraordinarily wide, and overwhelmingly enthusiastic, welcome accorded to *A Theory of Justice*. In the *New York Review of Books* (1972, Issue 3) for instance, in his notably uncritical 'Critical notice', the lifelong socialist Stuart Hampshire wrote:

> I think that this book is the most substantial and interesting contribution to moral philosophy since the war, at least if one thinks only of works written in English. It is a very persuasive book, being very well argued and carefully composed.

It presents, Hampshire continued,

> a noble, coherent, highly abstract picture of the fair society, as social democrats see it . . . This is certainly the model of social

justice that has governed the advocacy of R. H. Tawney and Richard Titmuss and that holds the Labour Party together.

Again, and similarly, the author of one of the first volumes in a new International Library of Welfare and Philosophy saw the implications of equating equality and social justice, liked them, and construed this as a licence to help himself to the premises from which they were presumed to follow. Having sketched a Rawlsian account of (social) justice as a (qualified) equality he remarks that one 'reason for linking equality and justice is that within the theory of justice one can [then] provide the necessary moral premise for adopting the principle of equal welfare as a prescriptive recommendation' (Weale 1978, p. 32).

The perfect put-down for this performance was provided long ago, probably before Weale was even born: 'The method of "postulating" what we want has many advantages; they are the same as the advantages of theft over honest toil' (B. A. W. Russell 1919, p. 17).

(b) It is easy to establish that equality and social justice are commonly equated. When, for instance, Section F of the British Association for the Advancement of Science devoted its annual meeting to 'Economics and equality' all concerned construed 'equality' to be, in this context at any rate, synonymous with 'justice'. Thus the editor of the resulting volume of papers observed in his Preface, as 'a given fact of life', that 'Inequality of all sorts has lost its legitimacy' (Jones 1976, p. 2). One representative contributor begins his article: 'Economic equality, with which this section is concerned this year, is one aspect of a wider theme of social justice' (ibid., p. 87).

What is indeed unusual about this volume is that, although some contributors are ready, without particular reason given, to rate any admitted evil as an instance of (social) injustice, others, or even the same contributors at other times, do bring themselves to pick out for this properly particular form of condemnation certain evils which really do constitute, in the most limited and conservative understanding, injustices.

Thus, although T. W. Hutchinson speaks of 'the social injustice of unemployment', while Tim Tutton thinks that 'There can be little doubt about the relevance of a high level of employment to the achievement of economic justice' (ibid., pp. 14 and 154),

Hutchinson does also condemn inflation, as it so rarely is condemned, as a (social) injustice (ibid., pp. 48 and 59). Even more unusually, and equally commendably, Harbury denounces 'the social injustice of taxing what are, in reality, negative investment incomes in an inflationary age' (ibid., p. 97).

Nowadays, Radical sociologists – and one sometimes has to wonder what other sorts there are – appear ever eager to misdescribe what is not racism and not violence as being in truth 'institutionalized racism' or 'institutionalized violence' (Flew 1985, pp. 11, 43, 51–2, 107 and 147). So it becomes salutary to identify both inflation and the taxation of negative incomes as being, what they certainly are, forms of institutionalized fraud.

It would be easy to extend indefinitely the list of quotations from British socialist sources showing some sort of near if not always perfect equation between on the one hand, the establishment of a general equality of welfare, and, on the other hand, a meeting of the demands of (social) justice. Such persons also take 'equality' to be as near as makes no matter synonymous with 'equity': an equitable distribution for them thus just is an equal distribution. For example: a leading Labour Member of Parliament, Mrs Barbara Castle, made a very characteristic statement in a debate on a Queen's Speech: 'Our complaint against the Government, and in particular the Prime Minister, is that brick by brick they have set out to create an unjust society' (*Hansard* for 6 November 1972: the then Prime Minister was a still slightly 'dry' Edward Heath).

In Townsend and Bosanquet 1980, a Fabian Society review of the two subsequent Labour administrations, the editors proclaim, in a Preface reprinted on the back cover, 'that the Labour Party can and should light a flame in a world of injustice and inequality'. Contributor after contributor to this volume speaks of 'socialist canons of equality and social justice', and of 'a more socially just and equal society' (ibid., pp. 131 and 228; also compare pp. 61 and 227). One author goes so far as to lay it down – without attempting to explain either what this would involve or why we should accept his assertion as true – that, in particular, 'Racial equality requires a society which is equal in all respects' (ibid., p. 151). Perhaps the strongest evidence that we are dealing with an equation is provided by a passage written by David Piachaud. It is a harshly confident denunciation: 'the Conservative government' – this time the first Thatcher administration – 'is renouncing the search for social justice' (ibid., p. 184).

That Piachaud is indeed assuming a substantial equivalence becomes clear just as soon as we consider how he would, were he reflecting 'in a cool hour', formulate his opposition. For he would have to say that he opposes the abominable Thatcherites because we reject the procrustean enforcement of equality; rather than – what would be an almost Hitlerian Big Lie – because we despise and disown old-fashioned, without prefix or suffix, justice. The same equivalence was accepted in the same completely confident and uncritical way in a 1982 statement *Community Benefit and Taxation* issued by the Laity Commission of the Roman Catholic Bishops' Conference of England and Wales: a statement which was, in this and other ways, totally typical of the pronouncements on social and political policy which continue to pour from all the mainstream Christian churches. (It was also, and equally typically, a client of the confusion to be considered in chapter nine, below; systematically collapsing any distinction between the reduction of inequality and the relief of real poverty.)

(ii)   The first puzzle in the present section 1 was how Hayek contrived to conclude 'that the people who habitually employ the phrase ['social justice'] simply do not themselves know what they mean by it'. The second is how, 'after careful consideration', he came 'to the conclusion that what I might have to say about . . . *A Theory of Justice* . . . would not assist in the pursuit of my immediate object, because the differences between us seemed more verbal than substantial' (Hayek 1976, pp. xii–xiii).

It is hard to escape the embarrassing discovery that Hayek's 'careful consideration' must have been confined to earlier articles by Rawls. Surely, and very understandably, and no doubt misled by the failure of reviewers to remark how far the book constituted a departure rather than a development from previous positions, Hayek must have excused himself from what for him, and not for him alone, would have been the extremely uncongenial labour of ploughing through those 600-plus pages?

Certainly the list of substantial and so much more than merely verbal differences between Hayek and the mature Rawls is long. When, for instance, has Hayek – as a true, classical liberal – ever failed to deny that all (social) goods either are or ought to be *distributed* or *assigned* by a hypostatized collective, Society? And when has he ever advocated that everything should 'be distributed equally unless an unequal distribution . . . is to everyone's advantage'? On the contrary: he has always insisted that he 'is against all attempts to impress upon society a deliberately chosen pattern of distribution, whether it be an order of equality or of inequality' (Hayek 1960, p. 87).

Again, consider how we should expect Hayek to react to a proposal 'to regard the distribution of natural talents as a common asset', with its corollary conclusion that 'Those who have been favoured by nature, whoever they are, may gain from their good fortune *only* on terms that improve the situation of those who have lost out' (Rawls 1971, p. 101: emphasis added). Had one of his enemies associated Hayek with this altogether uncharacteristic, mean-minded, dog-in-the-manger, totalitarian–collectivist principle his admirers would have had a right to be very indignant indeed. For Hayek has in fact repeatedly insisted, in *The Constitution of Liberty* and elsewhere, 'that the desirability of increasing the abilities and opportunities of any individual does not depend on whether the same can be done for others – provided, of course, that the others are not thereby deprived' (Hayek 1960, p. 88).

It is surely significant that the only passage from Rawls quoted in *The Mirage of Social Justice* comes from a 1963 essay on 'Constitutional liberty and the concept of justice'? There, and then, Rawls wrote that 'the principles of justice define the crucial constraints which institutions and joint activities must satisfy if persons engaging in them are to have no complaints against them. If these constraints are satisfied, the resulting distribution, whatever it is, may be accepted as just (or at least not unjust)' (Rawls 1963, p. 102). No wonder that, concentrating upon this very different and younger Rawls, Hayek could comment: 'This is more or less what I have been trying to argue in this chapter' (Hayek 1976, p. 100).

In a note Hayek adds a further comment: 'I am not aware that Professor Rawls' later more widely read work . . . contains a comparably clear statement of the main point' (ibid., p. 193). Mischievous readers may – since, most emphatically, it does nothing of the sort – be reminded of Kant's confession that he was 'not aware of possessing the literary talents of Hume'. Certainly we owe it to Daniel Bell to revive his wrongly dismissed judgment that, in *A Theory of Justice*, Rawls made 'the most comprehensive effort in modern philosophy to justify a socialist ethic' (quoted ibid., p. 183).

2 Three ideals of equality

Against the contention that 'Racial equality requires a society which is equal in all respects' it was, in the previous section 1, objected that the writer made no attempt 'to explain either what this would involve or why we should accept his assertion as true'. The insertion of this objection was no mere diversionary manœuvre. For the implementation of one ideal of equality in practice, or even in theory, may be incompatible with the realization of another.

(i) The first of the three different ideals of human equality to be distinguished here is often seen as a secularized version of something thought to be common to all the three main traditions of Mosaic theism: namely, the doctrine that all souls are of equal value in the eyes of God. It was a more particular variety of this general kind – an aspect of equality before the law – which was, very rightly, being demanded and conceded when in 1964 the US Supreme Court struck down a sentence for contempt against Mary Hamilton, a Black. She had refused to answer the public prosecutor of Alabama when he called her Mary and not, as he would have had she been white, Miss Hamilton (Pole 1978, pp. 340–1). It was this same first ideal of equality upon which the Scottish poet Burns was insisting when he wrote – with perhaps at least a suggestion of some regrettable, male chauvinist, sexism – (not a person is a person but) 'a man's a man for a' that'.

This first ideal of equality is essentially connected with the first of the three understandings of the word 'democracy' – distinguished in section 4 of chapter one, above. It is also from this sort of vision of human equality that, as we saw in chapter two, a universal equality of option rights may be, if not strictly deduced, at any rate derived; and, traditionally, has been. Although democracy in this first understanding is not essentially connected with any form of government, the associated ideal of human equality is perhaps most richly realized under regimes which are democratic in the second (not 'of the people' but 'by the people') understanding; especially in countries, such as Norway or New Zealand, where the total population is comparatively small.

Also, and much more importantly, the whole idea of government by consent has historically been derived from this first and most fundamental ideal of equality. Even though we cannot be altogether sure that his 'hes' were intended to embrace 'shes', there can be no better alternative to quoting simple yet magnificent words uttered by the 'russet-coated' Captain Rainborough in the Putney Debates of Parliament's New Model Army at the end of the English Civil War:

> Really I think that the poorest he that is in England hath a life to live as the greatest he; and therefore truly, Sir, I think it is clear, that every man that is to live under a government ought first by his own consent to put himself under that government; and I do believe that the poorest man in England is not at all bound to that government that he hath not had a voice to put himself under.
>
> (Firth 1891, I, p. 301)

(ii)   The second ideal of equality is always called equality of opportunity. But it would be much better, because less potentially misleading, to speak of 'fair and open competition for scarce opportunities' (Lloyd-Thomas 1977). This ideal is what was known to the great French Revolution of 1789 as that of *la carrière ouverte aux talents*. And for those revolutionaries it was an ideal to be applied primarily, if not perhaps exclusively, to public service appointments. The aim of the exercise always was that the scarce opportunities in question – opportunities to command armies, to become civil servants, or whatever else – should be awarded as prizes to the winners in fair and open competitions – competitions, that is, from which no one is excluded on any irrelevant grounds, and in which the organizers treat the contestants equally and without partisan prejudice.

(a)   This ideal was perfectly expressed in Article VI of the *Declaration of the Rights of Man and of the Citizen*:

> The law . . . should be the same to all . . . and all being equal in its sight, are equally eligible to all honors, places and employments, *according to their different abilities, without any other distinction than that created by their virtues and talents.*
>
> (emphasis added)

Clearly there was no thought of organizing an equal distribution of opportunities: for instance, by giving every soldier in turn his day as General of the Army. Had that been attempted the armies of the Republic would not have been so continuously successful in contests with the armies of the hereditary Dynasts!

The same proclamation should also make it clear that giving a fair and equal chance to all competitors does not mean ensuring that in fact every competitor is as likely to succeed as every other. Organizers are not by the ground rules of natural justice bound either to offset by handicapping or otherwise to neutralize every actual competitive edge making success in fact more likely or even certain. Whereas every advantage can be argued to be, not every advantage can be, an unfair advantage. Nor will it do to construe 'treating all potential contestants equally' as equalizing their actual chances of success – the probabilities, that is, that they will in fact succeed.

It is a paradoxical truth that the fact that the probabilities of winning are for this lot many times those for that lot is no proof at all that either had, in the appropriate sense, less than an equal chance. Indeed, if any confrontation is so arranged that all possible alternative outcomes are equiprobable, then what we have must be some kind of game of chance. In a perfect competition, the winners necessarily have to be the best performers. So, were the outcome in any such perfect competition to turn out to be a dead heat between all the participants, then that would make that 'competition' impotent to determine the allocation of scarce opportunities – or, indeed, of scarce anything else.

These fundamental points once taken, it becomes obvious that there can be no purchase for the application of this second ideal of equality save where there are among the potential contestants some actual inequalities – actual inequalities that are also allowed to be both relevant and legitimate. This observation cannot, of course, be made to yield any conclusions about which in particular may be admitted as legitimate or relevant and which may not. Yet, it does throw a somewhat sick light on one ruinous move in a much-commended article (B. Williams 1973).

(b) The very title, 'The idea of equality', is unfortunate. It suggests, what is false, that the key term is univocal. This suggestion is then followed through in the contention

that a system of allocation will fall short of *equality of opportunity* if the allocation of the good in question in fact works out unequally or disproportionately between different sections of society; if the unsuccessful sections are under a disadvantage which could be removed by further reform or social action.

(ibid., p. 245: emphasis added)

There is much to be learnt from this passage, though what is to be learnt is not what Williams set out to teach. In the first place, he has provided here a flagrant example of failure to make, in face of a vast and manifest difference, the corresponding crucial distinction. That is the distinction between, on the one hand, equality of opportunity, the second of the two ideals so far distinguished, and, on the other hand, the third, equality of outcome. Williams is, in effect, making his criterion for the latter his criterion for the former: 'a system of allocation will fall short of equality of opportunity *if the allocation of the good in question in fact works out unequally or disproportionately between different sections of society*' (emphasis now added).

Further lessons follow from the final proviso: 'if the unsuccessful sections are under a disadvantage which could be removed by further reform and social action'. For, almost if not quite without exception, every feature that in fact differentiates one identifiable human being from another must in principle be alterable, if not yet – or ever – in practice. Whatever is in fact determined by the environment theoretically could be altered by changing that. With appropriate alterations, the same applies to genetic constitutions and to their results. Science fiction can easily imagine a society in which all the babies come identical, as products of cloning. It is a situation that, as we remarked in chapter seven, too many professing social scientists and practising social engineers are inclined to assume already obtains. As for an identity of upbringing, visionaries from Plato onward have dreamed, or had nightmares, of a world in which all (or at least all members of one special caste) would, immediately from birth, be raised in one single uniform environment.

Williams himself proceeds: 'In these circumstances, where everything about a person is controllable, equality of opportunity and absolute equality seem to coincide; and this itself illustrates something about the notion of equality of opportunity' (ibid.,

p. 247). Certainly the final clause, after the semicolon, expresses a truth. Yet what this whole speculative exercise brings out is, not the ultimate coincidence of equality of opportunity with absolute equality (otherwise, equality of outcome or equality of condition), but the truth of what was being urged earlier about the purchase needed for any application of our second ideal – namely, that there have to be actual competitive edges not put down as unfair.

If there are to be scarce opportunities, and if these are to go to the winners of competitions, then some competitors have to enjoy competitive advantages, and some have to suffer competitive disadvantages. Furthermore, some of these advantages and disadvantages have to be authentically and legitimately theirs. So the truth is diametrically different. It is not that these two ideals must in the end coincide; but that they are, on the contrary, ultimately incompatible. This is so because, in so far as the outcomes are to be made the same for all regardless, there can be not only no incentive to compete but no scarce opportunities for which to struggle. The hypothesis requires that the attractions of anything that is inherently and incorrigibly scarce must be artificially offset by corresponding repulsions. Otherwise, there will emerge or remain that – supposedly – most obvious and infamous of evils, inequality.

(iii)   The previous subsection distinguished a second and a third ideal of equality: equality of opportunity, and equality of outcome. It also hinted at some of the costs and consequences of pursuing that third ideal. Already in chapter seven we saw more of those costs and consequences, in considering the pursuit of the same third ideal, but under the misdescription, 'social justice'. It will be an instructive reinforcement of these insights to see, in this final subsection of the present chapter, how Williams found himself forced to follow a road very similar to that later taken by Rawls.

The previous subsection showed that to follow Williams to the end would require the elimination of all those competitive advantages and disadvantages which alone make competition possible as a method of determining the allocation of what is scarce. The task now is to demonstrate what steps along this road are steps towards, namely, either the total abolition or, failing that, at least the radical delegitimatization of all those differences between individual human beings which might give rise to competitive advantages or disadvantages.

(a) There is a vast literature, notably neglected by Rawls, dealing with possible conflicts between ideals of liberty and ideals of equality (Nisbet 1974, pp. 116 ff). Between the first ideal of equality and the ideal of equal option rights for all there is, as we saw in chapter two, no conflict at all, but rather a close yet not logically necessary connection. The conflicts are with the second and still more with the third ideal of equality.

In the case of the second the extent of the conflicts will be a function of three variables: first, the nature and number of the competitions to which the ideal is to be applied; second, the stage or stages in the competitors' life-cycles at which these competitions are held; and, third, the competitive advantages or disadvantages which it is proposed to nullify or prevent 'by further reform or social action'.

If the relevant and approved competitions are to be held early in the life-cycles of the competitors, then the threat to the institution of the family must, all other things being equal, be greater. If the competitions for which equality of opportunity is mandated are confined to the public sector, and that sector is comparatively modest in size, then there would seem to be no possibilities of conflict at all. These arise only when 'equal opportunities' legislation is extended to cover all the activities of private individuals and private firms.

By the way: in considering its introduction it should be remembered, as it too rarely is, that – absent such legislation – private individuals and private firms are themselves bearing the costs of exercising their obnoxious and irrelevantly discriminatory preferences. They themselves, that is, suffer by hiring the less productive but racially, or sexually, or otherwise irrelevantly, preferred employee. Presumably this, rather than any superior virtue in 'capitalist' employers, is the main reason why, before the recent explosion of 'equal opportunity' and 'civil rights' legislation, Blacks in the USA were doing so much better in the private sector than with public or other 'non-profit' employers. (See Sowell 1975, ch. 6 and *passim*.)

(b) However, the serious and pervasive conflicts are between liberty and the third ideal of equality; the ideal which, it will be argued in chapter nine, may fairly be characterized, as in fact we have been characterizing it, as procrustean. Their present relevance arises from the fact that his commitment to this third ideal leads

Williams to set about the business of abolishing or delegitimizing differences between different individuals. Proceeding from the first of the two passages already quoted, he goes on to argue 'that one is not really offering equality of opportunity to Smith and Jones if one contents oneself with applying the same criteria to Smith as affected by favourable conditions and to Jones as affected by unfavourable but curable conditions' (B. Williams 1973, pp. 245–6).

From this Williams infers that curable competitive disadvantages – and presumably, by the same token, removable advantages – do not truly characterize or legitimately belong to those actual or potential competitors to whom they – what shall we say? – apply. He therefore delivers an Olympian ruling: 'Their identity, for these purposes, does not include their curable environment, which is itself unequal and a contributor of inequality.' Next, referring to his own stunningly high-handed proceedings, he comments: 'This abstraction of persons in themselves from unequal environments is a way, if not of regarding them as equal, at least of moving recognizably in that direction' (ibid., p. 246).

It is only after extending this approach, as consistency demands, to cover also alterable genetic constitutions that Williams begins to display a slight anxiety about the presuppositions thus revealed:

Here we might think that our notion of personal identity itself was beginning to give way; we might well wonder *who were* the people whose advantages were being discussed in this way . . . if one reached this stage of affairs, the individuals would be regarded as in all respects equal in themselves – for in themselves they would be, as it were, pure subjects or bearers of predicates, everything about them, including their genetic inheritance, being regarded as a fortuitous and changeable characteristic.

(ibid., pp. 246–7)

It is an impressive index of the enormously strong appeal which the procrustean ideal possesses for so many intellectuals in our time that the perception of such consequences does not, apparently, provoke Willliams – known by those who know him to be in general far from a fanatic – even to contemplate a reconsideration of his ultra-egalitarian commitment. It is a phenomenon which can best be compared, and is in fact commonly associated, with the persistence in socialist commitment of so many seemingly sincere democrats after they have come to realize that full socialism must ultimately and in practice prove incompatible with democracy, in the second ('by the people') understanding.

So reflect now, finally, upon the case of the comparably able Labour Minister who stated firmly in his last publication – the well-nicknamed 'Epistle to the Costa Ricans' – that 'A mixed economy is essential . . . complete state collectivism is without question incompatible with liberty and democracy' (Crosland 1975, p. 6). Yet he gave no indication either there or elsewhere of the point, if any, at which he himself would have to leave a party committed by its constitution to 'the public ownership of all the means of production, distribution, and exchange'; and, in practice, insisting on ever more and never less state-ownership. This is eventually to include, what Mill saw to be the most formidable of all threats to freedom, state monopoly in the supply of educational services (Mill 1859; and compare Flew 1987a). We can only infer that, for whatever reasons, both Williams and Crosland were entirely at one with:

> . . . the virtuous young lady of Kent
> Who said that she knew that it meant
> When men took her to dine
> Gave her cocktails and wine;
> She knew what it meant – but she went.

Chapter nine

Enemies of poverty, or of inequality?

A certain man . . . fell among thieves, which stripped him of his raiment, and wounded him, and departed, leaving him half dead . . . But a certain Samaritan, as he journeyed, came where he was: and when he saw him, he had compassion on him, and he went to him, and bound up his wounds . . . and brought him to an inn, and took care of him.

The Gospel according to St Luke
(AV: 10:30 and 33–4)

After this Theseus killed a man called Procrustes, who lived in what was known as Corydallus in Attica. This person forced passing travellers to lie down on a bed, and if any were too long for the bed he lopped off those parts of their bodies which protruded, while racking out the legs of the ones who were too short. This was why he was given the name of Procrustes [The Racker].

Diodorus Siculus,
The Library of History (IV 59, 5)

Some years ago now a journal circulating widely, perhaps mainly, among persons paid by and placed in the welfare state machine published an article by David Donnison. The editors had earlier and with reason selected him as then the most suitable spokesperson for contemporary social-democratic egalitarianism (Flew 1981, pp. 59–64). Under a challenging title, 'A radical strategy to help the poor?', Donnison began with a tribute to some of his professional colleagues, at once followed by a reproach for the still unenlightened vulgar:

From Charles Booth to Peter Townsend, some of Britain's ablest social scientists have devoted the best years of their lives to studying poverty and policies for the poor. The academic quality of their work may explain why their ideas take so long to make any impact on the thinking of ordinary people, and fail to generate any broadly based movement to eliminate poverty.

(*New Society* for 29 October 1981, p. 183)

The next paragraph raises the question: 'What do the British mean by "poverty"?' Referring to the interviewees' answers recorded in Townsend 1979 Donnison concluded, correctly, that 'scarcely anyone gave poverty the egalitarian, relative meaning ("It's when you can't have the things which everyone else has") which Townsend himself uses' (pp. 183–5). Yet Donnison seems not to see any of the implications of this not very surprising finding. For, in so far as Townsend is concerned with inequality rather than with poverty, as ordinarily understood, this must distance his work from that of Booth. And, given that this is true about Townsend, Donnison's rebuke to the benighted laity is like that of some supercilious Marxist–Leninist reproaching 'by the people' democrats for refusing to support Communist policies; explaining this refusal by referring to the supposed obtuse inability of the democrats to appreciate 'the academic quality' of the similar persuasive redefinition which allows him to describe Soviet Germany as the German Democratic Republic.

1 Procrusteans, or Good Samaritans?

The distinction which Donnison and Townsend are collapsing is not difficult. It is also of the very greatest importance, both theoretical and practical. Yet failures or refusals either to make it or to make anything of it have been and remain so persistent and so pervasive in most contemporary discussion that it is not extravagant to devote a whole, long chapter to reviewing the different theoretical implications and the different practical consequences of the alternatives involved. These always ought to be, yet all too often are not, firmly distinguished. For again and again, in all sorts of areas of practical policy, choices have to be made between equality and betterment. (See, for instance, Flew 1984b.) It really matters that everyone who has to make such choices should realize what and how much is at stake in their making. This review is also and incidentally bound to uncover some of the strong interests involved, and thus help to explain that reluctance to distinguish. It will become obvious, even if it was not obvious before, that sometimes we face a calculating refusal to distinguish rather than an innocent failure.

(i)   On the one side – call it the left – we have public policies intended to make the condition of all those subject to those policies in some respect (more) equal. One the other side – which must now be the right – are public policies aiming to ensure that none shall fall below some minimum level of whatever it may be. The objectives of this left are thus essentially and intentionally egalitarian, in a way in which those of this right are not. To borrow two images which were, from the victory in Europe onwards, part of the stock-in-trade of all Winston Churchill's domestic speeches, the aim of the second sort of policy is to provide a welfare-floor or a safety-net. Above this floor, this net, the sky can be the limit for individual effort. There are, or are to be, minima without maxima. The essential egalitarian aim, by contrast, is to bring and to maintain both floors and ceilings as near as may be the one to the other.

In thus proposing and supporting welfare-floor or safety-net policies Churchill could, and presumably did, think of himself as fulfilling one of the promises of the Atlantic Charter. (This he and Franklin Roosevelt had drawn up and signed during a 1941 conference held in a battleship on the North Atlantic. The substance as well as the style of the wartime commitment – a commitment to, among other things, 'Freedom from Want' – was far removed from the 'Security against Inequality' sought by one contributor to a May 1983 conference in the University of Waterloo.)

(ii)   It is, though common, wrong either to say or to suggest that anyone rejecting such an egalitarian ideal has to be, by that token, an inegalitarian. This is like saying that anyone who does not accept the classical Utilitarian thesis that the supreme good is the greatest happiness of the greatest number must, by that rejection, be committed to pursuing – as the sole, consequential alternative – the maximum misery of the maximum number.

(a)   Once again we have here something which ought to be too obvious to be even worth mentioning. Yet *The Pursuit of*

Inequality (Green 1981) is by no means the only work coming from a serious and non-partisan publisher which has nevertheless insisted upon this preposterous polemic misrepresentation. More significant perhaps than any such apoplectic and paranoiac book is the fact that so fairminded a commentator as Brian Walden could allow himself – shortly before his departure from Parliament and the Labour Party – to describe staunch opponents of the procrustean ideal as 'Jacobins of inequality'.

The fact that someone refuses to recognize equality of the present or perhaps of any other kind as either the greatest good, or even any sort of good at all, is simply not a warrant for inferring that they must cherish the corresponding inequality as the only alternative good-in-itself. For one excellent reason for rejecting ideals of equality is at the same time an equally good reason for rejecting ideals of inequality. It is that both treat mere relativities as goods-in-themselves. The classical Utilitarian, for one, must see it as perverse and preposterous to value for their own sakes the mere relativities of either equality or inequality: notwithstanding that, following Bentham, he is likely to be led by considerations of marginal utility to put some instrumental as opposed to intrinsic value upon the equalization of wealth and income: 'The more remote from equality are the shares . . . the less is the sum of felicity produced by those shares' (Bentham 1822–32, II, p. 27).

(b)   Policies of the first of the two sorts being distinguished in this section 1 are of their very nature directed towards that to which those of the second sort must equally essentially be indifferent: namely, relativities. This purely conceptual contention remains true notwithstanding that flesh-and-blood protagonists of the former may also happen to have – usually will in fact happen to have – some greater or lesser interest in the absolute levels at which their favourite equalities are eventually achieved; while those of the latter may permit, and maybe just as often will permit, the actual absolute levels of their required minima to be in whole or part first determined, and then from time to time redetermined, by reference to the higher and highest levels which are or could be currently enjoyed by other members of the target population.

The same purely conceptual contention remains true notwithstanding that public welfare-floor policies can in the real world be financed only by taxes on those (who would otherwise be) better off than the beneficiaries. They are, therefore, bound to result in some measure of equalization. Exactly how large or small this measure becomes will of course depend on who has to pay how much of the necessary tax-take; whether these taxes are proportionate or progressive and, if progressive, how steeply; and so on.

(iii)   Again, in the real world measures intended only or primarily to equalize may have the indirect and unintended effect of so discouraging the production of wealth that the previously worst off – who may or may not have been intended beneficiaries of these measures – in fact become as one result either worse off than they might otherwise have been or even worse off absolutely.

This is not the place to attempt a definitive answer to factual and very practical questions. It is sufficient, but also necessary, to say just enough to show that policies for promoting equality may in practice be in conflict with policies for abolishing truly scandalous poverty; the poverty, that is, not of purely relative deprivation but of absolute hardship.

(a)   Once this is appreciated it also becomes clear that those committed to the imposition of equality have an interest in concealing the difference between that objective and the abolition of the second sort of poverty. For they can scarcely fail to be aware that, whereas everyone is prepared at least to pay lip-service to the ideal of abolishing such truly scandalous poverty, there are many – perceived by the procrusteans themselves as *The Conservative Enemy* (Crosland 1962) – who do not even pretend to accept the ideal of an universal and forcibly imposed equality of outcome. How convenient it is, therefore, to conceal the difference between these two policy objectives, and to put it about that those who oppose the one (which is, admittedly, less than universally popular) are thereby revealing themselves to be heartlessly – indeed uncaringly and uncompassionately – indifferent towards the other.

Sometimes it seems that, by collapsing this and other crucial distinctions, enthusiastic egalitarians succeed in deceiving not only other people but also themselves. For instance, some years ago one of Britain's leading social scientists edited a volume of papers 'chosen to illustrate the approach and the achievement of the human sciences in theory and research concerning the ancient problem of nature and nurture' (Halsey 1977, p. 1). In a long, frequently technical Introduction to his often correspondingly technical selections he took it totally for granted that any reduction of inequality – inequality without prefix or suffix – is beyond dispute an intrinsic good (ibid., p. 25). It appears that the Professor of Social and Administrative Studies in the University of Oxford then just plain could not understand that opposition to his favoured measures for the enforcement of equality might be motivated by something other than 'malevolence' (ibid., p. 8).

(b) The practical point, which needs to be laboured, is that policies proposed – to quote Britain's latest Labour Chancellor – 'to make the rich howl in agony' will not necessarily benefit, and might actually harm, the previously worst off. Those unlovely and revealingly sadistic words were originally uttered in 1973 by Dennis Healey before a venomously applauding Party Conference.

When in 1974 he was introducing his first Budget in the House of Commons the case presented was, if less determinate, more decorous. As his justification for raising the top rates of tax to 83 per cent on earned and 98 per cent on investment income, he said: 'I believe that this type of redistribution through the tax system makes a major contribution to the health of the community, and I intend to go a great deal further before I have finished.' No doubt he saw himself as following the footsteps of Hugh Dalton who, in defence of his own first Budget in October 1945, had said that he proposed:

> to continue that steady advance toward economic and social equality which we have made during the war and which the Government firmly intends to continue in peacetime.

There can no longer be any question but that such extortionate rates of tax on higher incomes are fiscally counter-productive whatever the collectivistic benefits to 'the health of the community', and however great the envious and sadistic satisfactions for socialist militants. For both in the US and in the UK the collectors of taxes have reported that, since the making of substantial cuts in the highest rates, there has been a significant *increase* in the total tax-take from the top income percentiles.

It is worth quoting some of the perhaps surprising figures, all supplied by the appropriate official Treasury statisticians. In the US between 1981, the final year of the previous much higher rates, and 1985, the proportion of total income tax revenue coming from the top 5 per cent of incomes increased by 15.8 per cent; while that from the top 1 per cent *increased* still more, by 22.1 per cent. In the UK, in the last tax year of the Heath administration the proportion of income tax revenue supplied by the top 5 per cent of incomes was 28.6 per cent. This figure *dropped* to 24 per cent in the last tax year of the subsequent Labour administrations. But, despite or because of the removal of the former 83 per cent and 98 per cent rates under the first Thatcher administration, it *increased* to (an estimated) 27 per cent in the tax year 1986–7. (For more such figures and for details of their sources, see the Appendix to Bond 1988.)

About the impact of income taxation in general upon economic growth there is, no doubt, more room for honest and informed dispute. Yet there are several studies of apparently comparable countries showing that lower rates of taxation, especially of taxation falling directly upon incomes, correlate positively with higher rates of economic growth. So, even if the available evidence is insufficient definitively to establish any categorical conclusions, it is at least enough to confirm the suspicion that no one has actually found any good reason for believing that income taxation constitutes an exception to what is elsewhere a familiar and uncontentious general rule; namely, that taxes must at least tend to discourage, and subsidies to encourage, whatever is taxed or subsidized. (The point was made, with a characteristic pungency, by Rousseau in *The Social Contract*: 'Imposing a fine for work is a rather unusual way of abolishing idleness.')

Similar considerations apply to taxes on capital gains, even when these are indexed to offset inflationary distortions. Here, because capital gains taxes are in fact much less common than income taxes, there is less room for comparative international studies. What evidence there is nevertheless seems to confirm what we should have expected: namely, that such taxes tend to reduce the supply of capital available for financing high-risk ventures. Who, after all, will willingly put their capital at great risk if the corresponding possibility of gain is not equally great? Yet it is precisely (some of) the riskiest ventures which produce the most explosive economic growth. Certainly cuts in the rates of tax on capital gains in the USA have been followed by increases in the rates of economic growth; and the other way about.

All of which adds up to a strong case for concluding that, if what you want is indeed to improve the absolute rather than the relative condition of the less and the least advantaged, then you should go for overall growth, rather than for those confiscatory taxes on the more advantaged which give so much satisfaction to procrusteans. Even if it is not strictly true – to borrow words used by President Kennedy in recommending across-the-board cuts in income taxes – that 'a rising tide lifts all boats', still it does make larger resources available for possible transfer, whether voluntary or compulsory, to those who have not been lifted and cannot help themselves. A more recent convert to a remarkably similar view is Comrade Du Runsheng, a senior agricultural planner to the People's Republic of China. (Those concerned to conserve their US 'liberal' credentials will here have to think hard in hopes of discovering how all this differs quite fundamentally from the allegedly discredited 'trickle down effect' of ridiculous Reaganomics!):

> Our government promotes the policy that some people get rich first. Then we'll have the other people get rich. Our final purpose is to have all the people get rich.

(iv) In order to fix the desired distinction between two theoretically and practically very different policy objectives still more firmly in mind, let us draw upon the two epigraphs for chapter nine for the labels 'good Samaritan' and 'procrustean'.

(a) In view of the fact that the hero of the parable did the first aid with his own hands, and then financed the victim's further care out of his own private pocket, the former label may in the present context be too flattering. For in the public and strictly political case the good deeds are always to be tax-financed; while their advocates may often expect, and even try to ensure, that that finance will in fact be provided by other people. Notoriously 'the rich' – the most popular target for extractions – are always other people, and different from us; while, equally notoriously, the difference consists in their having, or being thought to have, more money!

In these days we need to put heavy emphasis upon the question: 'Who pays?' For it has become common political practice to abuse opponents as 'heartless', 'uncaring', and 'uncompassionate', while preening yourself and your associates upon your and their supposed possession of the opposite personal characteristics; and all this upon the sole ground that you and your party support further increases in state spending on welfare services, whereas your opponent and his (or hers) want to maintain some checks. Whatever the merits or demerits of such rival political positions, abuse in these terms commits a kind of category mistake. For the correct criteria for heartlessness, or for caring, or for compassion, are to be found among the reactions of individuals as individuals: in particular, in their willingness or unwillingness to make personal efforts; efforts drawing upon their own, private, resources.

The confusion on this count is so widespread and so complete that in *The Times* for 7 November 1984 a Member of Parliament sneered at two unnamed Ministers for allegedly interpolating into the parable a reference to 'the full wallet' of the Good Samaritan. Yet it was that Member's copy from which chapter 10, verse 35 had perhaps somehow been excised:

> And on the morrow he took out two pence, and gave them to the host, and said, 'Take care of him; and whatsoever thou spendest more, I, when I come back again, will repay thee.'

(b)   As we have just seen, the first of the two suggested labels is often, in its implications of personal and sacrificial generosity, far too kind. The second is much less friendly, yet in that very unfriendliness completely apt. For in a picturesque way it epitomizes the third ideal of equality; equality of eventual condition, equality of outcome. And the reference to the legendary innkeeper Procrustes underlines the second essential point; that this particular ideal is one to be attained by social engineering and by exercises of state power rather than self-imposed upon devoted volunteers.

If there are anywhere egalitarians who actually do begin by equalizing themselves – perhaps by surrendering their persons and property to a kibbutz – and who after that try to persuade others to do the same, *without at any stage appealing for the enforcement of their ideal by the state*, then it is obvious that it would be utterly unfair to pin on them the unfriendly label 'procrusteans'. But these possible people are not the actual egalitarians whose ideal we have been considering. For, as we saw in earlier chapters, the reason why our actual procrusteans persist in identifying the imposition of their ideal with the pursuit of (social) justice just is to justify its imposition by the public power.

In the present perspective it becomes easy to appreciate that the welfare state is no more essentially procrustean than it is essentially an institution for meeting the antecedently just claims of its beneficiaries. When – to refer again to the Iron Chancellor – Bismarck inaugurated a system of national insurance in Imperial Germany this did no doubt constitute, in effect, a modest measure of equalization. But that was not its purpose, and its proponents certainly had no thought of eventually equalizing the conditions of the Junkers with those of the factory workers or the farm labourers.

The case is the same with the provision of educational and health services. There is nothing essentially procrustean about the public provision of such services, free at the point of consumption, for those unable to pay. Procrusteanism begins when, and in so far as, such services are offered without charge to all; and without any tax relief for those choosing to make their own independent provision. It is in full possession when and only when all provision has to be uniform and monopolistic; on the grounds that, at least in these areas, no one must do either better or worse than anyone else, whether for themselves or for their children.

2 Procrusteanism and monopoly provision

What is to liberals perhaps the most repellent face of procrusteanism is revealed when those who choose to abandon their claims on such publicly provided services by paying twice, both through taxes and privately, are then denounced, with malign and mindless fury, as 'queue-crashers'. Since they have, by their withdrawal, without harming anyone in front, enabled everyone behind to move up a place, this preposterous charge constitutes the diametric opposite of the truth.

Nevertheless the fact that it is made, and has been constantly reiterated by persons who have elsewhere shown signs of intelligence and understanding, must be significant. For no one, surely, would present an argument so egregiously perverse and manifestly worthless if they had anything less disreputable to offer?

Confronted by a situation which seemingly reduces procrusteans to apoplectic irrationality, the sensible Samaritan will want to explore the possibilities of further relieving the pressure on publicly provided facilities by offering some tax relief to encourage more people to make their own private arrangements. Yet that, of course, is the rub. For this Samaritan response, like the original offence of the person abused as a 'queue-crasher', steps away from monopoly. And any move away from monopoly – and, in particular, any move away from state monopoly – engages with powerful opposing interests, both ideological and material. It should not be surprising therefore, that those eager to defend or extend such monopoly become willing, in desperate defiance of all reason and truth, to pretend that escapers necessarily worsen the situation of those left behind. How else, after all, is their support to be recruited to a cause which is in truth irrelevant or even contrary to their own most immediate interests?

What then are the ideological and material interests favouring monopoly? These are of three theoretically distinguishable but in practice closely connected kinds: first, commitment to the procrustean ideal for its own sake; second, the imperatives of socialist doctrine; and, third, intrinsically unideological – indeed extremely material – labour union, producer interests.

(i) Anyone escaping from any imposed equality must as such offend the procrustean, and that offence will be the greater the more it promises to be followed by further 'home runs'. Any procrustean, furthermore, is almost bound to be also and simultaneously a socialist in the Clause IV sense. For his desired equalities of condition scarcely could be imposed without state monopoly provision of all relevant goods and services; notwithstanding that such socialist, state monopoly provision still by no means guarantees the realization of the procrustean dream. It is, that is to say, though surely a necessary most certainly not a sufficient condition; just as a pluralist and competitive economy would seem to be a necessary but equally clearly not a sufficient condition of a pluralist and competitive political culture.

We perhaps need now to explain, parenthetically, that, from its foundation, Clause IV of the Constitution of the Labour Party, a clause which used to be printed on every membership card, stated that the primary aim was to secure the public ownership of 'all the means of production, distribution and exchange'. In 1958, the year in which the German Social Democrats abandoned their own parallel commitment to total socialism, Hugh Gaitskell as Leader tried unsuccessfully to persuade his own Party Conference to adopt a New Economic Policy, and to limit the scope of Clause IV to what he called – tacitly borrowing a phrase from Lenin – 'the commanding heights of the economy'.

Gaitskell in fact succeeded in securing only an insubstantial amendment. Since it is nowadays so often said, both by mendacious apologists and by media wiseacres, that the Labour Party either never really was or at any rate no longer is, in this understanding, socialist, it becomes just worth quoting from Clause IV, as so amended:

> to secure for the workers by hand or by brain the full fruits of
> their industry and the most equitable distribution thereof that
> may be possible, upon the basis of the common ownership of the
> means of production, distribution and exchange.

(ii) Just as socialism is bound to attract procrusteans, so socialists will naturally pick out procrusteans as possible allies. In the first place, equalization may be seen as, as it were, the specialty of the house. In face of all the accumulating experience of 'actually existing socialism', not only in the USSR but now in so many other countries also, there is no longer much prospect of persuading any sceptical and openminded enquirer that socialism promises either an end to scarcity or a universal improvement in the quality of life. (It would, for instance, be hard to find in northwest Europe any scandals of uninhibited industrial pollution comparable with the worst, or even the average, which I have myself experienced in Poland and Czechoslovakia.)

Suppose, however, that we are prepared, as so significantly many of our procrusteans appear to be, to ignore the vast inequalities, not only in power but also in privilege and perquisites, between, on the one hand, the masses and, on the other, the *Nomenklatura* (Voslensky 1984). Then perhaps we can plausibly commend socialism as facilitating, even if not necessarily guaranteeing, some desired forms of equalization.

But, at a deeper level, there is a firmer, more theoretical foundation for alliance. For, as we saw in chapter seven, the same drive to delegitimize all the differentiating characteristics of individual human beings is needed, both to justify the Manna-from-Heaven assumption that all wealth is always ultimately the property of the collective; and to remove every possible ground for any claims that the deserts and entitlements of different individuals are in any way different and, therefore, unequal.

(iii) There is no need to labour long in order to discover reasons why many of the loudest and most persistent voices calling both for equal and for exclusively public provision come from those trade unions whose members are most involved.

Part of the story, of course, is that the vast majority of union officials in Britain are, for whatever reasons, already socialists by conviction. It would nevertheless be naive not to go on to notice the urgings of more direct and material interests among the rank and file. There is, for a start, no shortage of evidence showing both how management in any monopoly operations, whether public or private, unharried by any threat from competition, can and will tolerate or even encourage overmanning, restrictive practices, and slovenly work; and how resistance to inflationary wage claims by monopoly employers, and especially perhaps by monopoly public employers, is almost always weaker than that by competing and bankruptable private employers.

For anyone who has been living the eighties in Britain the most instructive and relevant reference is, however, to the wholesale and systematic opposition, both of the unions and of their creature party, to every move to put out to competitive tender particular services currently supplied either by the NHS or by local authorities. Had the General Secretaries and the Executives of the relevant unions, people in a much better position to know than most of the rest of us, truly believed that, because public monopoly employers 'do not have to make a profit', they and their employees always, or even typically, supply better and/or cheaper services than any possible private competitor, then they would have welcomed rather than opposed all such moves. For these would have been seen as promising to provide the electorate with a compellingly persuasive demonstration of the superiority of socialism.

The Wealth of Nations contains several astringent observations of how employers will rarely come together, even for 'merriment and diversion', without their associations resulting in some conspiracy to restrict competition, and hence to exploit the consumer. Since employees too are human, we have to expect the same of labour unions. We are in both cases sometimes disappointed. But not often.

So when leaders of public sector labour unions demand – in the name, naturally, of 'equality and social justice' – state monopoly in the supply of health, education, or other services, then – in words borrowed from the most formidable of England's political thinkers – it is easy to recognize 'the benefit that proceedeth from such darkness, and to whom it accrueth' (Hobbes 1651, XLVII).

3 Distracting aims within the Poverty Lobby

Section 1 developed the theoretical distinction between procrustean and Samaritan objectives. It proceeded to show that in practice policies directed towards one of these will often obstruct the attainment of the other. Section 2 argued that the first, securing *equality in provision*, must conflict with a third, securing whatever *quality of provision* best satisfies each individual consumer. This was because, in order to achieve the desired uniformity, the procrustean is bound to favour monopoly. But the sovereign way to secure the different objective of satisfying every individual consumer is to have competing suppliers; suppliers competing precisely if not only because they all have a strong personal interest in catering for as many consumers as they can.

(i)   The present section 3 is concerned with confusions between procrustean and Samaritan objectives among those who constitute what calls itself, and is called, the Poverty Lobby. Already at the very beginning of this chapter we saw how two leading members – both professing social scientists – systematically collapse that distinction.

Before his election as a Member of Parliament, in the Labour interest, Frank Field had already become well known and respected as Director of the Child Poverty Action Group. We might therefore have expected, at least so long as he held that previous position, that his concerns would be primarily if not exclusively Samaritan. In fact he always has been, as he still is, more inclined to talk about inequality than about poverty. For instance, although Sir Keith Joseph as Minister for Social Services in the 1970–4 Heath administration popularized the idea of 'cycles of deprivation', Field prefers, in continuing that discussion, to speak of 'cycles of inequality'. Indeed, he seems not to notice that he is thus significantly and constantly misreporting Sir Keith (Field 1973).

(a)   It must have been shortly before his election that Field, as a self-appointed Master of the Hounds, summoned various associates to a rich hunt. The resulting book bears words from R. H. Tawney in bold print on its dust-jacket. These describe 'the problem of poverty' as 'what thoughtful poor people call with equal justice the problem of riches' (Field 1979). In his Introduction the editor promises to explain and to justify these words. In fact he makes little or no attempt to redeem that promise. Thus he does not even begin to calculate whether the total after-tax income presently being received by whomever he chooses to define as rich would be sufficient to cover all the transfer payments necessary to abolish everything which he would rate as poverty; much less to estimate the implications for the basic and continuing business of wealth creation of still heavier taxation on higher incomes.

Had Field actually taken the trouble to make such calculations – as he surely would have done were his prime concern a Samaritan longing to raise up the poor, rather than a procrustean passion to grind down the rich – then we can be quite sure that his own estimates of new money available to his Chancellor Robin Hood would have been grotesquely optimistic. For all the income figures which he does give here (ibid., pp. 50–6) must, since this is not something which he sees fit to specify one way or the other, be presumed to be figures for income before tax. But, at the time when he and other contributors were writing for Field 1979, the top rates were those introduced in 1974 by Dennis Healey's first Budget: namely, a massive 83 per cent on earned and a confiscatory 98 per cent on investment income.

Field's own failure to take account of current tax extractions in his argument for intensifying 'Labour's war against inequality' – presumably by some still further increase in those extractions – seems, shamefully, to be par for the course in this Poverty Lobby. (See, for instance, Townsend and Bosanquet 1980; in which, by never even mentioning those top tax rates, professing social scientists permit themselves to dismiss, without supporting evidence or argument, the 'myth' of heavy taxation on the rich.)

That systematic failure, the frequent though less systematic failure to specify what if any corrections have been made for inflation (Field 1979, pp. 6 and 8), and – at least when in the heat of the political kitchen – the willingness to contrast the weekly take-home pay of potential supporters with before-tax annual incomes of the class enemy, all combine to suggest that there should perhaps be some redirection of Field's complaint that certain (other) academics 'have abandoned scholarship in order to become campaigners, drawing conclusions from the data which do not stand up to careful scrutiny' (ibid., p. 101).

(b)   As a whole Field's Introduction is much more interested in 'the kind of society Labour is in business to create' (ibid., p. 6), and in capturing major procrustean campaign objectives, than in any different and narrower Samaritan ends. Generally it is for Field 'the whole network of unjustifiable and unjustified privileges which disfigure the face of British society' rather than any recalcitrant local pockets of real poverty that provide the target of choice (ibid., p. 3). Perhaps that is his backhanded reason for claiming:

> For those contributors who work in what has become known as the 'poverty lobby', it is the first conscious attempt to extend the framework in which they campaign. And, because this move will be misunderstood, it is important to spell out the reasons for the change.
>
> (ibid., p. 2)

But then, instead of this promised and needed explication, what we actually get first is what purports to be an answer to those who object to making general 'distributional questions the stuff of politics'. This purported answer concludes, with no very obvious relevance: 'Again, as Tawney remarked, when the liner is sinking and the passengers leave for the life boats, there is no place for distinguishing between first and second-class passengers' (ibid., p. 2). After that we are unhelpfully assured:

> The initial step in the long haul back to a society where our economic appetites are once more subordinate to moral principles is to ensure a much wider and more informed debate about the society in which we live, and it is hoped that the reports on the rich will contribute to this development.
> (ibid., p. 3: it is, by the way, never revealed to what particular past period Field would have us heave ourselves back)

Neither of these two remarks, nor the subsequent ideological tirade, does anything to explain, much less to justify, Field's final and supposedly recapitulatory sentence: 'Justice for today's poor is as linked to "the problem of riches" as it was when Tawney delivered that inaugural lecture sixty-five years ago' (ibid., p. 9).

(ii) We shall, it seems, have to investigate for ourselves the reasons which Field and his friends might have offered, but did not. In the present context the word 'problem' has to be understood in the sense implying that there is a wrong to be righted. In the alternative sense it implies that there is an explanation to be found and a theoretical question to be answered (Flew 1976, ch. 4). So why is it apparently thought that the supposed twin evils of riches and of poverty are so connected that the abolition of either must involve the abolition of the other?

(a) There are two reasons, both unsound but one much more important and fundamental than the other. The slighter of the two takes off from the observation that the comparative expressions 'the richer' and 'the better off' constitute such correlatives of the expressions 'the poorer' and 'the worse off' that, where there is no application for either of the first pair, there necessarily cannot be any application for the corresponding member of the second pair. Yet of course this purely formal and semantic truth does not carry the substantial implication that, as a matter of universal fact, those who actually are richer and better off have caused and are causing those who actually are poorer and worse off to be as they so unfortunately are; nor, indeed, the other way about.

In any particular case in which either or both of these particular causal propositions does or do happen to be true, this contingent fact of its or their truth needs to be demonstrated by direct appeal to the evidence in that selfsame particular case. Thanks, however, to the pre-eminent force of the falsifying, negative, *particular* instance we can already know that all *general* theories of this kind are untrue. Section 1 of chapter three, above, took note of one of these, applying to countries: namely, Third World Dependency Theory. Applied to individuals, albeit individuals here considered only as members of classes, the most famous specimen surfaces first in *The Poverty of Philosophy*:

> From day to day it thus becomes clearer that the production relations in which the bourgeoisie move have . . . a dual character . . . in the self-same relations in which wealth is produced, poverty is produced also . . . these relations produce bourgeois wealth, i.e., the wealth of the bourgeois class, only . . . by producing an ever growing proletariat.
>
> (Marx 1847, p. 104)

By the way: in view of the fact that many outside the strict Marxist–Leninist obedience continue to concede the obituary claim of Engels that Marx was a social scientist equal in stature to Darwin in biology, it is worth pointing out that Marx himself, years before he made this Immiseration Thesis one of the centrepieces of *Capital*, knew that it was not true of the paradigm case of the United Kingdom. His revealing first reaction was persistently to misrepresent the Budget speech in which Gladstone had stated and relished the opposite truth. Then in *Capital* itself Marx simply suppresses, without attempting to challenge, the falsifying statistical evidence. (See, for instance, Felix 1983, pp. 160–1 and Wolfe 1967, pp. 322–3; and compare Flew 1984a, III 2, and Schwartzschild 1986, *passim.*) *So war dieser Mann der Wissenschaft* [Thus was this man of science]!

(b)   The far more important and far more fundamental reason why Field and so many others believe that there must be a causally necessary connection between the perceived problems of riches and of poverty is that all their enquiries and recommendations presuppose, first, that there is always and only some fixed quantity of wealth available; and hence, second, that the only way in which those perceived as poor can possibly become better off is by receiving some sort of handout (to be first taken from somebody else). Believing this, they are also and further inclined to assume that the total amounts of wealth which will be available in the future will not be significantly affected by the amounts and manner of such projected takings.

These assumptions are widespread well beyond the bounds of the domestic Poverty Lobby. For they also both pervade and misguide most of the campaign documents of those who, while claiming to put the Third World First, refuse to attend to the case for concluding that government to government handouts are typically wasted or worse than wasted; often going to strengthen governments which are in fact themselves the main obstacles to the economic advancement of their subjects (Bauer 1976, 1981, and 1984). Again, similar assumptions nowadays infect and misguide almost every statement made on behalf of any of the mainstream Christian churches. (See, for instance, Anderson 1984, Block 1983 and 1986, and Flew 1986b.) But here we concentrate upon the significance of the name chosen for one of the elements in the domestic Poverty Lobby.

For the description 'Low Pay Unit' is very suggestive. It suggests, as is presumably intended, that the object of the exercise should be to ensure that those who are at present paid precious little for doing whatever they are doing should be paid more to go on doing the same. It also encourages, whether or not this too is intended, a further false assumption; namely that, absent minimum wage legislation, or some equivalent governmental intervention, none of the individuals who are at present low paid will ever go on to earn more. Since almost all economists, and indeed almost everyone else who has ever examined the evidence, believe that such legislation makes for more unemployment (W. Williams 1982, ch. 3); and since even low-paid jobs are incontestably preferable to no jobs at all, and may themselves become a step on the road to better things, it would, surely, be better to conceive the problem as one not of low pay but of low earnings? In this more positive perspective we shall begin to ask, not how the employers of the presently low paid are to be forced to pay more for the same; but how the presently low paid are to be helped to fit themselves to increase their earnings.

No doubt the poor, at least in the strained and limited sense of persons who are simply unable to help themselves to a minimum standard of living, will always be both with us and with our descendants, if only because no human society will ever escape all the accidents and afflictions to which all flesh is heir. So there will always have to be handouts for those thus afflicted; handouts which every Samaritan, and indeed every one of us as a potential victim of disabling afflictions, will wish to make as generous as possible. But handouts of their very nature involve dependency; and dependency is something which all who put a high value upon self-respect, both for themselves and for others, must want to minimize.

This requires that we approach every problem of poverty in a dynamic and forward-looking way, paralleling that suggested in the proposed replacement of the Low Pay Unit by a Low Earnings Unit. Because effective demand tends to increase supply, the open-ended and unconditional provision of welfare handouts must itself tend to increase that dependency which valuers of self-respect perceive as one of the worst aspects of the real evil of (not 'relative deprivation' but) poverty.

It is, in the main, because, ignoring these truths, they adopted a statically redistributive, handout approach, similar to that favoured by the British Poverty Lobby, that various very lavishly financed US poverty programmes have in their effects been often disappointing and sometimes counter-productive. Anyone who really is concerned to abolish poverty, rather than either to promote socialism or to realize the procrustean ideal, now categorically must take to mind the lessons of *Losing Ground: American Social Policy 1950–1980* (Murray 1984).

The approach of our Poverty Lobby, as we have just seen in the particular case of the Low Pay Unit, is misguided by two false presuppositions: first, that there is always and only some fixed quantity of wealth available for (re)distribution; and hence, second, that the sole solution for the poverty of those perceived as poor is for them to acquire some increment of income by transfer from somebody else. The most famous as well as probably the most influential formulation of assumptions of this sort is to be found in the first two paragraphs of Book II of Mill's *Principles of Political Economy*:

> The laws and conditions of the production of wealth partake of the character of physical truths. There is nothing optional or arbitrary in them. . . . It is not so with the Distribution of Wealth. That is a matter of human institution solely. The things once there, mankind, individually or collectively, can do with them as they like. They can place them at the disposal of whomsoever they please, and on whatever terms. Further, in the social state, in every state except total solitude, any disposal whatever of them can only take place by the consent of society, or rather of those who dispose of its active force.
>
> (Mill 1848, II, pp. 199–200)

Since wealth is produced by and sometimes even consists in human actions there cannot, strictly speaking, be any natural laws of its production. For, as we saw in chapter one, whatever is determined by a true law of nature must be physically necessitated. So, although there can be and are in human conduct regularities which may sometimes make prediction possible, behaviour which is physically necessitated cannot constitute action (Flew 1985, ch. 4). Among the regularities which do indeed make prediction possible are those guaranteeing that, all other things being equal, if an existing stock of wealth is redistributed without reference to antecedent claims of ownership, then much less will be produced in the future. This is the trite truth which Lenin had rediscovered when he at last replaced the principles of what had then to be qualified as 'War Communism' by those of his New Economic Policy. (See, for instance, Heller and Nekrich 1986.)

Earlier chapters have attacked the Manna-from-Heaven assumptions of redistributionist theoreticians upon, in the main, moral grounds. The primary objection has been that these theoreticians have rushed on to recommend more or less drastic (future) redistributions without even attempting first to show that those from whom wealth or income is to be forcibly taken are not really entitled to (that part of) their (present) holdings. But there is also, as has been suggested throughout the present chapter, the objection of prudence. For, whatever may have been true of Lenin and his party:

> it needs no economist to tell *us* that if in any country the products of a living civilization were treated as the Bedouins treat the products of a dead civilization, the swift result would be fatal to that civilization . . . poverty, famine, and death.
>
> (George 1890, p. 437: emphasis added)

Continuing his criticism of the passage previously quoted from Mill, the author of *The Science of Political Economy* indicates the prudential crux:

> But the things on which the natural laws of distribution exert their control are not things already produced, but things which are being, or are yet to be, produced.
>
> (ibid., p. 438)

(iii)   Field, as the previous two subsections have surely shown, misrepresents what is in fact a procrustean drive for general equalization, and in particular for grinding down the rich, as if it were a required rational development of a different, narrower, authentically Samaritan concern for the relief or prevention of poverty. This Field does, it must be reiterated, without good or even any reasons given.

Townsend 1979, the enormous book which we earlier saw Donnison commending for its allegedly elevated 'academic quality', makes little pretence to any Samaritan concern for the relief of actual hardship. If he does indeed have such a concern, it is one which regularly takes second place to procrustean and socialist commitments.

Certainly we hear much of Townsend's lifelong desire for a 'wider distribution of land, property and other assets'; something which, he tells us, can be achieved by (among other things) 'extending public ownership' (ibid., p. 925). But in his 'academic quality' he does not condescend either to explain how concentration of ownership in the hands of the state constitutes a 'wider distribution'; or to notice what for socialists must be the embarrassing consequence of insisting that it does. (It is that this insistence necessarily discredits all those well-publicized researches purporting to show that, even in countries blessed with substantial public sectors, many if not most people possess no capitals worth speaking of.)

Misled by these different, distracting commitments, Townsend insists on devising factitious criteria which enable him, to his own satisfaction, to demonstrate the unbelievable conclusion that 15 million people, or more than a quarter of the whole UK population, live in poverty or 'on the margins of poverty'; or, rather, that they did in 1968–9, when his data were first put on file (ibid., pp. 301–2; and cf. p. 275). Since no one is going to believe that there were even then so many living in what the despised laity would recognize as scandalous poverty, Townsend thus guaranteed that the eventual publication of his report would not give rise to any kind of crusade against that smaller but actual scandal which he chose not to investigate.

His vast exaggeration of the extent of the problem also effectively excused Townsend from the labour of excogitating any immediately practical policies. Instead he confined himself to ritual calls for a total, all-purpose, and hence in practice inevitably totalitarian and perhaps impoverishing, socialist 'transformation of work organization and social relations'.

It is a sad pity that he did not put the Rowntree Trust's generous research grant to a better and, one presumes, its intended use. An excellent and peculiarly appropriate model would have been Rowntree 1901. For it was Seebohm Rowntree's revelations about truly scandalous poverty in York at the turn of the century which did so much to prepare politicians and public for the attacks on that evil launched by the great reforming Liberal administration of 1906. It is a wry yet salutary reflection that the time which elapsed between the publication of Rowntree's book and the election of that administration was exactly half that between the collection of Townsend's interview data and the eventual appearance of his monster report.

(iv) Perhaps the most striking demonstration of the difficulty which so many seem to find in grasping and keeping hold of the distinction between procrustean and Samaritan policies is provided by two well-reviewed and widely circulating books enquiring into 'the morality of political violence, or really, political violence of the Left' (Honderich 1976, p. vii: it is, one supposes, taken totally for granted that any violence perceived as 'right-wing' is always and altogether without excuse).

(a) Honderich starts with what he insists on presenting as facts not of poverty but of inequality: 'the worst-off tenth now living in each of the developed societies will have considerably shorter lives than the individuals in the best-off tenth'; while, 'On average, males in Gabon die well before what is regarded as middle age in Britain.' Thus, 'There arises the question of the possibility of any real change, either in the inequalities of lifetime within developed societies or in the inequalities of lifetime between developed and less developed societies' (ibid., pp. 4, 5, and 6).

Although Honderich consistently says developed, without qualification, we are, I think, always intended tacitly to exclude the never-mentioned socialist societies. Here, as so often in similar works, inequalities within the lands of 'actually existing socialism', and the actual conditions of the worst off in socialist societies, are systematically ignored. Such significant neglects must not be overlooked if the claim is that these are moral considerations (and therefore to be applied universally). For everyone sincerely committed to a world war on want, rather than to exploiting the facts of poverty (in non-socialist countries) as one more handy stick with which to beat the bourgeois, will be eager to study *The Poverty of Communism* (Eberstadt 1988).

But it is only after starting with all the emphasis on relativities, and upon these exclusively in non-socialist countries, that Honderich – apparently as an afterthought – turns his attention to the absolute rather than the merely relative conditions of the worst off:

the facts of inequality . . . claim our attention not only because they consist in *inequalities*. It is not merely that some people have less, but that they have *so little*, judged in an absolute rather than a comparative way.

(ibid., p. 10)

What emerges . . . is that what we must have is a principle or a pair or a set of principles which give importance to the avoiding of both distress and inequality . . . Obviously a perfect equality of suffering leaves much to be desired.

(1976, p. 38)

We ought, nevertheless, to accord a word of welcome to that afterthought observation. For it expressed an insight which has not, it seems, been vouchsafed to all. Thus, in an editorial contribution to Townsend and Bosanquet 1980, entitled simply 'Health', we are taught that 'There is a basic *inequality* between the state of illness or injury, and the state of health. Prevention aims to reduce this inequality' (p. 219: emphasis added)! But now, if the evil really was the inequality as such, then an equally good and sometimes swifter and more available remedy would be to ensure that everyone else was afflicted with the same disease, or suffered the same sort of injury.

It is indeed obvious that 'a perfect equality of suffering leaves' not merely much but almost everything to be desired. Nevertheless we must not allow the consequent chorus of agreement to conceal a most remarkable fact. This is that it is in terms of two actual or alleged evils, neither one reducible to the other, that Honderich formulates his own negative neo-Utilitarianism: 'that we should always act in such a way as to produce *that state of affairs which most avoids inequality and distress*'. The manifesto is forthwith glossed: 'this attitude . . . is the fundamental part of the most common of all reflective moralities' (Honderich 1976, p. 24).

Whatever the merits of such a negative neo-Utilitarianism, a moment's thought about the implications of introducing inequality as a second independent bad, whether or not it is fully co-equal with the first, must at once dispose of the suggestion that Honderich is merely reformulating classical Utilitarianism; or indeed any other very common 'reflective moral system'. For classical Utilitarianism spoke only of the greatest happiness of the greatest number. Concentrating upon the maximization of aggregate satisfactions, it had nothing to say about equal distribution as a separate and independent good; although its spokespersons have, as we saw earlier, often maintained that equality may in fact be one means by which to reach their own sole supreme end. But this instrumental consideration, important though it is, cannot support a separate principle of the badness of inequality as such. It does not, therefore, offer obstacles to those inequalities which either impose no costs upon anyone else or which may turn out to be necessary as incentives to the achieving of the Utilitarian supreme good.

By contrast, Honderich's own first system, since it condemns all inequalities as in themselves bad, requires that such incentives be conceded only grudgingly, if at all – traded-off after hard bargaining against whatever decrease in 'distress and suffering' they make possible. For the same reason an adherent of this allegedly 'most common of all reflective moralities' must insist that, even in a society or a world in which no one was afflicted by 'deprivation, distress and suffering', it would still be at least presumptively bad if anyone became or remained in any way substantially better off than anyone else.

The same refusal to separate Samaritan from procrustean ends combines with the fury and vehemence of his partisanship to prevent Honderich, as it prevents so many other left-wing activists, from admitting that most of those abominated as greedy and heartless Thatcherites, while rejecting the latter, endorse the former. In 1980, for instance, at much the same time as Penguin Books published Honderich's paperback, *Violence for Equality*, the Selsdon Group issued its *Beginner's Guide to Public Expenditure Cuts*. This inner circle within the Conservative Party is regularly described by the media as 'ultra right-wing', and sometimes commended by members as 'so dry as to be positively crisp'. Yet it too insisted:

> Only by cutting out some state activities altogether can this or any government concentrate on that very limited list – defence . . . guaranteeing a minimum standard of life to the poorest – of activities which . . . only the state can perform. The last-mentioned is, of course, not the least important duty of the state.

(p. 7)

(b)   After all this it is curious to notice that in Honderich 1980, the later and more popular version of Honderich 1976, despite what is perhaps an even more frequent employment of the word 'equality', its referent is apparently no longer alleged to be good in itself, but only good as a means to a different end. In the earlier book, Honderich had written as a rich-hunting procrustean: 'There are economies, as satisfactory as ours, which are without the rich' (1976, p. 85).

Waiving possible questions about the satisfactoriness of the state of the British economy in 1976, notice that Honderich 1980 advances under the suggestively threatening title *Violence for Equality*. Nevertheless it is here that the author formulates what he persists in calling the 'Principle of Equality' in words making it tolerably plain that it is not in fact equality but the relief of distress which is now supposed to be for him the true value: 'What is required is that we should improve the lot of . . . those in distress . . . The principle is against distress and hence any inequality which causes it' (1980, pp. 54–5).

Certainly, Honderich continues: 'This preferable policy will make for a movement towards equality of well-being . . . Also it may be that a necessary means to this end will involve reducing the well-being of the better-off' (ibid., p. 55). But equality is no longer to be pursued for its own sake, as an intended objective. At least in words, therefore, Honderich is here abandoning the procrustean ideal. Later the words become even more emphatic: 'the end of the Principle of Equality . . . is not to get people *on a level*, some level or other. It is not, strictly speaking, to reduce inequality . . . The end is . . . to improve the lot of the badly off' (ibid., p. 138).

But now, if that is and always has been his game, why does he still so perversely insist that it has to be systematically misdescribed? And, having in his previous book himself accepted and recommended equality as an end, how does he now muster the effrontery to accuse of 'a certain amount of propaganda and self-deception' those of us who have all along maintained that many people are indeed devoted to the imposition of equality as a good in itself (ibid., p. 137)? The kindest comparison possible is with the performance of the White Knight:

> But I was thinking of a plan,
> To dye one's whiskers green,

And always use so large a fan,
That they could not be seen.

(Carroll 1872, ch. 8)

4 A sting in the tail

The kindest is, nevertheless, perhaps too kind. For Honderich's hectoring readiness to attribute his own faults to opponents of his now disowned procrusteanism suggests that he too may once have succumbed to the attractions of collapsing the distinction between the two different policy objectives distinguished in section 3, above.

I will not be so mean as to refuse to share my own prize specimen of such propagandist collapsing. It came in a private letter from one who in my and his young day was awarded First Class Honours in the School of Politics, Philosophy, and Economics at the University of Oxford, and who has since become among professing social scientists one of the most prominent procrusteans: 'It *is* arguable that bad housing, squalor, pollution, ignorance, etc. etc. are "good". But unless you are prepared to argue that case you must be an egalitarian . . .'

At the beginning of chapter eight, after refuting claims that procrusteans are executing the mandates of a kind of justice, we regretted that 'Since the propaganda advantages of these pretences are so enormous, and since the attractions of self-images as disinterested crusaders after justice are so great, it would be unrealistic to expect much immediate response to appeals for truth in advertising' (p. 167). Earlier, section 1 of chapter six pointed out another strong attraction which this false identification has for procrusteans. It gives them their knock-down answer to the otherwise intractable objection: ' "By what right . . . are you planning to impose your individual and personal ideal upon everyone, by collective force?" ' (p. 126).

But, to provide the necessary basis for this satisfactorily decisive riposte, the word 'justice' has to be construed here in the strong and particular sense: the sense in which persons must morally deserve or be otherwise morally entitled to whatever is to be justly given to or justly imposed upon them. The author of *Social Justice* realized that he needed to employ the word in that stronger and more particular sense: 'We are, perhaps, fortunate that we have lost one of the senses which the term had for the Greeks, the sense in which justice was equivalent to virtue in general . . .' (D. Miller 1976, p. 17).

But what Miller and so many others fail or refuse to recognize is that the same element in the stronger conception of justice which warrants the decisive answer to that otherwise intractable objection also and necessarily supports what for many is bound to be a most uncomfortable demand: 'Take what you like', as God says in the Spanish proverb, 'take it; and pay for it.' Certainly this demand has to be extremely uncomfortable for all those procrusteans – and their name is Legion – who are, by their own stated standards, conspicuously underdeprived.

'There is', as *The Road to Serfdom* says, 'all the difference in the world between demanding that a desirable state of affairs should be brought about by the authorities, or even being willing to submit provided everyone else is made to do the same, and the readiness to do what one thinks right oneself at the sacrifice of one's own desires . . .' (Hayek 1944, p. 157). So long, however, as we are talking only of some private and personal ideal, there can be all manner of more or less creditable reasons for not undertaking such self-sacrifice immediately and voluntarily. The case is, however, altogether different if the sacrifice is demanded by justice. It now becomes imperative to insist that, if and in so far as equality of outcome truly is so mandated, then all those who are at present holding anything more than their perfectly (or approximately) equal share are thereby and necessarily in possession of stolen property; and, most shameful of all, but equally necessarily, property stolen from others worse off than themselves.

If once this sting in the tail becomes widely appreciated, we may expect to hear rather less talk of equality of outcome as the manifest mandate of (social) justice, and fewer furiously self-righteous denunciations of opponents as, *ex officio*, committed enemies of (unqualified) justice. That will be the day!

Bibliography

This list is intended to provide all necessary particulars of the books from which quotations are made in the text above. For works first published in earlier centuries and for some others the dates given in the text are those of first publication, though the page references are to the more recent editions. The more usual alternative practice both irritates some and encourages anachronistic misconceptions in others! Both dates are given in the reference list, the date of the original publication in square brackets and the date of the edition used in round parentheses. It must also be noted here that the translations from Greek, Latin, and French used in the text above are not always those of the books listed below.

Ackerman, B., *Social Justice and the Liberal State*, New Haven, Conn.: Yale University Press, 1980.

American Law Institute, *Model Penal Code: Official Draft*, Washington, DC: American Law Institute, 1962.

Anderson, D., (ed.) *The Kindness that Kills*, London: SPCK, 1984.

Aquinas, [*c.* 1225–74] *Summa Theologica*, translated by the Fathers of the English Dominican Province, London: Burns Oates & Washbourne, 1926.

Aristotle, [384–322 BC] *Politics*, translated by H. Rackham, Cambridge, Mass. and London: Harvard University Press and Heinemann, 1977.
Rhetoric, translated by J. H. Freese, Cambridge, Mass. and London: Harvard University Press and Heinemann, 1980.
Nicomachean Ethics, translated by H. Rackham, Cambridge, Mass. and London: Harvard University Press and Heinemann, 1982.

Austin, J. L., *Sense and Sensibilia*, Oxford: Clarendon, 1962.
Philosophical Papers, 2nd edn, Oxford: Clarendon, 1970.

Bambrough, R., 'Plato's political analogies', in R. Bambrough (ed.) *Plato, Popper and Politics*, Cambridge and New York: Heffer and Barnes & Noble, 1967.

Barry, B., *The Liberal Theory of Justice*, Oxford: Oxford University Press, 1973.

Bauer, P., *Dissent on Development*, Cambridge, Mass.: Harvard University Press, 1976.
Equality, the Third World and Economic Delusion, London: Weidenfeld & Nicolson, 1981.
Reality and Rhetoric: Studies in the Economics of Development, Cambridge, Mass.: Harvard University Press, 1984.

Benn, S., 'Human rights – for whom and for what?', in E. Kamenka and A. E-S. Tay (eds) *Human Rights*, London: Edward Arnold, 1978.

Bentham, J., [1789] *An Introduction to the Principles of Morals and Legislation*, edited by J. H. Burns and H. L. A. Hart, London: Methuen, 1982.
[1816] *Anarchical Fallacies*, in J. Bowring (ed.) *The Collected Works of Jeremy Bentham* (London and Edinburgh: Simpkin Marshall, and Tait, 1841.
[1822–32] 'Leading principles of a constitutional code', in F. Rosen and J. H. Burns (eds) *Constitutional Code*, Oxford: Clarendon, 1983.

Berlin, I., 'Equality', *Proceedings of the Aristotelian Society*, 1955–6, new series vol. 56, pp. 301–26.
Four Essays on Liberty, Oxford: Oxford University Press, 1969.

Blackstone, W., [1765] *Commentaries on the Laws of England*, London: Cadell & Butterworth, 1825.

Bloch, S. and Reddaway, P., *Russia's Political Hospitals*, London: Futura, 1978.

Block, W., *Focus: On Economics and the Canadian Bishops*, Vancouver, BC: Fraser Institute, 1983.
The US Bishops and their Critics, Vancouver, BC: Fraser Institute, 1986.

Bond, J., *Personal Taxes for the Nineties*, London: Centre for Policy Studies, 1988.

Boorse, C., 'On the distinction between disease and illness', *Philosophy and Public Affairs*, 1975, vol. 5, no. 1, pp. 49–68.

Bradley, F. H., [1894] 'Some remarks about punishment', in his *Collected Papers*, Oxford: Clarendon, 1935.

Brandt, R. B., (ed.) *Social Justice*, Englewood Cliffs, NJ: Prentice Hall, 1965.

Brittan, S., 'The economic contradictions of democracy', in J. W. Alexander (ed.) *The Political Economy of Change*, Oxford: Oxford University Press, 1975.

Butler, S., *Erewhon*, ed. P. Mudford, Harmondsworth: Penguin, 1970.

Cardoso, F. H. and Faletto, E., *Dependency and Development in Latin America*, Berkeley, Calif.: California University Press, 1979.

Carroll, L., [1872] *Through the Looking Glass*, in *The Complete Works of Lewis Carroll*, London: Nonsuch, 1939.

Chernyshevsky, N. G., *What is to be done?* translated by B. R. Tucker and introduced by E. H. Carr, New York: Vintage, 1961.

Chomsky, N., *American Power and the New Mandarins*, Harmondsworth: Penguin, 1969.

Confucius, [559–471 BC] *The Analects*, translated by W. Soothill, Taiyuanfu, Shansi: Soothill, 1910.
Conquest, R., *The Great Terror*, London: Macmillan, 1968.
    The Harvest of Sorrow: Soviet Collectivization and the Terror Famine, Oxford: Oxford University Press, 1986.
Corwin, E. S., *The Higher Law Background of American Constitutional Law*, Ithaca, NY: Great Seal, 1955.
Crosland, C. A. R., *The Conservative Enemy*, London: Cape, 1962.
    Social Democracy in Europe, London: Fabian Society, 1975.
Crossman, R. H. S., *Plato Today*, New York: Oxford University Press, 1939.
Daniels, N., (ed.) *Reading Rawls*, Oxford: Blackwell, 1975.
Davis, B. D., *Storm over Biology*, Buffalo, NY: Prometheus, 1986.
Day, J. P. de C., *Liberty and Justice*, London: Croom Helm, 1987.
De Reuck, A. V. S. and Porter, R., *The Mentally Abnormal Offender*, Boston, Mass.: Little, Brown, 1968.
Descartes, R., [1591–1650] *Philosophical Works*, translated and edited by E. S. Haldane and G. R. T. Ross, Cambridge: Cambridge University Press, 1931.
Deutscher, I., *The Prophet Unarmed*, New York: Vintage, 1965.
Dworkin, R., *Taking Rights Seriously*, Cambridge, Mass.: Harvard University Press, 1977.
Eberstadt, N., *The Poverty of Communism*, New Brunswick, NJ: Transaction, 1988.
Felix, D., *Marx as Politician*, Carbondale, Ill.: Southern Illinois University Press, 1983.
Field, F., *Unequal Britain*, London: Arrow, 1973.
    (ed.) *The Wealth Report*, London: Routledge & Kegan Paul, 1979.
Firth, C. H., (ed.) *The Clarke Papers*, London: Clarendon for the Camden Society, 1891.
Flew, A. G. N. 'On the interpretation of Hume', and 'On not deriving ought from is', in W. D. Hudson (ed.) *The Is/Ought Question*, London and New York: Macmillan and St Martin's, 1969, pp. 64–9 and 135–43.
    An Introduction to Western Philosophy, London and Indianapolis, Ind.: Thames & Hudson and Bobbs-Merrill, 1971.
    Crime or Disease?, London: Macmillan, 1973a.
    'What Socrates should have said to Thrasymachus', in C. F. Carter (ed.) *Skepticism and Moral Principles*, Evanston, Ill.: New University Press, 1973b.
    'In defence of reformism', in H. Hawton (ed.) *Question Seven*, London: Pemberton, 1974.
    Thinking about Thinking, London: Collins Fontana, 1975.
    Sociology, Equality and Education, London: Macmillan, 1976.
    A Rational Animal, Oxford: Clarendon, 1978.
    'Russell's judgement on Bolshevism', in G. W. Roberts (ed.) *Bertrand Russell Memorial Volume*, London: Allen & Unwin, 1979.
    The Politics of Procrustes, Buffalo, NY: Prometheus, 1981.
    'A strong programme for the sociology of belief', *Inquiry* (Oslo), 1982, vol. 25, pp. 365–78.

'Mental health, mental disease, and mental illness: "the Medical Model" ', in P. Bean (ed.) *Mental Illness: Changes and Trends*, New York: Wiley, 1983a.

'Legitimacy and the gadfly challenge', in *Philosophical Quarterly*, 1983b, vol. 33, no. 130, pp. 84–9.

'Justice: real or social', *Social Philosophy and Policy*, 1983c, vol. 1, no. 1, pp. 151–71.

Darwinian Evolution, London: Paladin, 1984a.

'The concept of human betterment', in K. Boulding (ed.) *The Economics of Human Betterment*, London: Macmillan, 1984b.

Thinking About Social Thinking, Oxford: Blackwell, 1985.

David Hume: Philosopher of Moral Science, Oxford: Blackwell, 1986a.

'An ungodly muddle', *Encounter*, 1986b, vol. 67, no. 3, pp. 74–6.

Power to the Parents: Reversing Educational Decline, London: Sherwood, 1987a.

The Logic of Mortality, Oxford: Blackwell, 1987b.

'Brainwashing, deprogramming and mental health', in *Reason Papers No. 13*, Santa Barbara, Calif.: Reason Foundation, 1988.

Flew, A. G. N. and Vesey, G., *Agency and Necessity*, Oxford: Blackwell, 1987.

France, A., *Le Lys Rouge*, Paris, 1894.

Frankena, W., 'The concept of social justice', in Brandt, *Social Justice*, 1965; also in Daniels (ed.) *Reading Rawls*, 1975.

Freud, S., *New Introductory Lectures on Psychoanalysis*, London: Hogarth, 1933.

Friedman, M. and R., *Capitalism and Freedom*, Chicago: Chicago University Press, 1962.

Free to Choose, London: Secker & Warburg, 1980.

Gaitskell, H., *Socialism and Nationalization*, London: Fabian Society, 1956.

Galbraith, J. K., *The Affluent Society*, New York: Houghton Mifflin, 1958.

George, H., *The Science of Political Economy*, New York: Doubleday, 1890.

Gewirth, A., *Reason and Morality*, Chicago: Chicago University Press, 1978.

Gibbs, B., *Freedom and Liberation*, Brighton: Sussex University Press, 1976.

Gray, J., *Liberalism*, Milton Keynes: Open University Press, 1986.

Green, P., *The Pursuit of Inequality*, Oxford: Robertson, 1981.

Grotius, H., [1625] *The Law of War and Peace*, translated by F. W. Kelsey and introduced by J. B. Scott, Indianapolis, Ind.: Bobbs-Merrill, 1925.

Halsey, A. H., *Heredity and Environment*, London: Methuen, 1977.

Halstead, B., 'The New Left's assault on science', *The Salisbury Review*, 1987, vol. 5, no. 2, pp. 37–9.

Hamilton, A., Madison, J. and Jay, J., [1788] *The Federalist Papers*, edited by C. Rossiter, New York: New American Library, 1961.

Hampshire, S. N., 'A critical notice of *A Theory of Justice*', *New York Review of Books*, 1972.

Hare, R. M., 'Critical notice of *A Theory of Justice*', *Philosophical Quarterly*, 1973, vol. 23, pp. 144–55 and 241–52.

Harrington, M., *The Twilight of American Capitalism*, New York: Simon & Schuster/Touchstone, 1977.

Harris, R. and Seldon, A., *Over-ruled on Welfare*, London: Institute for Economic Affairs, 1979.

Welfare without the State, London: Institute of Economic Affairs, 1987.

Harrison, L. E., *Underdevelopment is a State of Mind*, Lanham, Md.: Madison, 1985.

Hart, H., 'Are there any natural rights', *Philosophical Review*, 1955, vol. 64, pp. 175–91.

Hartley, L. P., *Facial Justice*, London: Hamilton, 1960.

Hayek, F. A., *The Road to Serfdom*, London: Routledge & Kegan Paul, 1944.

The Constitution of Liberty, London: Routledge & Kegan Paul, 1960.

Studies in Philosophy, Politics and Economics, London: Routledge & Kegan Paul, 1967.

The Mirage of Social Justice, London: Routledge & Kegan Paul, 1976.

New Studies in Philosophy, Politics, Economics and the History of Ideas London: Routledge & Kegan Paul, 1978.

Hegel, G. W. F., [1830] *Hegel's Logic*, translated by W. Wallace, Oxford: Clarendon, 1975.

Heller, M. and Nekrich, A. M., *Utopia in Power: The History of the Soviet Union from 1917 to the Present*, New York: Summit, 1986.

Hobbes, T., [1651] *Leviathan*, in W. Molesworth (ed.) *The English Works of Thomas Hobbes*, London: Bohm, 1839–40.

Honderich, T., *Three Essays on Political Violence*, Oxford: Blackwell, 1976.

Violence for Equality, Harmondsworth: Penguin, 1980.

Honoré, A. M., 'Social justice', in R. S. Summers (ed.) *Essays in Legal Philosophy*, Berkeley, Calif.: California University Press, 1968.

Hook, S., *Revolution, Reform and Social Justice*, New York: New York University Press, 1975.

Housman, A. E., *Juvenalis Saturae*, rev. edn, Cambridge: Cambridge University Press, 1931.

Hume, D., [1739–40] *A Treatise of Human Nature*, 2nd edn, edited by L. A. Selby-Bigge and revised by P. H. Nidditch, Oxford: Clarendon, 1978.

[1748] *An Enquiry Concerning Human Understanding*, in *Hume's Enquiries* 3rd edn, edited by L. A. Selby-Bigge and revised by P. H. Nidditch, Oxford: Clarendon, 1975.

Essays Moral Political and Literary, edited by E. F. Miller, Indianapolis, Ind.: Liberty Classics, 1985.

Huxley, A., *Brave New World*, London: Chatto & Windus, 1931.

Eyeless in Gaza, New York: Harper & Row, 1936.

Jencks, C. *et al.*, *Inequality*, London: Allen Lane, 1973.

Jensen, A., *Genetics and Education*, London: Methuen, 1972.

Jones, A., (ed.) *Economics and Equality*, Oxford: Philip Alan, 1976.

Kant, I., [1785] *Groundwork of the Metaphysic of Morals*, translated by H. J. Paton as *The Moral Law*, London: Hutchinson, 1949.

Laity Commission of the Roman Catholic Bishops' Conference of England and Wales *Community, Benefit and Taxation*, London: Laity Commission, 1982.

Lenin, V. I., [1902] *What is to be Done?*, translated by S. V. and P. Utechin, London: Panther, 1970.

[1922] *Our Revolution*, in *The Essentials of Lenin*, no translator named, London: Lawrence & Wishart, 1967.

Letwin, W. (ed.), *Against Equality*, London: Macmillan, 1983.

Lewis, C. S., [1954] 'The humanitarian theory of punishment', in his *Undeceptions*, London: Bles, 1972.

Lindsay, A. D., *The Two Moralities*, London: Eyre & Spottiswoode, 1940.

Lloyd-Thomas, D. A., 'Competitive equality of opportunity', *Mind*, 1977, vol. 86, no. 343, pp. 388–404.

Locke, J., [1690a] *An Essay concerning Human Understanding*, edited by P. H. Nidditch, Oxford: Clarendon, 1975.

[1690b] *Two Treatises of Government*, edited by P. Laslett, Cambridge: Cambridge University Press, 1960.

Macdiarmid, H., *Selected Poems*, edited by D. Craig and J. Manson, Harmondsworth: Penguin, 1970.

McDonald, J., *Rousseau and the French Revolution: 1762–1791*, London: Athlone, 1965.

Mandeville, B. de, [1725] *The Fable of the Bees*, Harmondsworth: Penguin, 1970.

Marx, K., [1843] 'On the Jewish question', in *Marx: Early Writings*, Harmondsworth: Penguin, 1975.

[1844] *The Economic and Philosophical Manuscripts of 1844*, translated by M. Milligan and edited by D. K. Struik, New York: International, 1964.

[1847] *The Poverty of Philosophy*, no translator named, London: Lawrence & Wishart, 1936.

[1875] *Critique of the Gotha Programme*, vol. II, in K. Marx and F. Engels *Selected Works*, no translators, named Moscow: FLPH, 1969.

Matson, W., 'What Rawls calls justice', in *The Occasional Review*, San Diego, Calif.: World Research, 1978, issue 8/9, pp. 45–57.

Menninger, K., *The Crime of Punishment*, New York: Viking, 1968.

Mill, J. S., [1848] *Principles of Political Economy with some of their Applications to Social Philosophy*, edited by V. W. Bladen and J. M. Robson, Toronto and London: Toronto University Press and Routledge & Kegan Paul, 1965.

[1859] *On Liberty*, in Mill, *Utilitarianism*, 1910.

[1861] *Utilitarianism, Liberty and Representative Government*, London and New York: J. N. Dent and Dutton, 1910.

Miller, D., *Social Justice*, Oxford: Oxford University Press, 1976.

Miller, F. D., 'The state and the community in Aristotle's politics', in *Reason Papers No. 1*, Santa Barbara, Calif.: Reason Foundation, 1974.

Milton, J., (1649) *The Tenure of Kings and Magistrates*.

Minogue, K., *The Liberal Mind*, London: Methuen, 1963.

Moore, G. E., *Principia Ethica*, Cambridge: Cambridge University Press, 1903.

Moss, R., *Chile's Marxist Experiment*, London: David & Charles, 1973.

Muir, R., *In the Opinion of Robert Muir, Jr., in the Matter of Karen Quinlan: An Alleged Incompetent*. Super. A. N. J., Chancery Division, Morris Company, C–201–75 10 November, 1975.

Murray, C., *Losing Ground: American Social Policy 1950–1980*, New York: Basic, 1984.

Nielsen, K., 'In defence of radicalism', in H. Hawton (ed.), *Question Seven*, London: Pemberton, 1974.
'Impediments to radical egalitarianism', *American Philosophical Quarterly*, 1981, vol. 18, pp. 121–9.

Nisbet, R., 'The pursuit of equality', *The Public Interest*, 1974, vol. 35, pp. 103–20; repr. in Letwin, *Against Equality*, 1983, but, remarkably, not in Daniels 1975.
'The fatal ambivalence of an idea', *Encounter*, 1976, no. 6, pp. 10–21.

Novak, M., *The Spirit of Democratic Capitalism*, New York: Simon & Schuster, 1982.

Nozick, R., *Anarchy, State and Utopia*, New York and Oxford: Basic and Blackwell, 1975.

Orwell, G., *1984*, London: Secker & Warburg, 1950.

Paine, T., [1791–2] *The Rights of Man*, Harmondsworth: Penguin, 1984.

Palmer, F., (ed.) *Anti-Racism: An Assault on Education and Value*, London: Sherwood, 1987.

Pinel, P., [1806] *A Treatise on Insanity*, New York: Hafner, 1962.

Plato, [*c*.428–*c*.348 BC] *The Republic*, translated by P. Shorey, Cambridge, Mass. and London: Harvard University Press and Heinemann, Loeb vol. I: 1930, Loeb vol. II: 1935.
The Laws translated by R. B. Bury, London and Cambridge, Mass.: Heinemann and Harvard University Press, two Loeb volumes, 1926.

Pole, J. R., *The Pursuit of Equality in American History*, Berkeley, Calif.: and London: California University Press, 1978.

Popper, K. R., *The Poverty of Historicism*, London: Routledge & Kegan Paul, 1957.
The Open Society and its Enemies, 5th edn, London: Routledge & Kegan Paul, 1966.
Objective Knowledge, Oxford: Clarendon, 1979.

Raphael, D. D., 'Conservative and prosthetic justice', *Political Studies*, 1964; and repr. in A. de Crespigny and A. Werthheimer (eds.) *Contemporary Political Theory*, New York: Atherton, 1970.
'The rights of man and the rights of the citizen', in D. D. Raphael (ed.) *Political Theory and the Rights of Man*, Bloomington, Ind.: Indiana University Press, 1967.

Rawls, J., 'Justice as fairness', *The Philosophical Review*, 1958, vol. 67, pp. 164–94.
'Constitutional liberty and the concept of justice', in J. R. Pennock (ed.) *Nomos*, New York: Lieber-Atherton, 1963.
A Theory of Justice, Cambridge, Mass. and Oxford: Harvard University Press and Clarendon, 1971.
Report of the Royal Commission on Capital Punishment, London: HMSO, 1953.
Report of the Royal Commission on the Law Relating to Mental Illness and Mental Deficiency, London: HMSO, 1957.
Reznek, L., *The Nature of Disease*, London: Routledge & Kegan Paul, 1987.
Richardson, H., (ed.) *New Religions and Mental Health*, New York and Toronto: Mellen, 1980.
Richardson, K. and Spears, D. (eds.), *Race, Culture and Intelligence*, Harmondsworth: Penguin, 1972.
Ross, A., *On Law and Justice*, Berkeley, Calif.: California University Press, 1959.
Ross, W. D., *The Right and the Good*, Oxford: Clarendon, 1930.
Rothbard, M., *Egalitarianism as a Revolt against Nature*, Washington, DC: Libertarian Review Press, 1976.
Rousseau, J. J., [1762] *The Social Contract, and other Discourses* translated and introduced by G. D. H. Cole, London and New York: Dent and Dutton, 1978. Be warned that it is only the 1978 3rd edn which, at very long last, prints these various works in the order of their first composition.
Rowntree, S., *Poverty, a Study of Town Life*, London: Macmillan, 1901.
Russell, B. A. W., *An Introduction to Mathematical Philosophy*, London: Allen & Unwin, 1919.
A History of Western Philosophy, London: Allen & Unwin, 1945.
Russell, P., (1987) 'Nozick, need and charity', *The Journal of Applied Philosophy*, 1987, vol. 4, no. 2, pp. 205–16.
Sacks, J., *Wealth and Poverty: a Jewish Analysis*, London: Social Affairs Unit, 1984.
Schopenhauer, A., [1841] *On the Basis of Morality*, translated by E. R. J. Payne, Indianapolis, Ind.: Bobbs-Merrill, 1965.
Schwartzschild, L., [1948] *The Red Prussian*, new edition with introduction by A. G. N. Flew, London: Pickwick, 1986.
Searle, J. R., 'How to derive *ought* from *is*', reprinted in W. D. Hudson (ed.) *The Is/Ought Question*, London and New York: Macmillan and St Martin's Press, 1969.
Seldon, A., *Charge*, London: Temple Smith, 1977.
Shafarevitch, I., (1980) *The Socialist Phenomenon*, New York: Harper & Row, 1980.
Siculus, Diodorus [first century BC], *The Library of History*, translated by C. H. Oldfather, C. L. Sherman and R. M. Geer, London: Heinemann (Twelve volumes with various dates), vol. 12, 1967.
Sidgwick, H., *The Methods of Ethics*, 6th edn, London: Macmillan, 1901.

Singer, P., *Marx*, New York: Hill & Wang, 1980.

Skinner, B. F., *Walden Two*, New York: Macmillan, 1948.

Beyond Freedom and Dignity, New York: Knopf, 1971.

Smith, A., [1759] *The Theory of the Moral Sentiments*, edited by D. D. Raphael and A. L. Macfie, Oxford: Clarendon, 1976.

[1776] *An Inquiry into the Nature and Causes of the Wealth of Nations*, edited by R. H. Campbell, A. S. Skinner and W. B. Todd, Indianapolis, Ind.: Liberty Press, 1981.

Sowell, T., *Race and Economics*, New York and London: Longman, 1975.

Ethnic America, New York: Basic, 1981.

Stephen,. J. F. *Liberty, Equality and Fraternity*, London: Smith & Elder, 1873.

A Digest of the Criminal Law, 6th edn, London: Macmillan, 1904.

Stevenson, C. L. 'Persuasive definitions', *Mind*, 1938, repr. with revisions in *Ethics and Language* New Haven, Conn.: Yale University Press, 1944, vol. 47, pp. 331–50.

Sumner, W. G., [1883] 'The forgotten man', in *The Forgotten Man and Other Essays*, edited by A. G. Keller, New Haven, Conn.: Yale University Press, 1919.

Talmon, J. L., *The Origins of Totalitarian Democracy*, London and New York: Secker & Warburg and Praeger, 1952.

Thucydides, [471–401 BC] *A History of the Pelopponesian War*, translated by R. Crawley, London and New York: Dent and Dutton, 1950.

Tolstoy, L., [1909] *The Law of Love and the Law of Violence*, translated by M. K. Tolstoy, New York: Holt, Rinehart, Winston, 1970.

Townsend, P., *Poverty in the United Kingdom*, Harmondsworth: Penguin, 1979.

Townsend, P. and Bosanquet, N. (eds.), *Labour and Equality*, London: Heinemann, 1980.

Trotsky, L.,*The Revolution Betrayed*, translated by Max Eastman, Garden City, NY: Doubleday, 1937.

Tucker, R. C. (ed.), *The Lenin Anthology*, New York: W. W. Norton, 1975.

Vieira, E., 'Rights and the American Constitution', *The Georgia Law Review*, 1979, vol. 13, no. 4, pp. 1447–1500.

Voslensky, M., *Nomenklatura*, London: Bodley Head, 1984.

Weale, D., *Equality and Social Policy*, London: Routledge & Kegan Paul, 1978.

Williams, B., 'The idea of equality', in Williams, B., *Problems of the Self*, Cambridge: Cambridge University Press, 1973.

Williams, W., *The State against Blacks*, New York: McGraw Hill, 1982.

Wittfogel, K. A., *Oriental Despotism: A Comparative Study of Total Power*, New York: Random House, Vintage edn., 1981.

Wolfe, B., *Marxism: One Hundred Years in the Life of a Doctrine*, London: Chapman & Hall, 1967.

Three who Made a Revolution, New York: Stein & Day, 1984.

Wootton, B., *Social Science and Social Pathology*, London: Allen & Unwin, 1967.

Zamiatin, E., *We*, translated by G. Z. Zilbourg, New York: Dutton, 1924.

Name index

The intention is to include all but only the names of the flesh-and-blood people mentioned; and therefore to exclude gods, legendary figures, and characters in works of fiction.

Ackerman, B. 140–1
Allende, S. 22
Anderson, D. 199
Aquinas, Saint Thomas 52
Aristotle 52, 84, 100, 124, 133, 135–9, 141–3, 150–1
Attlee, C.R. 21
Austin, J.L. 9, 20, 35–6, 127

Bambrough, R. 111
Barry, B. 140
Bauer, P. 53, 199
Bazelon, Judge 96
Bell, D. 173–4
Benn, S. 34
Bentham, J. 27–9, 36–7, 78, 80, 185
Berlin, I. 5, 9, 55, 72, 74–5, 77, 87, 139, 142
Bismarck, O. von 124, 191
Blackstone, W. 43–4
Bloch, S. 98–9
Block, W. 199
Bond, J. 188
Boorse, C. 101–3
Booth, C. 183
Bosanquet, N. 171, 196, 205
Bradley, F.H. 107
Brezhnev, L. 132
Brittan, S. 134

Burns, R. 174
Bury, J.B. 8
Butler, S. 92

Cantor, G. 7
Cardoso, F.H. 53
Carroll, L. 208
Castle, B. 171
Castro, F. 78
Charles II, King 49
Chernyshevsky, N.G. 48
Chomsky, N. 22
Churchill, W.S. 49, 184
Cicero, M.T. 36
Confucius 39
Conquest, R. 89
Cooper, A.A. 49
Copernicus, N. 31
Corwin, E.S. 49
Crosland, C.A.R. 181, 186

Dalton, H. 187
Daniels, N. 140
Deng Xiaoping 89
Davis, B.D. 145
De Reuck, A.V.S. 106
Descartes, R. 12, 32
Deutscher, I. 93
Diderot, D. 61
Diodorus Siculus 182

Donnison, D.V. 182–3, 202, 208
Du Runsheng 189
Dworkin, R. 28–9, 141
Dylan, R. 145

Eberstadt, N. 204
Engels, F. 199
Epinay, Madame d' 55

Faletto, E. 53
Felix, D. 199
Field, F. 195–8, 202
Firth, C.H. 175
Forester, C.S. 139
France, A. 6
Frankena, W. 135
Freud, S. 15, 98, 161
Friedman, M. 23

Halsey, A.H. 145, 186–7
Halstead, B. 145
Hamilton, M. 174
Hampshire, S.N. 154, 158, 169
Harbury, C.D. 171
Hare, R.M. 119, 146
Harrington, M. 157
Harris, R. 125
Harrison, L.E. 53
Hart, H.L.A. 39–40
Hartley, L.P. 145
Hayek, F.A. 23, 72, 113, 152, 162, 165, 168, 172–3, 209
Healey, D. 187, 196
Heath, E. 171, 188, 195
Hegel, G.W.F. 64
Heller, M. 68, 89, 202
Helvetius, C.-A. 5–6
Hitler, A. 47–8, 65, 71, 102, 172
Hobbes, T. 5, 49, 53, 195
Ho Chi Minh 78
Honderich, T. 204–7
Honoré, A.M. 33
Hook, S. 48
Housman, A.E. 151
Hume, D. 4, 10, 12, 16, 31–2, 34–5, 45, 49, 86–7, 127, 163
Hutchinson, T.W. 170–1
Huxley, A. 69, 145

James II, King 49–50
Jefferson, T. 41
Jencks, C. 144
Jensen, A. 162
Jerome, J.K. 145
Jones, A. 170
Joseph, K. 23, 195

Kadar, J. 21–2, 86
Kant, I. 31, 44–5, 173
Kemal, M. 46
Kennedy, J.F. 189
Kharume, A. 21–2, 86
Khruschev, N. 104
Kolakowski, L. 3

Lehrer, T. 111
Lenin, V.I. 7, 22–3, 39, 47–8, 56, 70, 73, 78, 87, 113–15, 193, 202
Lewis, C.S. 108
Lincoln, A. 20, 46
Lindsay, A.D. 124
Lloyd-Thomas, D.A. 175
Locke, J. 10, 12–14, 27, 29, 33, 42, 47–51, 53
Loucks, J. 42–3
Luther, M. 77

Macdiarmid, H. 47
McDonald, J. 48
McNaghten, D. 95
Mandeville, B. de 111
Marcuse, H. 70
Marx, G. 38
Marx, K. 23, 70, 73, 85–8, 111, 113–15, 121, 130, 148, 198–9
Mary (of William and Mary) 50
Matson, W. 120
Maudsley, H. 105
Menninger, K. 97, 168
Mill, J.S. 8, 26, 72, 76, 85, 122, 127, 181, 201–2
Miller, D. 159, 209
Miller, F.D. 137
Milton, J. 7
Minogue, K. 109–10
Montesquieu, C.-L. de S. 50
Moore, G.E. 31, 35

Moss, R. 22
Muir, R. 42
Murray, C. 201

Napoleon 153
Nekrich, A.M. 68, 98, 202
Newton, I. 31
Nielsen, K. 113, 166–7
Nisbet, R. 122, 153, 179
Novak, M. 53
Nozick, R. 121, 128, 140–1, 159

Orwell, G. 70, 145

Paine, T. 25
Palmer, F. 164
Piachaud, D. 171–2
Pinel, P. 94
Plato 30, 33, 71–4, 76–7, 90, 92–3,
   111, 114–15, 119–20, 127–38,
   143, 161, 164
Pole, J.R. 174
Popper, K.R. 31, 127
Posidonius 8
Pot, P. 71

Quinlan, K.A. 42

Rainborough, T. 175
Raphael, D.D. 124
Rawls, J. 78, 119–28, 133–43,
   146–61, 167, 172–4, 178–9
Reagan, R. 189
Reddaway, P. 98–9
Reznek, L. 102–6
Richardson, H. 98
Richardson, K. 163–4
Riefenstahl, L. 67
Robespierre, M. 78
Roosevelt, F.D. 47, 184
Ross, A. 142
Ross, W.D. 124
Rothbard, M. 150
Rousseau, J.-J. 47–68, 93, 122, 125,
   147, 188
Rowntree, S. 203–4
Russell, B.A.W. 47–8, 55, 170

Russell, P. 125
Ryle, G. 3

Saint-Just, L.A. de 78
Schopenhauer, A. 44
Schumpeter, J.A. 72
Schwartzschild, L. 199
Searle, J.R. 34
Seldon, A. 125
Shafarevitch, I. 68
Shakespeare, W. 56
Sidgwick, H. 122, 142
Singer, P. 8
Skinner, B.F. 14–19, 90, 149–50
Smith, A. 53, 88, 126, 159–60, 194
Snezhnevsky, A.V. 104
Socrates 90, 93, 128–30, 164
Somerville, Judge 94
Sowell, T. 164, 179
Spears, D. 164
Stalin, J.V. 13, 130, 157
Steele, C. 105–6
Stephen, J.F. 95, 97, 142
Stevenson, C.L. 69–70
Sumner, W.G. 168

Talmon, J.L. 48
Tawney, R.H. 153, 170, 196–7
Thatcher, M. 172, 188, 206
Themistocles 138
Titmuss, R. 153, 170
Tolstoy, L. 89, 115
Townsend, P. 171, 183, 196, 202–5
Travers, R. 106
Trotsky, L. 78, 88, 93
Tucker, R.S. 48
Tutton, T. 170

Ulpianus, D. 120

Vesey, G. 9
Vieira, E. 24
Vitus, Saint 14
Voslensky, M. 193

Walden, B. 185
Wallace, E. 166
Wayne, J. 126

Weale, D. 170
Weil, S. 109–10
William (Dutch William) 50
Williams, B. 176–8, 180–1
Williams, W. 200

Wittfogel, K.A. 68, 88
Wolfe, B. 48, 199
Wootton, B. 97, 103

Zamiatin, E. 144–5, 156